Transplanting Hope:
My life – Someone
Else's Heart

Dea Family!
Thank you so much for your support!
Hope you enjoy the book!

Kristy Thackeray

Kristy Thackeray

Transplanting Hope: My life – Someone Else's Heart
Copyright © 2016 by Kristy Thackeray

A portion of the proceeds from this book will be used to start a foundation to help donor families. For more information please contact Kristy via Facebook, Twitter or by visting her website www.kristythackeray.com

*I have tried to recreate events, locales and conversations from my memories of them. In order to maintain anonymity in some instances, I have changed the names of individuals and places and may have changed some identifying characteristics and details such as physical properties, occupations and places of residence.

ISBN-13: 978-1530777631
ISBN-10: 1530777631

Cover artwork by Jenn Llewellyn
Edited by Lea Storry at Our Family Lines

Printed by Createspace in the USA

DEDICATION

This book is dedicated in loving memory to:
Dawn Marie Tremblay
May 26, 1973 – May 25, 1996
You are my hero and my angel. This all started when you shared your heart with me.

And to our unknown hero who gave Shaylynn, our daughter, the gift of life on January 23, 2004.
We are so grateful to you and your family.

We would like to thank all donor families who have saved countless lives with their generosity.

This book is also dedicated to every individual who is on the transplant list and waiting.

To every transplant recipient, take care of your gift of life.
To every single person who has ever experienced dealing with the medical system, I hope my book encourages you to keep going and gives you inspiration. You are your best medical advocator.

CONTENTS

ACKNOWLEDGMENTS

There are so many people in my life who have inspired me. Please don't be offended if I forgot your name – you are definitely not forgotten in prayer.

To the Tremblay family: you'll never truly know how much and how often I think of all of you. Coral and Remi, both of you are like my second set of parents and I can't tell you enough times how thankful I am for receiving Dawn's heart. I know I say this to you often but words cannot express how grateful I am to your daughter. I know that my life wouldn't have been possible if it weren't for Dawn. Heather, you're the sister I never had. I love you. To Dawn's extended family, from her cousins, to aunts and uncles, to grandparents, you're always in my prayers and thoughts.

As a mother, I can't imagine the loss Coral and Remi have felt over the last 20 years and how many times they wished for one more day with Dawn or even one more moment; to imagine what she would have been like now and to hear her voice one more time. I will never forget when Dawn's parents told me that if things would have been a bit different, Dawn and I would have been good friends.

To Dawn's friends (those I've met and those I haven't): I think about all of you a lot. I can't imagine what those days and hours would have been like during and after the accident. You're always in my heart (literally) as I carry Dawn's heart with me and I'm humbled at how much she was loved by all of you.

To Shaylynn's donor family: I wish so badly we could meet. I would give you all hugs and hold you tight. I'm so thankful for your decision to donate your child's organs. We think about you constantly and January 23, 2004 is a day we dedicate to you. We love you.

Thank you to my mom and dad, Margo and Blaine Plotsky. You two are always my biggest supporters even when we don't see eye-to-eye on things (especially in regards to some of my decisions in life). The one constant is that you believe in me and my potential. Thank you for constantly pushing me to be the best I can be. My drive to succeed and compassionate nature are traits I have thanks to the both of you. Thank you and I love you very much. To my brother Billy, thank you for being you. You're the best big brother a sister could ever wish for. Thanks for always being there for me. I know I can always count on you. We don't say this often but I love you.

To my Aunty Terry and Uncle Steve: you were both such an important part of my story and advocated for me all the time. Thank you for loving me like your third daughter. To my cousins Leanne and Rob: thank you for sharing your home with us when we came to Calgary for my many medical appointments. Jen and Mike: thank you so much for your love and support throughout the years. I love you all.

Thank you to Shaylynn and McKayla. You're both my miracle babies. I never imagined I would have twins. You're definitely the light in my life and I love you two so much. I look forward to what the rest of our lives have in store for us. I'm always here for you no matter what and I'm so grateful to call you my daughters. I'm proud of both of you and the young women you're becoming.

Wade, thank you for loving me as I am. You came into our lives and completed our family. Thank you for showing the girls what it means to be a dad. Thank you for continually supporting my dreams. You believed in me from the beginning. I know we'll never stray from our vows even when times are tough. I will never stop believing in us as a family. I love you.

To my mother- and father-in-law: thank you for believing in my story and loving me like a daughter.

To my friends: thank you for allowing me to use your names. Each one of you played a very important role in my story.

To my editor Lea, at Our Family Lines, I'll never forget the first time we met at your Chinook Learning Services memoir writing class. Thanks for teaching me the ins and outs of writing. Thank you so much for taking all my words on the page and making them sound amazing, while still keeping my voice in the story. I loved chuckling at our silly banter while completing edits. Thanks for the Starbucks too! Thank you for believing in my story and encouraging me along the way.

Jen Llewellyn thank you so much for doing my first tattoo. You made the experience relaxing and painless and also made my tattoo amazing. Thank you for providing the artwork for the front and back cover. You took exactly what I saw and made it a reality – perfect.

I would like to acknowledge the Medicine Hat News, the Calgary Herald and Glamour magazine for providing permission to reprint news articles and photos.

I saw a lot of medical doctors over the years but here are a few I'd like to acknowledge: Dr. Giuffre, Dr. Harder, Dr. Patton, Dr. Coe, Dr. Mullen, Dr. Isaac, Dr. Ghatage, Dr. Sader and Dr. Hak. Each one of you holds a special place in my life and I think about all of you often. I have definitely had a great team of medical professionals always looking after my health.

I would like to thank the team of health care professionals that have provided Shaylynn with amazing care. Dr. Greenway, we couldn't have asked for a better doctor. Kelly and Norma: you are both amazing nurses! Keep up the fantastic work.

God: I'm humbled and in awe of your amazing power and grace. Every day I make it my mission to become more like Jesus. There's an event in the Bible that I marvel at every time I read it: John 13 "Jesus washes his disciples' feet." Could you imagine washing the feet of someone who will betray you in your biggest time of need? According to John 13, Jesus washed the feet of the individual who was going to lead him to be crucified on the cross. I want to have a heart just like Jesus and love people in a self-sacrificing way. I'm grateful that you have allowed me to give you all my life each and every day.

Dawn: Thank you for talking to your family about organ and tissue donation. Thank you so much for giving me your heart on your birthday. Your birthday, May 26, has become a much bigger deal than my own birthday. We celebrate my transplant anniversary but more importantly, your day. I love you very much.

To every donor family: your stories do matter. Share them with the world. We need more families like you because organ donation starts with you.

To transplant recipients: as you live your life after your transplant, never forget who made it possible. When life is hard, stay hopeful but when life is good, always remain humble for the person whose organ you have is giving you the life they never got to experience. Always, always remember they were and are loved and missed by many.

To those who say you'll never donate an organ or tissue, think about this – if you ever needed a transplant would you take it? If so, then you should be willing to give it too.

FOREWORD

Foreword by Dr. Michael Giuffre
   Pediatric Cardiologist
   Clinical Professor of Pediatrics and Cardiac Sciences
   Faculty of Medicine, University of Calgary
   Calgary, Alberta, Canada

Kristy has written a deeply moving book that conveys a factual and emotional sharing of her life, a life that is fraught with highs and lows, a life that embodies the journey into the medical world of transplantation medicine. Kristy has portrayed a life that has become an exquisite complexity. Her ability to share both her hope and her courage throughout the detailed heart transplant journey makes for a compelling read.

Her acknowledgement of the marvels of the surgical and medical care, that is required in having and maintaining a successful cardiac transplantation, is surpassed only by the accompaniment of an ongoing story of the deep personal consequences of the transplantation, to not only herself, but to all of those that surround Kristy. The misfortunate trappings of an often inadequate "medical system of care" is inherent in the story, with silos of medical care doing their best, but inevitably lead to a non-integrated disjointed care plan that should be deeply troubling to most caregivers throughout the world.

Kristy's narrative has the rare quality of being raw and honest as the complexities of her personal story begin in childhood and adolescence and then continue through an ongoing chronology toward her current life. She is both critical and compelling in her writing style, as she acknowledges those people who were so important in various stages of her life. The role of her support teams were very evident, with family playing a pivotal role, as both her parents and her older brother Billy in particular, proved to be the underpinnings of her hope, during her consistently wavering physical and emotional wellbeing. Kristy relays beautifully the overall feelings of contentment and love for her twin girls and husband, yet also portrays the ongoing trepidation in her daughters co-journey into heart transplantation.

Kristy came into my life and my pediatric cardiology practice as a young child, accompanied by her parents, more than twenty years ago. This was a time when cardiac transplantation was still in its infancy. The knowledge base for the various types of cardiomyopathy and their associated genetics was only at a rudimentary stage.

The learning's in transplant medicine have been tremendous over these last twenty years, with documented improvements achieved in both survival and quality of life parameters. The transplant protocols for the members of the medical and surgical teams involved in heart transplant today are more inclusive, sophisticated and encompassing. Great amounts of transplant expertise have amassed and ongoing research in rejection and treatment refinements is ongoing. Those that participate in transplant medicine are rightfully proud and devote their lives to ongoing improvements that are commendable. Kristy seems most grateful for most of the medical and surgical care she has received.

In this book, Kristy is however not subtle in pointing out, not only those caregivers that were special, but also those caregivers that need improvement. There is an underlying call for general improvements in transplantation medicine that should accompany the new and improved protocols and sophistications of the surgical and medical teams. Many aspects of Kristy's disclosed health care journey prove out that we have a long way to go in bettering the patient's journey. Kristy has a loved one's heart beating inside her, a gift from Dawn, the daughter of the heart donor's family. They too are eloquent in pointing out the deficiencies within the medical system that profoundly affected them and the ongoing detrimental consequences.

Kristy and her family, throughout the narrative, impart an important message of hope. The message is sent to those that support the patient, the patient or receiver of medical care and finally to the deliverer of medical or surgical care. This message becomes clearer as the transplantation story unfolds. That message is that hope needs to be ever present and is an inherent part of any person's journey into illness, sickness and health. The absolute necessity of Kristy's need for both "hope" was also accompanied by a whopping dose of "courage" and the massive role that the patient's support team, in Kristy's case her family, play in creating and maintaining this essential lifeline. Kristy's circle of support, was indeed wide, and included her relatives, friends and her donor family.

As a physician, you often get snippets of a patient's journey, and this insight may be improved when the patient-physician relationship is thriving and longitudinal. Seldom do we receive an opportunity to gain such detailed insights into the patients and their families' perspective during their heath-care journey. I do wish that I could have read this book by Kristy earlier in my medical career and not near the end, as I think it would have made me a better, more insightful doctor. Kristy has had so many doctors and nurses in her life through this journey and she has touched many of them with her spirit, hope and courage. I am so honored that Kristy asked me to read her story and write a brief forward.

Finally, to me this book exemplifies the current state of the medical system that society seems to blandly accept, a medical system that forces the patients to navigate and advocate for themselves. This is often in a setting of the patient or family being in a situation without adequate knowledge of how the system works or without a set of tools that would help the navigation or advocacy process. With advancement we have effectively dehumanized the patient. Healthcare has evolved toward "silos of care", inside the "system of care" that is delivered largely inside of these complex institutions, largely hospitals, and called a "healthcare system". The patient and family is expected to fit in or find their way and this is generally difficult to navigate and not at all "kind" to the patient and their family.

I hope that we can move back toward family centered and home health care. We need to allow the patient physician relationship to lead the way toward healthcare being brought to the patient, the medical home, instead of having the patient navigate the silos of health care that exist inside expensive institutes of care.

CHAPTER ONE

I'm one of them

It was a cold January morning in 1996. I woke early to start packing for the long week ahead. My parents and I were leaving our family acreage just outside of Medicine Hat, Alberta for the big city of Edmonton. After a year and a half of hospitals, needles and many doctors, we finally had the answers we had long been waiting for. I had been diagnosed with restrictive cardiomyopathy, a rare condition where the muscle around the heart becomes stiff and restricts the heart from expanding fully to let enough blood into its chambers. In short: a disease of the heart that restricts it from pumping. People with this condition often need heart transplants. I was one of them.

Before my name could be added to the organ transplant waiting list, there were several tests I had to go through. The transplant assessment takes approximately one week and involves many tests and many visits from the cardiologist. I was going to Edmonton for transplant assessment because I needed a heart transplant at age 14.

WAIT...

Let me back up a little and tell you a bit more about myself. I am the youngest daughter (the only daughter, born in the spring of 1982) to Blaine and Margo Plotsky, who were married in Medicine Hat in 1975. I have one brother, Billy, who was born in 1979. We grew up on a 240 acre farm with a coulee (valley) and a creek running through it, just outside of the Medicine Hat city limits. When I was 10 years old, we moved from one acreage to another. Our family made the decision to move across the coulee to the other side of the farm to be closer to my grandma. When my paternal Grandpa Bill passed away in 1987, his wife, my Grandma Jackie, was completely heartbroken and devastated. So in 1992, we sold our house and built a new one. I remember moving into our new home in the fall of the next year and how it smelled of fresh paint and the green rug didn't even have a footprint embedded in it yet. I consider this house my childhood home and it has a special place in my heart. Our dogs, Chuck (a yellow lab) and Tinker (a shih-tzu), loved this house too because it was close to the coulee and creek: places great for sniffing and running wild.

Life was pretty simple when I was a young child and I had a lot of fun. My dad's siblings and their children also lived on the farm so Billy and I were lucky to be surrounded by family. I was fortunate to be living so close to extended family. The time I spent with my cousins as a child is unforgettable. I definitely think life was different for us farm folk because we never locked our doors at night and the keys to our trucks remained in the ignition or under the visor.

Even though we lived on the border of the city limits, my brother and I went to a rural school in a small Alberta town named Seven Persons.

"Why is it called Seven Persons?" strangers always asked me.

"I don't know," I always replied. But I always got the same response.

"Is it called Seven Persons because that's how many people live there?"

Seriously, I have no idea how the town name came about but what I do know for sure is that I have many fond memories of the place and the country school Billy and I attended. We rode the bus there every day because it was a good 20 kilometres from our farm.

It was in early 1995 when I was 13 that my life started to drastically change. I was sick a lot after starting Grade Seven and missing a lot of school. I was always tired and some days I would wake up to find my eyelids so swollen that I couldn't open them. It was scary and the inflammation was so bad that I couldn't see. I would lay on the couch worrying that I was going blind. I thought maybe I had some type of eye infection that I couldn't get rid of. It would take hours before I could open my eyes completely. On the mornings when I couldn't pry my eyes open, I lay on the couch. My eyes felt so heavy and I had no energy at all. I didn't go to school because there was no point: I couldn't see the chalk board. If my parents had to go to work, I spent time with one of my two sets of great-grandparents. I feel fortunate that I had that time with them.

As the days passed and my missed school days turned into weeks, mom and dad decided to seek advice from a pediatrician. Dr. Hendrik Hak was a really good pediatrician in Medicine Hat. He had a sterling reputation and listened to our concerns. I soon got to know him well because we kept coming back to see him every couple of weeks. My school was extremely understanding in respect to me being absent so many days and my friends were kind and helped me catch up on the days I was well enough to return. Nevertheless, I was gone so many days that I missed writing the Grade Seven final exams. How could I concentrate on exams when I didn't know what was wrong with my body? I didn't know when we were going to get some answers but I kept my hopes high. However, every time we saw the doctor there were more questions than answers. Dr. Hak wasn't sure what was making my eyes swell. I also felt nauseous and had no energy.

The day everything changed will always be with me: May 29, 1995. I remember it like it was yesterday. The morning sky was unbelievably bright and blue and there was still a noticeable chill in the spring air, a reminder that winter had just passed. I loved the smell of the morning air and the sounds of birds chirping in the distance and plus, this particular day was special. I had a big project due for my Grade Seven language arts class. We had to write and give mock wedding speeches and my job was to toast the bride and groom. My project group agreed we should all dress the part so we asked Mariposa, a clothing store in Medicine Hat, if it would kindly lend the girls dresses for the day. The shop graciously agreed and it was a lot of fun putting on the formal wear that morning. My speech turned out well and I remember the feeling of accomplishment after our group completed the project. I had been planning this day for a long time and I was ecstatic I wasn't sick.

After lunch, things took a terrible turn for the worse. It was during French class when my leg started to hurt. It was excruciating. My leg was throbbing and the pain was shooting up and down. I had felt well at the beginning of class so I didn't worry too much about the pain. As a child my brother and I would get these unbelievable leg pains which we called "ankles." To us, it felt like someone was tearing our muscles off our bones. Sometimes our legs were so bad that the only way to relieve the ache was to have the other person sit on the hurting leg. If I was at home alone, I positioned Chuck to lie on my leg. I became an expert with my leg pains and soon realized the less movement that I made with my leg, the less it hurt. But in French class, having a classmate sit on my leg was definitely not an option.

Shortly after my leg started to hurt, my vision blurred and I heard an awful ringing in my ears. The teacher was writing on the chalkboard as I carefully made my way to her.

"Can I please go to the sick room?" I asked, trying to concentrate on not fainting. All I wanted to do was lie down somewhere, preferably at home. I hated not feeling well around other people because I always felt like a burden. I always tried to hide being ill in hopes the feeling dissipated.

"Yes, you may go to the sick room," she replied softly.

I slowly walked to the sick room, stopping at the principal's office to make a quick phone call to mom. I prayed that she would answer and pick me up, but unfortunately she was at her job as a nursing aid. I couldn't get a hold of her. I would have called dad to get me (he owned an electrical company) but he didn't have a cell phone. That meant I would have to wait until school ended and take the bus home. It would be a long, excruciating ride when I wasn't feeling the best.

In the sick room, I sat on the bed and looked at the clock; the fuzzy numbers said 1:35 p.m. I knew I only had two hours to rest before school was over. I closed my eyes and slept right until home bell blared. My girlfriend Candia was kind enough to come see me and make sure I had heard the signal that school was over. I still wasn't feeling great but we walked back to class and she helped me retrieve my belongings. Together we walked to the bus at the front of the school. We took different buses so we parted ways. I sat with my cousin on that long bus ride home. It was the longest ride of my life. I was concentrating on not get sick or fainting. I sat with my head leaned against the backrest and then closed my eyes and fixated my thoughts on arriving home and crawling into bed. Across the aisle sat two of my classmates.

"Kristy, you don't look so good," one said sympathetically.

"I know. I am not feeling well."

As those words left my mouth so did the food I had eaten earlier. I threw up all over myself. It could have been an embarrassing situation but at this point, I was too sick to care. My classmate kindly handed me a napkin. I didn't make any eye contact with him and took the serviette and carefully wiped my face. Then I sank down in my seat, patiently waiting for the terrible bus ride to be over. I was praying to God with all my might that I wouldn't throw up again.

I had felt so ill that when I got off the bus and arrived home, I didn't even have the energy to make it to my own bedroom downstairs. Instead, I lay on my parents' bed. When mom got home from work she checked on me immediately. For the next couple of hours she rushed between her bedroom to check on me and the kitchen to check on supper. Dad hadn't returned home from work yet.

That night was awful. I threw up every twenty minutes. I was so dehydrated that I eventually started to throw up stomach acid. It burned and I absolutely hated the taste and smell of it. Even the thought of it today makes me want to throw up. As I lay squirming in my parents' bed, I thought up some crazy idea that I had fish poisoning. My parents and I had gone fishing the evening before and maybe one of the fish I touched gave me something. Possible, right? Every time I started dozing off, I dreamt about fishing and being poisoned. Perhaps I got salmonella.

Mom grew more concerned because I had not stopped throwing up so she took me to emergency at the Medicine Hat Regional Hospital. We arrived at about 10 o'clock at night and were given a room quickly. We stayed in emergency for several hours before being discharged. The doctors gave me morphine through intravenous (IV), to help relax me and take away the pain in my stomach and the pain in my legs that I had had earlier that day.

"If she's still sick in the morning, Mrs. Plotsky, please bring her back to emergency," said a doctor. Mom nodded.

"As if," I thought to myself. I'd be better by morning. Really, it must just be some kind of stomach bug. A 24-hour flu that would be out of my system as soon as it arrived.

That morning I woke up with my eyes so swollen I could barely open them. On top of it all, the nausea was still there. Great. That meant another hospital trip. Mom and I drove back to emergency. There was definitely something wrong with me.

The ER department admitted me immediately and started the process of running tests. My blood was taken and a series of scans and tests were done. After about an hour, the blood results came back and showed that my albumin, a main protein of human blood plasma, was significantly low, which could indicate why my eyes were swelling and why I was getting sick all the time. We didn't know why my albumin was low and the doctors in Medicine Hat were stunned. Three days later, Dr. Hak transferred me to the Alberta Children's Hospital in Calgary, Alberta.

My parents drove me the three hours to Calgary to be admitted and my life changed forever. At the time, the Alberta Children's Hospital was located off of 17th Avenue South West. (This is the old hospital. A new children's hospital was built in 2006.) I recall the sounds of a busy emergency department when I first walked through the hospital doors. There were the sounds of blood pressure monitors beeping, doctor's names being paged over the intercom and kids crying in the waiting room. The various noises were overwhelming and the unfamiliar scene of a busy emergency was frightening. I wanted nothing more than to go home. But I couldn't and neither could my parents. Thankfully, while I was in the hospital, they stayed with family in the city. My brother, 15 at the time and still in school, stayed home to take care of our dogs and house.

In the two weeks that I was at Children's, we saw many different doctors. First, I saw a cardiologist, a heart doctor, and then gastroenterologist, an internal medicine doctor that specializes in diseases of the digestive tract. The team of physicians responsible for my care contacted cardiology because they thought my illness had something to do with the heart. Then the team decided it was not heart related so cardiology was then not involved in my care. The team consulted with oncology, cancer specialists, and then it was decided that I didn't have cancer. Finally, after a few weeks of many needles, tests and different specialists, doctors diagnosed me with lymphangiectasia, a disorder of the lymph vessels.

"Kristy, you have lymphangiectasia," the doctor told me, sounding somewhat thrilled that we had finally come to a conclusion and, perhaps, even solved the mystery of the sick girl from Medicine Hat. Lymphangiectasia is a disorder characterized by chronic diarrhea and loss of proteins, such as albumin, from the digestive tract. It occurs when lymph vessels supplying the lining of the small intestine are blocked. It's a disease that even the most brilliant physicians don't know exactly what it's all about. What we knew for sure was that lymphangiectasia was extremely rare.

Well, this would explain why my albumin was low. The physicians at the Alberta Children's Hospital were completely bewildered that I had this disorder because the usual symptoms the disease presented didn't occur for me. The only typical symptoms I was showing were low albumin and swollen eyes. According to medical text books then, a person with lymphangiectasia should have swelling in many different areas of the body, not just the eyes. I should have looked like the Goodyear Blimp. It was also noted in the medical literature that people who have lymphangiectasia can live with the disease for up to five years from the time of diagnosis. Therefore, the end result was that I was probably going to die within five years. What! I only have five years to live? Surely there was a mistake, especially because I wasn't showing the exact symptoms.

The doctors wanted to be absolutely sure that I had lymphangiectasia and wanted to perform a biopsy. A biopsy is a surgical procedure where a physician makes an incision near the area of tissue he/she would like to biopsy. In my case, the doctor wanted to biopsy my lymphatic system. The lymphatic system is part of the immune system that has vessels that carry fluid towards the heart. The lymphatic system also aids in helping the immune system by filtering out and destroying pathogens (bad stuff).

My biopsy was scheduled for August 1995. It would be my first significant medical procedure and I'd receive IV anesthetic and be put to sleep. It was going to be the first surgery in a series of surgeries to come.

***

It was biopsy week. We travelled to Calgary a few days early to enjoy some time with family. We went to Callaway Park, an amusement park, for a day filled with fun. It was too bad we had to leave the park earlier than expected because a construction worker accidentally cut the power line to the area. Luckily, we weren't on a ride at the time! (Some people got stuck on the log ride.)

The next day we arrived at the Alberta Children's Hospital. I was tired of seeing doctors already but I was hopeful that the biopsy would provide some much needed answers. Before the procedure, the doctors informed me that an incision was going to be about 2-3 inches below my right breast. Then it was go time.

I don't recall how I felt my first time under anesthetic but I was aware that my body didn't take well to it. The medical staff almost lost me on the operating table that day. My heart started pumping irregularly and my blood pressure was way above my normal. Once the doctors got everything under control, it was surgery as usual.

CHAPTER TWO

Girl on the other side of the curtain

BEEP. BEEP. BEEP. BEEP. BEEP.

I woke up after the surgery to the sound of my IV pump beeping. Loudly. I couldn't move because it hurt too much. The right side of my chest, just under my breast, was heavy and throbbing. I knew that was exactly where the doctors had made the incision.

The curtain was pulled between the rooms, making me aware I was probably sharing a room with someone. I didn't see my parents anywhere in sight. I felt scared at first that they weren't there to greet me but then I felt anger because I thought they should be there to greet me after surgery.

My IV pump was still going off. I had tubes in my stomach and every flinch I made, I could feel them. The pain was unbelievable and I couldn't comprehend that this was my new reality. Finally, I heard a voice… but it wasn't a familiar voice. It was a voice yelling. Yelling at me. Someone wasn't happy with me.

"Shut that fucking machine off!" screamed a girl. "Someone shut it off before I kick your ass."

Oh my! The voice scared me as she screeched about my IV pump but what could I do? I couldn't even move to find the buzzer for the nurse. There was no way I could defend myself if she decided to do what she was threatening to do. I didn't know what to do so all I did was cry. The tears poured down my face as I prayed and lipped the words, "Please God, help me."

He answered my prayer because a couple of minutes later, a nurse entered the room. As quiet as possible, I whispered to her about the girl on the other side of the curtain. In the midst of my story, my parents walked in. Not too long after, I was transferred to a different room and although I was in a lot of pain and could hardly move, my new roommate was much, much nicer. It might have been because she thought my family was a bit crazy.

It was getting late and I was readying myself for bed. I was going to brush my teeth and then go to sleep. Mom and my cousin Leanne were with me during the day and usually stayed until I was tucked securely in bed. Leanne was a dental hygienist at the time and saw an opportunity to teach both me and my roommate about brushing our teeth properly. (I think Leanne wanted to make sure her cousin had gleaming pearly whites.) My roommate and I sat on our beds with mirrors and our toothbrushes while Leanne went through her dental spiel.

Then I lifted my toothbrush topped with toothpaste to my mouth. Leanne got into demonstration mode and took her hand and folded it over my brushing hand and we started to brush together. She told me to "swish" the toothbrush from side-to-side and helped me make the movement. However, as she was saying "swish" and making the tooth brush swish, some toothpaste flecks sprayed out of my mouth and into her hair. Mom started laughing and then all of a sudden... Leanne grabbed a baby powder bottle and shook it at mom. Then mom grabbed a bottle of baby powder and before you could count to 10, there was baby powder everywhere. My roommate and I sat on our beds and laughed wildly.

The next morning, the curtains in my room were incredibly dusty. Except, it wasn't really dust. The room smelled good though.

When Leanne wasn't giving oral hygiene lessons or spraying baby powder on my mom, she was singing. Some days she would take the hospital curtains, drape them over her head like she was Julie Andrews in the movie The Sound of Music, and sing, "these are a few of my favourite things." These moments are a few of my favourite memories now. Back then, the funny moments lightened up the hospital room I shared with the other girl. I think about her often. She was about my age, maybe a year older, and had something terribly wrong with her pancreas. I wonder what happened to her.

After a few days in the hospital passed and I was able to move around, the first thing I did was look at my scar. (Examining my incision would become a ritual for me after each surgery.) I slowly lifted my arm and stared down at the scar. I had a very visible scar that started under my right breast and continued towards my back, under my armpit. The scar was flaming red with black woven in and out of it: the stitches. It was a perfectly straight line about 8 inches long. It was definitely longer than the doctors said it would be. I was shocked about the length. Seriously, they said it would be about three inches. This was much, much bigger! It made me think that maybe the surgery didn't go as planned. Amazingly, this is one of my least noticeable scars to date and in fact, a lot of people don't even know I have it. (Today, the skin above and below my scar is numb to touch, perhaps it's because the physicians had to cut some of the nerve endings where the incision was made.)

The first few days after my surgery, I just lay in bed while mom and dad sat in the room with me. It was around day three when I thought I could sit up in a chair for a while.

"May I sit in a chair?" I asked the nurse.

"Sure, Kristy," she said. "We'll put you in this chair over here." The nurse pointed to a chair at the right side of the bed. With her help, I gingerly positioned my legs until they dangled over the bed. The nurse and I then carefully brought me to a standing position. This is when I noticed how bad my scar hurt. When I went to straighten up, I realized that it was not an option. It was painful. Straightening my back hurt because I was stretching and pulling the scar. I also had draining tubes in my chest that were attached to the front of my body to drain air and fluids from the area around the incision. I realized I would probably be walking with a hunch for a few weeks.

The nurse and I shuffled slowly to the right of the bed, like a slow-motion ballroom dance couple. Finally, I got to the chair. Holding a pillow tightly against my chest, I deeply and slowly exhaled.

"What a relief," I thought to myself as I sunk into the chair. I was a little lightheaded but I enjoyed the moment of sitting. It was moments like this, sitting in a chair after surgery, that I would think about how thankful I was for mom and dad and the people who loved me. I sat in the chair for about 30 minutes before I was exhausted. I turned my head towards mom and asked her to get the nurse. Mom quietly left the room and minutes later, returned with my nurse trailing behind. We arranged for my transfer back to bed but during the commotion of moving IV poles and clearing a path to the bed, a sharp pain pierced my lungs. Every time I took a breath, pain stabbed me in the chest. Amidst gasping for air, I started screaming.

"I can't breathe! I can't breathe!"

The pain was stabbing me with every breath I took. I yelled in agony and tears welled up in my eyes.

"Okay, Kristy, okay," said the nurse as she calmly pushed the call button for help. "It looks like one of your chest tubes has come loose. We need to get you back into bed."

Dad was asked to leave so that the nurse could open my gown and tend to the detached drain tube.

The nurse somehow got me back into bed but I still couldn't breathe. I was scared and thought this was going to be the end for me. I laid there screaming for my life. Screaming for help. Screaming for my dad. If I was going to die then I wanted to see him one last time.

Immediately, two nurses rushed into my room and began working on repairing the loose chest tube. The pain was something I had never in my life felt before and it came with every single breath. The torment never dulled and I couldn't inhale fully. My eyelids were closed as tight as possible but tears were able to sneak their way through. As I exhaled the short amount of breath I had, I was stopped short again by piercing, stabbing pain. Trying to take my mind off my misery, one nurse encouraged me to talk about my dog Tinker.

"What kind of dog is he?" asked the nurse.

"He eee's a shih tzu," I sobbed while trying desperately to catch my breath in-between severe pain bouts.

"Kristy, on the count of three, we need you to hold your breath and hold very still. Okay?" said the nurse.

I opened my eyes, blinking slightly. Everything was blurry. I thought this was it. I wasn't going to live through this. Given the pain I was feeling, I assumed it was exactly what hell would feel like. I looked up at the nurse and quickly nodded my head up and down.

"One. Two. Three," she counted. I held my breath and at that moment, I prayed to God, "Help Me!" Moments later, a profound sense of peace came over my body. I was breathing without strain. The nurses were unable to repair the chest tube and had completely removed it. That day is marked on my memory. I will never forget it. Mom, dad and I even talk about it now and then. I can't imagine how I was able to endure that kind of agony. Honestly, I can't even find the words to describe the detail of what that pain felt like. It was a frightening day for me and my parents and I realized how quickly things can change.

About two weeks later, I was discharged from the hospital. The doctors informed us that my lymphatic system was unbelievably out of control. The biopsy confirmed that I did indeed have lymphangiectasia. Shamefully, I admit a part of me was thankful that I wasn't diagnosed with cancer. (I was worried about having chemotherapy and potentially losing my hair.) The discharge chart instructed I follow a strict diet upon release from the hospital. I was put on a low fat diet to help my body better absorb the fat I ate. The maximum amount of fat I could have in a day was 25 grams. If you think about it, one trip to Burger King would go beyond the maximum fat I could have in a day. My new way of eating was something our entire family would have to get used too. Some of these changes weren't going to be easy.

Another change was I had to take an oil called MCT oil. MCT stands for medium-chain triglyceride, which is a special oil that helps the process of breaking down the fat in the body. To put it pure and simple, I thought MCT oil tasted disgusting and wanted to throw-up every time I had to take it. (The thought of it makes me feel nauseous today.) I hated MCT and yet I was supposed to take two tablespoons a day. Despite the oil and the adjustments, I was happy I finally knew what was wrong with me and I could have my life back.

When we returned home, we started living by my new diet. Mom immediately switched from our regular two per cent milk, to skim milk. My paternal Great Grandma Crockford started to cook with the MCT oil. She made low fat butterhorns, which were actually delicious. When I went out with friends, I had a salad while they had hamburgers. It was very hard to get used to eating differently but I thought it was a small change to make for my health when I looked at the bigger picture.

I started Grade Eight in September 1995, attending full-time. I did miss some classes as I was making trips to Calgary to see my doctors.

However, even with the diagnosis of lymphangiectasia and my low fat diet, I was still getting sick and not feeling well. It seemed like we were missing a significant piece of the puzzle and my health kept deteriorating. With a series of more tests and scans at Children's in Calgary, my heart was finally ruled back in as a problem and we were scheduled to meet with the hospital's cardiology department. I met with Dr. Michael Giuffre and his colleagues Dr. Joyce Harder and resident doctor Dr. David Patton. The three cardiologists were working collaboratively with each other to find out what was wrong with my heart. No one had any answers at this point and I didn't know if I was going to live or die. Not knowing was sometimes the hardest part but then there was the waiting. I would soon learn that the waiting was the toughest.

In order to get an idea of what was going on with my heart, the cardiologists wanted to do a biopsy of my heart. A heart biopsy, also known as a cardiac catheterization, is where doctors insert a catheter (a tube) into a main artery and it's passed to the heart. In children, the catheter is inserted in the groin area through a vessel into the main artery. Once the catheter is inserted, the physician gently pushes the catheter, which has wire coil inside the tube, up towards the heart. Sometimes the patient is awake for the biopsy because anesthetic can be used to numb the area of the groin where the catheter is inserted. In my situation, I was put under general anesthetic and therefore, not awake for the procedure. A cardiac catheterization can confirm the presence of a heart problem; determine the severity of the heart disease and is used to assess the heart prior to heart surgery.

I went in for my cardiac cath, as I called it, on December 1, 1995. After the biopsy, you're required to lie flat on your back for four hours post procedure. This is due to the fact that the area in the groin where the tube is inserted is a main artery. Getting up too soon after the biopsy won't allow enough time for the small incision site to heal. (You can pass out in a matter of seconds if you bleed from that area.) I don't remember much about my first cardiac cath but I know there were concerns about how I would react to the anesthetic because my last experience with it didn't go so well.

I had the biopsy and then laid flat for four hours, counting down each hour. I was groggy from the anesthetic and so I slept a good part of the time. I also watched TV and visited with my parents. It seemed like the four hours would never pass. They did however and the next day I was discharged from the hospital. We left Calgary and made the three hour trek home without any new information about my prognosis from the doctors. Back at home, my leg and groin area were sore from the biopsy for the next week.

My next appointment in Calgary provided us with some answers. Apparently, the biopsy of my heart showed that it was being restricted from pumping. My cardiologists were certain that the lining around my heart was too tight and therefore, restraining the heart from pumping. The cardiologists felt that if we removed the lining, then my heart would be able to pump normally again. They also felt that it would cure the lymphangiectasia, which was now thought to be secondary to the heart problem. Removing the lining around my heart meant I would be cured. I would be healthy once again and able to eat whatever I pleased. No more low fat salad dressing. Ahh! The thought of having Chinese food again made me drool. Being cured also meant I wouldn't miss anymore school. No more hospitals – what an amazing thought!

Unfortunately, removing the lining meant open heart surgery. That was a troublesome thought. It meant cutting open my chest and exposing my heart so doctors could access the valves, muscles and arteries of the vessel. A physician would saw through my sternum because my heart rested beneath it. The sternum is the organ's skeletal armor and the central bone to which the ribs are attached.

This surgery would mark my first open heart surgery and I hoped, my last. When my cardiologist provided me with all the details, I was extremely uneasy and thought maybe the results of removing the lining wouldn't be in my favour. With much deliberation my team, including my doctors, my parents and me, decided it was a viable option. Open heart surgery it was but I couldn't fight a nagging feeling that there was more to my health problems than just a tight lining around my heart. Intuition or instinct, there was definitely something in the back of my mind constantly reminding me that this surgery was not going to help and we had a much bigger problem on our hands. Despite my reluctance, the surgery was scheduled for December 11, about 10 days after my biopsy.

I went home to wait for the procedure date. I fought my anxiety by telling myself open heart surgery could be the cure I was looking for. Over the next week, I did everything in my power to focus on the one positive outcome of the surgery: getting healthy. Everything else was just background noise and me being negative. My week at home was serene as I prepared myself for another surgery.

CHAPTER THREE

10...9...8

It's a long drive to Calgary when you're facing life-changing surgery. I passed the time in the vehicle by reading magazines like Teen Beat and drawing. Once at the hospital, it kind of felt like a second home. I met lots of new people but I did miss my own home on the acreage and was clinging to my memories of my last week there. I missed Tinker incredibly. He was my best friend in the whole entire world and understood me like nobody else. Since it was December, we were getting closer and closer to Christmas. I couldn't wait to get this surgery over and done with and get home to spend the holidays with my dog and family.

Preparation for the surgery took about three hours. My parents completed the usual paperwork consenting to the procedure after reading about the risks involved. My blood was drawn and my IV started. I entered the patient room of the hospital where I was meeting with the nurse. My stomach growled like a monster that hadn't eaten a thing in days... and I really haven't. I had been fasting since midnight the night before. I wasn't allowed to eat or drink after 12 a.m. prior to my surgery because I would be under general anesthetic. (It relaxes the digestive tract and airway muscles.) After the meeting with the nurse, I was transferred from the Alberta Children's Hospital to the Foothills Medical Centre, the largest hospital in Calgary, where my surgery was going to take place.

After arriving at the Foothills, I was greeted by another nurse who helped get me ready for my surgery. I slipped into the cold faded blue hospital gown, getting a shock from the static spark made by the fabric and dry Calgary air. As I was being prepped, I wondered what it would be like to be normal again: to be like all my friends. I knew I would have a long recovery from this surgery, probably similar to the one I had in August, but I was thrilled to be able to return to school in January and start a new year: 1996. The new year was going to be different and if all went well, I would be back in Medicine Hat in time for Christmas and living my life again. A quick jab of my intuition broke into my positive thoughts and reminded me, once again, that something more was wrong with me. That the problem wasn't only the lining around my heart. I could only pray that I was wrong and the doctors were right.

"Okay Kristy, if you are ready we can head down to the OR," the nurse said as she opened the curtain to my room. "They have called for you."

"I'm ready," I said quietly. I looked at mom and then at dad and stood up. We gave each other the usual hug and kiss and off I went on a stretcher to the operating room.

A team of doctors greeted me as I entered the OR. They tried to make me feel comfortable by engaging in small talk. I knew I was in great hands with cardiac surgeon Dr. Bhardwaj doing my surgery, as he was a fantastic surgeon. That is why my surgery was done at the Foothills Hospital.

The OR felt like a freezer and smelled of rubbing alcohol and disinfectant. The air in the room felt different and made it hard for me to breathe. I sometimes imagined this is what it would be like in outer space. I always wondered how nurses and doctors can do this every day. I was always amazed at how it seemed like just another day at the office for them. It was not like that for the patient: me. (Every time I visit an operating room, I'm fascinated by the different smells, the happy people and the many shiny instruments used to perform medical miracles.) Each OR experience is different for each patient but the one thing that remains the same is the uncertainty and, of course, the freezing cold temperature.

My skin stiffened as it made first contact with the chilly stainless steel operating table. I was not going anywhere now. (Except to sleep.)

The anesthesiologist hit my vein with the first jab. Wow.

"You're good," I said calmly, trying hard not to move. "I have bad veins so good job getting it the first poke."

The anesthesiologist turned his head in my direction.

"You're right," he replied. "You do have bad veins. They wanted to hide on me. I'm glad I didn't have to poke you twice. Okay, Kristy, that should do it. You can relax."

Now came the sleep part.

"I'm going to set this mask gently on your face," said the anesthesiologist. "Breathe directly into the mask and soon you should start to feel sleepy."

I nodded to let him know I had heard him. It was hard to talk with the mask on my face and air blowing directly at me through the mask. Despite the distractions, I needed to concentrate. It was this moment that I had a silent conversation with God. I had begun talking about death with him. I told him about my feelings of helplessness and having no control. I asked God to provide my parents with strength to deal with the uncertainty that lied ahead. Here I was, lying on a cold hard metal operating table, and within seconds I would be asleep and the doctors would begin cutting open my chest cavity. I reflected on my past surgery in August and vividly remember the chest tubes, the pain and the time it took for my scar to heal. This was the moment that was the hardest for me. I didn't know how I would wake up, what I would wake up to, and if there would be pain. I asked God to be with me and the doctors and then I started my ritual of counting backwards in my head, 10... 9... 8...

My eyes were blinking like crazy and keep squeezing shut. My eyelids are heavy and it was hard to open them. Was the surgery done? What was happening? There was an enormous amount of preparation for surgery and it takes a long time to get to the operating table but once the surgery is over, you feel like you've only been asleep for an hour. I knew better though. These surgeries can take longer than expected. I felt a tight squeeze or maybe a hug around my arm and then a few seconds later a slow release. I realized it was the blood pressure monitor. I also realized I can't talk; the endotracheal tube (also known as a breathing tube) is in my mouth.

The breathing tube helps keep my airways open and helped me breathe during surgery. There were chest tubes attached to the front of my chest. I was worried about these tubes because of my last terrifying experience of having one come loose and the pain it caused. Oddly enough, this was not how I expected to wake up. I guess I expected cheering and jumping from my family and my doctors, especially if the surgery was going to cure me. I tried desperately to make myself comfortable on the bed. Unbelievably, not one person was there to greet me when I woke up. But something else bothered me more than not having an entourage. Something that didn't feel right. I felt it in my gut. Was it because my chest was sore and throbbing? That must be it. I didn't feel right because of the fresh incision. This scar will be much more noticeable. I was sleepy and weak. I looked around and I realized I was in ICU. Hours passed by slowly but because I was so drowsy, I drifted in and out of sleep. People came to see how I was doing. I really didn't know. I was in some pain and couldn't eat because of the endotracheal tube (a tube inserted into my windpipe). Every now and then a family member swabbed my lips with water using a pink foam tip brush. Family came to visit me, including my brother and our cousin. My cousin had a Dr Pepper lip smacker and the smell reminded me of the soft drink. I thought to myself, "I'm so thirsty I could eat the lip smacker."

It had been at least four days now since the surgery and I hadn't received any answers. Nobody told me anything but then again, I was pretty drowsy and might not understand what was being said.

About a day later I was stable. I was transferred from the Foothill's ICU, to the Alberta Children's Hospital ICU. Time didn't speed up here. It dragged on and on.

One thing that helped me forget where I was (for a few minutes) were gifts my family left me. I have the greatest family in the entire world and shortly after my surgery they presented me with a basket full of wrapped presents. Each present had a little Post-it note with a short but sweet saying that represented the gift. While I was in ICU, I opened one present a day and the notes provided me with a positive message. I received some nice things like socks along with the message that said:

Woolly socks to keep you cozy from head to toe. Get better! We love you!

I liked magazines at the time and I got a few of those, plus a nice message:

Teen fashion and gossip to keep you in touch! We love you!

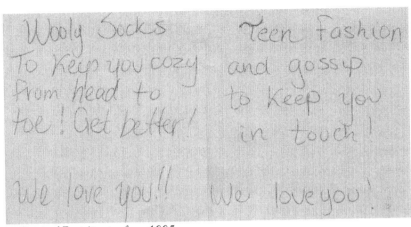

Original Post-it notes from 1995.

I get more visitors coming into my dark room. Everybody who came to see me tried to be quiet. My Great Aunt Carol stopped in on a day when I was particularly restless. I hated being restless, especially when I had company. It was that not-wanting-to-be-sick-in-front-of-people feeling. I really didn't want to be a burden. Really. My Great Aunt Carol could tell I was having a bad day and tried her best to make me comfortable. She rubbed my back and swabbed my lips. I loved having visitors but felt terrible that I wasn't able to be good company.

I couldn't talk to anyone because I was still intubated. I flagged mom down by using my hands to signal I wanted to write something. She raised the head of my bed slightly and handed me a piece of paper and a pen. My hand trembled as I grasped the pen and scribbled, "Am I healed?"

Mom gently brushed her hand over my forehead, sweeping back hair that had fallen in my eyes, and replied, "We have to wait until the doctor comes in, Kristy."

This didn't seem right to me. That gut feeling that the surgery wouldn't cure me, crept up on me again: a nauseating wave of anxiety.

Later, a nurse quickly, but quietly, entered my room and told me and mom that the breathing tube was coming out. (Good news!) It was the last apparatus to be removed from my body, other than my IV. The removal of the breathing tube was uncomfortable, accompanied by minor pain in my throat, but considering what I had been through already, it wasn't too much for me. Besides, if we were counting, this was my second major surgery. I was an old pro by now.

The first words I spoke were, "Mom, so, am I cured?"

Complete silence filled the room before mom said, "Kristy, I haven't spoken with the doctors yet so we just have to wait until we hear from them."

I called her bluff, but only in my head. I didn't say anything out loud because I didn't want to hurt her feelings. I knew she was lying. I knew she had spoken with the doctors. If you knew my mom, you would know what I was talking about. She was a Momma Bear and protected her young. After any surgery I had, including biopsies, she was talking to the doctors right away to find out what they knew, even if there was nothing to report. Mom was not the kind of mother who sat and waited for the doctors to come to her. She went to them. I knew she had already met with them. What was keeping her from telling me what they had said?

Meanwhile, a couple of days passed and I was able to complete my scar ritual. I stared down at it and it, flaming red, stared right back at me. I was overwhelmed with how noticeable it was and wondered if I would ever be comfortable wearing a bathing suit again. This scar was definitely going to be hard to hide. It was a line from my lower abdomen to my upper chest, positioned perfectly between my breasts. I had two small holes, about one inch thick by half an inch tall, which was covered with gauze. The holes were where the tubes were placed to drain my chest. Funny, during my first surgery the chest tubes were so painful and hurt when they were taken out. But I didn't remember these chest tubes being removed. I guess it was because I was sleepy the first few days after the second surgery.

I had to patiently wait to talk to the doctors and that was hard. My intuition crept over me and covered me like a hospital blanket. It was not going away. Later that day, Dr. Giuffre, the cardiologist I had been waiting to speak with, came by. I asked him right away, "So, am I healed?"

His reply was calm but not reassuring, "Kristy, we need to talk.

Once you are in a room we will talk."

His words stuck in my head and I started to analyze the situation. It didn't sound good.

Eventually, I was transferred out of ICU and moved to the U Cluster (a unit in the hospital). I settled into my new room, hoping I wouldn't have to stay there long. I was feeling much better by this time, even more awake than in previous days. It seemed like every hour I was getting my strength back. I was even using a wheelchair when we went out to the courtyard or to the cafeteria. My Aunty Terry (dad's sister and also a nurse) took some time off work to help us out during the surgery. Having her around was great fun. She made me laugh a lot and she also gave my parents a break, when they needed it. I spilled some hot chocolate on myself in the cafeteria one time and my aunt, who didn't want me to feel bad, spilled some on herself too. That moment was a bright spot for me.

Aunty Terry was with me and my parents when Dr. Giuffre came to talk to me. He walked into my room, happy to see me as usual, and said, "Kristy, let's go talk with your family, okay?"

I nodded my head. I just wanted to know if I was cured or what was wrong with me. Mom pushed me in the wheelchair to a room with five chairs arranged in a circle. Mom, Dad, Aunty Terry, Dr. Giuffre and Dr. Harder sat in the chairs while I sat in the wheelchair. Dr. Giuffre sat next to Dr. Harder, directly diagonal from me. We looked like we were crowded around a camp fire. Unfortunately, there was no camp fire.

We sat in silence for at least five minutes before anyone spoke. You seriously could have heard a pin drop. Dr. Giuffre finally broke the quiet by reviewing my medical situation thus far. He spoke clearly and confidently and was intent on not missing one piece of information. He reminisced on what we had originally thought was wrong with me and defined what wasn't wrong with me. He wasn't getting to the part I wanted to know though.

"Spill it!" I demanded in my head to the doctor. "Tell me what's wrong. Now!"

Instead, I stayed quiet and tried to follow his words. He moved on to how we thought my heart was restricted from pumping and how removing the lining would help. He said Dr. Harder was adamant about the heart lining and was excited about the outcome of the operation but...

I hung onto the word but. In the dictionary the word but is used in the beginning or end of a sentence to introduce something that's true or contrary to what has just been said. I took this *but* to mean the latter: contrary to what Dr. Giuffre had just said. This meant the lining around my heart was not the problem?

"Kristy, when Dr. Bhardwaj went in to remove the lining around your heart, he was very disheartened and shocked when he found that your heart is much enlarged," he paused and then slowly continued.

"Kristy, your heart is very sick and you require a heart transplant. The only option we have now is to put you on the transplant waiting list, for a heart transplant."

Seriously, did I hear him correctly? I needed a heart transplant? The room was quiet. It was like we were frozen in time. I wished we could go back a couple of minutes before I heard the words *heart transplant*.

Dr. Giuffre slowly repeated the words, heart transplant, several times. He made it clear that there were no options for me other than receiving a new heart. Dr. Giuffre also made it clear that in the end, it was my decision to agree to being put on the transplant waiting list. He said I was the boss and the doctors were part of my team, my pack of wolves.

"We are a pack of wolves and you are the pack leader," he said.

"Whatever you choose to do, is what we will do."

I felt the tears starting to form and I tried hard to stop them from falling. It was no use and they came down like a waterfall. I could hear sniffles from my aunt, who was noticeably crying. I looked at dad and he was white like he had seen a ghost. Mom had tears trickling down her face. Something inside told me that they had known what the doctor was going to tell me and they had needed time to digest the information before letting me in on my fate. I was only 13 years old. Having a heart transplant was a major decision for someone that young. I felt as though I was having an out of body experience. Maybe I was stuck in a bad dream.

But I wasn't.

Dr. Giuffre explained to me that the heart was a muscle in the body and it knew no race and no sexual orientation. However, the donor of the heart that I would hopefully receive must be an identical match in terms of blood type and size in order for the transplant to be successful. There were many tests that organs go through in order to be considered for donation. I would also have to go through numerous tests before I could be put on the transplant list.

I thought the worst had already happened. I needed a new heart. Then another thought entered my mind: someone had to give me the heart. Someone had to die so I could live. I couldn't handle the thought of someone dying and having their heart inside my body. Why should I live and they die and who gets to decide that?

When I voiced my concerns about someone dying for me to live, Dr. Giuffre told me that the only way for someone to be considered a heart donor was that the individual must be confirmed brain dead by a physician. I didn't understand what Dr. Giuffre meant when he said brain dead but then he explained it to me. He said being brain dead meant when the brain lost function and was no longer active. When a patient was pronounced brain dead, their brain had ceased function, however, their organs still functioned as if they were on a heart-lung machine.

The information was all new to me. Before now, I hadn't even known you could donate your organs. It was something I had never thought about. I felt ashamed for being so selfish, never giving a thought to organ donation and knowing there must be others like me waiting for new hearts. I quietly pondered what Dr. Giuffre had told me and asked myself if I would donate my organs to someone in my position. I was trying to look at it from a different point of view. I realized I would definitely donate my organs, especially if it meant saving a life.

"What would I need my organs for if I was going to die anyway," I thought to myself.

Despite my reasoning, I was aware it was going to take some time before I fully understood what I had to go through. I also think, at this moment, I was still in the denial stage and didn't comprehend that my heart was that sick. It was hard to believe when you can't see it.

Dr. Giuffre then gave me a name for what I had: restrictive cardiomyopathy, a rare heart disease that restricts the heart from pumping. The only cure... a heart transplant. Dr. Giuffre said he would arrange for my assessment in Edmonton right away and then I would be put on the waiting list for a heart. It was crucial we did the assessment as soon as possible because restrictive cardiomyopathy cases usually died within one year of diagnoses. We didn't know how much time I had left because we didn't know exactly when the first symptoms of the disease had presented. There would be no warning if my time ran out. If it did, it would be sudden and I would just die.

Restrictive cardiomyopathy is an incredibly rare heart disease and at this time, in the mid-90s, there was barely any information on it. What we did know then was it wasn't hereditary and so didn't run in families. Due to the rarity of the disease and the diagnosis of lymphangetasia, Dr. Giuffre was seeking a second opinion from the Mayo Clinic, a world class health institution in Rochester, Minnesota.

We returned to my room and everything was the same. Except completely different. Now I needed a heart transplant. I needed to wait... wait for someone to die to save my life. In my head I thought about the moments before we went into the room with Dr. Giuffre and after we left. Did I come out a different person? I wanted so badly to know what was wrong with me. Now I knew and now I didn't want to know. I wish I had some kind of time machine that sent me back to when I was healthy, or at least I thought I was healthy. Never in my wildest dreams did I think I would need a new heart. Geesh. I mean I knew I felt crummy often but to need a new heart? The doctors must not be looking properly. Was I really that sick??

I was lost in my thoughts when a knock at the door brought me back to earth. I looked up and my nurse was standing there. She apologized for interrupting and wondered if a couple of doctors, who were currently completing their residency, could come in and examine me and perhaps listen to my heart. Without hesitation I agreed. Secretly, I was hoping that the residents would find that there was nothing wrong with me and prove Dr. Giuffre wrong.

The doctors patiently waited outside of my room while each one got to examine me and listen to my heart. Doctor after doctor came in until I realized there was now a line-up of at least 10 doctors waiting to get the chance to listen to my sick heart. I was overwhelmed and I still didn't understand what all the hype was about. The news of needing a new heart and now the line-up of resident doctors outside my door was becoming way too much to handle. My parents could see I was starting to fade away. I love my family to pieces because it was during these moments when things are so hard that they find humour – or a really amazing way to cheer me up. We decided that if any doctor wanted to listen to my heart, he or she would have to pay up: 25 cents. We put up a sign with a little penny jar that I had received as gift and set it up at the front of my room. Oh my goodness! Before I knew it, I had a jar full of quarters.

Later that night, I had a nice break from all the medical staff, just enough time to make a few important phone calls to my brother and grandparents. It was weird that they already knew all the important information about me. This led me to conclude what I already knew: my parents knew all along. For some reason, the thought of them telling everyone for me actually relieved me in some small way. It took the burden off my shoulders of having to share the life-changing news. Sitting on that payphone, talking to my grandma and hearing her cry as she told me everything would be all right, was very difficult. I knew grandma would have changed places with me if she could and I was sad that there was nothing either of us could say that would change the situation. I think I had another out of body experience then. I tried hard not to look at my parents, who were standing a few metres away from me. They tried to be so positive for me, only focusing on one day at a time.

The hospital was quiet around me while I listened to Grandma Jackie. For a few seconds I lifted my head and directed my eyes off the hospital floor. Everything was the same: the same as the night before. I looked around some more. Nothing had changed. Absolutely nothing. It was amazing and I realized life went on even though I felt terrible inside. People who were in that area of the hospital had no idea what I was going through and, at the same time, I had no idea what they were going through. Was this the worst that it was going to get or was there something worse about to come? I tried to imagine something worse and then it hit me like a punch in the gut – oh right – someone has to die for me to live.

I hung up the phone with grandma and called a few friends in Medicine Hat. Their lives were carrying on too and without me. It almost felt like they didn't care. Did they not know I was sick? Then again, perhaps I was overreacting. Maybe a heart transplant wasn't such a big deal? The more I repeated that in my head, the more I wanted to cry. It seemed like it was no big deal for everyone else, except for my family and me. Were we being too dramatic?

After I made all the necessary phone calls, I quietly returned to my room.

When I entered, I saw a little bag of candy with a note and .25 cents taped to it. Dr. Giuffre must have heard that I was charging doctors and left me a treat in my room.

"Kristy, see you Saturday. Don't eat too much candy," the note said.

Note from Dr. Giuffre.

Earlier that Friday, Dr. Giuffre gave me a pass. I would spend the weekend out of the hospital but I would have to check in with him before I was officially discharged. Hopefully I'd be back in Medicine Hat soon. I sure missed Tinker. I had a photo of my dogs thanks to my Aunty Terry. She gave me a picture of Tinker and Chuck to keep by my hospital bedside. On the back of the picture it says, "Kristy, we miss you. Hurry home."

Me with Dr. Giuffre during a clinic visit.

CHAPTER FOUR

Christmas questions

It's Sunday and after being discharged from hospital, I was standing at the entrance of a Calgary Costco. The cold December air snaked its way through the open door and crowd of people until it reached me. I shivered. Christmas was only two weeks away and the song *Silver Bells* was being played over the store's intercom. I love Christmas. It's my favorite time of year. Finally I saw my entourage approaching the entrance. My family and I are making a quick shopping trip before driving home to Medicine Hat. I can't wait to get home and see Tinker, although I was already exhausted from standing a short five minutes.

"I'm tired and still a little sore from the surgery," I said quietly, trying not to burden anyone.

"Kristy, do you want to get in the shopping cart?" asked my cousin Rob (always so generous). "I could push you?"

"What a great idea," I said as I climbed into the cart with a little help from mom. Rob was hilarious driving me around in that shopping cart. He was pretending to crash every corner we turned. While hurtling through the aisles we pretended I was a race car driver. I was having fun but I had noticed prior to lifting myself into the shopping cart, that my foot was tingly. I didn't want to make a big deal out of nothing and so I kept it to myself. Eventually, the tingling sensation became unbearable and I had to say something.

"Mom, I can't feel my foot. It feels really numb."

I pulled off my shoe and sock and to everyone's shock (including mine) my foot was as white as snow. By the look on everyone's face, I knew my snow-white foot was not normal.

"Kristy, I think we better take you back to the children's hospital to have that checked out," mom said, looking at me and then at my Aunt Terry. Everyone said I should go back to emergency and make sure something wasn't seriously wrong. Part of me agreed that we should go back to the hospital but then another part was angry. I was upset with myself for showing them my foot. It was probably nothing. We should drive home and if my foot doesn't get better, then we can visit the Medicine Hat hospital.

After making our way to the checkout and paying for our items, dad brought the car to the front entrance. I stepped outside while a blizzard blew snow around me, and said goodbye to my Aunt Terry, Uncle Steve and my cousins Leanne and Rob. Then I climbed into the vehicle. We drove back to the hospital in silence.

It was a terrible car ride. I felt like a prisoner who had escaped from jail and had just been caught. I felt like my freedom was being taken away. When we pulled into the emergency parking area at the Alberta Children's Hospital, there was a knot in my stomach and a lump in my throat. I tried not to cry because I didn't want my parents to see me upset.

We told the physicians in the emergency department that I had a cardiac biopsy the beginning of December and two weeks ago I had just undergone open heart surgery to remove the lining around my heart. We shared what that surgery had concluded – I needed a heart transplant. Well, I'm sure you know what happened: I was admitted that day. By this time, I severely dreaded hospitals, especially as a patient.

After I was admitted, numerous tests were ordered and performed. The tests confirmed I had a blood clot in my heart. It was a serious situation. The doctor informed us that if this blood clot moved one inch in any direction, it could kill me. The medication I needed to dilute the clot would have to be flown in from Edmonton and cost $20,000.00. (My family didn't have to pay the high price tag on the medication, it was covered by Alberta health care, and to this day I can't believe that medication to save someone's life, costs that much. We are so fortunate in Canada that our medical system doesn't require patients to come up with that kind of money.) Unfortunately, there was no guarantee the expensive drug would even work but it was our only hope. I went back into ICU.

This was an incredibly low time for me in my life, but I was fortunate because I always had my family. Santa Claus also came to visit while I was in ICU. Seeing Santa sure brightened my day. While I was visiting with him, the clot in my heart moved, which caused severe chest pains, and I turned grey. Santa had to leave my bedside so the doctors and nurses could tend to my health.

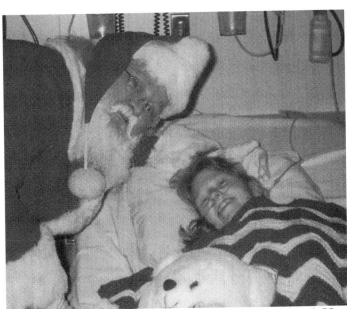

Getting my picture taken with Santa Claus at the Alberta Children's Hospital. My mom told me that when he left my bedside he was in tears.

The blood clot in my heart slowly started to dissolve and several days later there was talk about transferring me to the Medicine Hat hospital so I could be closer to home if I had to be in the hospital over Christmas. But there was a problem with that plan because I was still on heparin drip to dilute the blood clot. Heparin drip is a medication, an anticoagulant, that stops blood from clotting. It's given to patients through IV and therefore patients need to be watched carefully. Too much heparin or too little can be deadly. Because I was still on the drip, doctors in Calgary were leery about discharging me given my previous history of having blood clots. We needed to be careful although the only thing I wanted for Christmas was to be home for the holidays.

The doctors in Calgary talked with the doctors in Medicine Hat and I was allowed to be discharged from the Alberta Children's Hospital and flown to the Medicine Hat hospital where I would be admitted and observed carefully while I continued with heparin drip. At this time, the Medicine Hat hospital didn't have much experience with young children on heparin drip so precautions had to be taken but I was positive that nothing bad would happen. I felt extremely confident being in the Medicine Hat medical professionals' hands. My trip was arranged and I was looking forward to being "home" for Christmas.

Mom and dad left Calgary a few hours prior to me and drove to Medicine Hat. They met me at the Medicine Hat Regional Hospital when I arrived in the ambulance. (My airplane landed at the airport and there was an ambulance waiting to transport me to the hospital.) I was immediately taken to ICU where the nurse started checking my IV and vitals. I spent the next few days in ICU before finally being transferred to a room. I was so relieved to be back in my home town. I really needed to see familiar surroundings and faces, especially while the news of needing a heart transplant sank in.

My time in the hospital wasn't quiet time: my story became news. While my family gathered around my dimly lit room, reporters and camera men were there too asking questions and taking photos. The big news was about the Medicine Hat girl who may be spending Christmas in the hospital.

My story made the front page of the local Medicine Hat paper. Mom handed me a copy of the article with the headline:

Christmas in Hospital for Hat Girl.

I really didn't like the picture of me that went along with the article. I was half smiling…or frowning (not sure which, maybe both?). The magazine I had been reading while the photographer was snapping pictures, was opened to a full page advertisement of Jockey underwear. (We laugh about this picture today.) In any event, I thought the newspaper article was well-written, even though it was hard to believe it was about me. Thankfully, the headline turned out to be wrong. On December 22, 1995, with only three days until Christmas, I found out that I was going to be discharged the next day.

This was my first interview after hearing the news I needed a heart transplant.
Printed with permission from the Medicine Hat News.

I was lucky I didn't have to spend the holidays in the hospital and I was discharged two days before Christmas. I was ecstatic to see Tinker and he gave me so many kisses and wagged his tail so hard I thought it might fall off. Just to squeeze him in my arms made my day.

Some sadness did catch up to me. Before Christmas dinner at Grandma Jackie's, my brother and I started arguing about something. I can't say I was in the best spirits and I have to admit, I was feeling sorry for myself and a little envious of everyone else. I was jealous that everyone around me was healthy. Their hearts were all in perfect working order. Why was I the one who had to have a heart problem?

No one else had to worry about dying. Just me. I started to cry and my brother couldn't figure out what was wrong with me. Mom said that I had been through a lot in the past few months and crying was only normal. I think that was one of the few times I broke down in front of my parents. I wanted to be so strong for them and for everyone but sometimes I just couldn't do it.

When we got to grandma's house everyone treated me as normal as possible, although I knew everyone was scared. What were they scared of? I realized that needing a new heart wasn't the scary part: it was thinking about the surgery and getting a new heart in time. The moment a heart became available, what would those few moments be like for me and my family and what would it be like for the family on the other side? It was a lot to think about and at times I really couldn't wrap my brain around it. I felt sad thinking how I would triumph over another family's immense loss. It's amazing how a grieving family, going through the most tragic time of their lives, can be so selfless and think about saving the life of someone else. What an incredible gift.

After I had been home for a few days, we realized the stairs were becoming a bit of an issue for me. It was too much exertion for me to go up and down and down and up. I was also starting to feel more tired as the days passed. We didn't want to put any extra strain on my heart so a bedroom was arranged on the main floor of our walk-out bungalow. It was getting to the point when I couldn't do much and I had to take it easy. My life was put on hold and for how long, nobody knew.

It was the Christmas of 1995 that I realized how fortunate I was to have such a close family. It occurred to me that not many families get together because so many things pull them apart. My family was strong and I was lucky to be a part of them. The little things about them started to make me happy and realize how blessed I was. Grandma's house was never silent during the holidays and our house smelled so good from mom's cooking. Christmas Day was fantastic because after my immediate family opened gifts, both sets of grandparents came for tea. This was the opportunity for me and my brother to show off all our cool Christmas presents. The best gift for me was being home.

After the craziness of the holidays died down, mom had to go back to work as did dad. When they were at their jobs, I stayed at Aunty Terry and Uncle Steve's home or with my grandparents. To be honest, sometimes it was more fun staying with family then to be at school. It was definitely more fun than being in the hospital. Before I knew it, Christmas was over and we were planning our trip to Edmonton for my transplant assessment.

The start to 1996 looked a lot different than what I had imagined a couple of months before. Instead of planning to go back to school with my friends, I was planning a trip to Edmonton. I was still going to have tests, but not the kind most 14 year olds write.

On January 4, Dr. Giuffre received a reply to his letter to the Rochester Mayo Clinic. Dr. James B. Seward, a doctor in cardiovascular disease at the Mayo, confirmed the lymphangiectasia was secondary to the restrictive cardiomyopathy. He wrote: *Lymphangiectasia is very rare and I cannot recall a specific association of restrictive cardiomyopathy in that disease. However, it is apparent that a chronic congestive syndrome can exist in the presence of restrictive cardiomyopathy, which probably increases some of the manifestations of the lymphangiectasia.*

Dr. Giuffre showed mom and dad Dr. Seward's letter and they were relieved with what they read. It was the heart causing the lymphangiectasia, which meant a heart transplant was a viable option for me. If the lymphangiectasia hadn't been secondary to the restrictive cardiomyopathy, then we wouldn't have been put on the transplant list. The lymphangiectasia had a prognosis of five years and a transplant wouldn't have solved anything.

As you know, before my name could be added to the organ transplant waiting list, I needed to go through several tests for the transplant assessment. The assessment took approximately one week and involved many examinations and many visits from the cardiologist and other specialists such as a nephrologist (kidney doctor) and pulmonologist (lung doctor). It was a cold January morning when I woke early to start packing for Edmonton. It was going to be a long week ahead of me but after a year and half of hospitals, needles, and many doctors, we finally had the answer to a long unanswered question.

We left for the Alberta capital on January 15, 1996 and arrived at Jim and Bev's house that evening. They were extended family and even though I didn't know them well, Grandma Jackie said they were nice and would love to have us stay with them. Bev and Jim's daughter Jody was staying with them too and had set the basement up as her own little suite. This is where my parents slept. I slept downstairs in Jody's son's room. Jody's son was only three at the time and it was nice to have a little kid running around the house to take my mind off things. He knew every single Jim Carrey movie by heart and he loved Garth Brooks. I have to say I became quite attached to the whole family. I started calling Jim "Grumpy Jim" or "Jimbo" and we sure had our share of laughs. Even though my parents and I were settled in at a great home, we were still scared about what was coming with the new doctors. All I knew is that my new doctor's name was Dr. Coe.

I was shy and when first meeting a new physician, it took me some time to get comfortable with the person. After a while, you get to know him or her so it's hard to change to another doctor you don't know. This reminded me of Dr. Hak in Medicine Hat, who originally transferred me to Calgary and the Alberta Children's Hospital. The children's hospital was scary at first but we met Dr. Giuffre and we got to know him. We loved him and didn't want a new doctor. In fact, I didn't even want to be in another new city let alone another new hospital. I hated the new and only wanted the old but I had no choice.

The day came for assessment and we headed to Edmonton's University of Alberta Hospital. I was surprised by the place. It didn't look like a hospital once you were inside. On the main floor, you could look up and it had all these windows that made it appear like an apartment building. (There were some signs it was a hospital. The wall colours were a bit dreary and I wasn't used to seeing adults who were sick too.) The U of A had an atrium in the cafeteria and from here, you could see the elevator going up and down to all five floors of the hospital. It was big.

We headed to check in for my blood work and to meet the new doctor. Linda, the heart transplant coordinator, greeted us. She was the one helping us with the assessment and at first she came off a bit strong. The coordinator was blunt, to the point, and didn't sugar coat anything. I don't really know what I had been expecting. I certainly didn't think the hospital staff was going to bow down to me and say, "Oh, here is the girl from Medicine Hat who needs a heart transplant. Treat her extra well." But the atmosphere could have been warmer. I know they must go through this kind of thing all the time but the assessment process was new for me.

Linda began filling in all the necessary paper work and asked me a simple question.

"Kristy, do you want to have a heart transplant?"

"No, I do not want to have a heart transplant," I replied, confused as to why she would even ask me that. Our conversation ended and my parents and I went on to meet Dr. Coe at the cardiology clinic.

The first time I met Dr. Coe, he was wearing green OR scrubs. He spoke calmly and with reassuring tone. (Mom usually did the talking while I just sat and listened.) He told us about the transplant itself and what exactly would happen. Dr. Coe encouraged me to meet with other people my age who had received heart transplants. He thought it was a good opportunity to talk to people like myself and also to see how the family dealt with life after transplant. My parents thought it would be a good idea as well. As it turned out, while we were in Edmonton for the assessment, a family was there with their daughter, who had undergone a heart transplant not long ago. We agreed to meet the night before we left Edmonton.

The girl made an impression on me. I was blown away by her strength and courage. The things she had gone through seemed so hard but she made it seem like going through a heart transplant was easy. I found myself staring at her, envious of how brave she was and wanting to trade places. She was already well on her way to a regular life with school and friends while I had lots of medical mountains to climb.

The visit with the girl was helpful but tough. Looking back, I think I didn't want to hear any success stories because I wasn't a success yet. During my assessment in Edmonton, the transplant team tasked me with writing an essay on what death meant to me. I no longer have a copy of those words. It's too bad because I would like to read what I thought death was all about at aged 13.

CHAPTER FIVE

Opposite of Normal

When January 18 finally arrived, it meant the transplant assessment and our week in Edmonton was over. We were ready to go home to Medicine Hat. We left that night for Calgary and stayed in the city at my cousin's house. The next day, we rolled into Medicine Hat. Life seemed to be going okay. I was keeping up with school through distance learning and attending classes when my health allowed me to go. I had to take it a little easier than usual and cut back on activities that I may have participated in prior to being sick like going for bikes rides and hiking through the coulee.

I was now on medication to help my heart including diltiazem for blood pressure, baby aspirin, warfarin (brand name Coumadin) to decrease developing blood clots, and furosemide (brand name Lasix) to reduce fluid in my body. I took the medication in the morning and afternoon and it didn't bother me too much. I didn't like taking pills in front of my friends but I really had no choice. It was important for me to take the medication on time and as directed by the doctor.

We were seeing Dr. Hak in Medicine Hat on a regular basis, about every week, and we spoke to both Dr. Giuffre and Dr. Coe often. I received a setback late January when we learned I hadn't been listed on the transplant waiting list. Why? I had been assessed as not ready for the big commitment. It stemmed from the answer I gave Linda when she asked if I wanted a heart transplant. As you know, I replied no. Not because I wasn't ready, but because it was a confusing and stupid question. Receiving an organ is a lifelong, ongoing commitment. During visits with doctors, they explained a heart transplant isn't like putting a new engine in your car. Receiving an organ actually requires much more maintenance, it's life changing. When I answered Linda's question, I took it literally: did I want a new heart? Of course a new heart wasn't something I wanted, but it was something I needed.

I didn't realize my future heart was tied to this one question. I felt bad. I guess I should have agreed but in my opinion, who in their right mind would answer yes? We had talked to Dr. Coe about our concerns with how Linda was handling our situation and how we felt she was a little to blunt and sometimes came off rude. Dr. Coe reassured us that Linda was in no way trying to be abrasive; she was just doing her job. Linda really wanted me to understand all aspects of having a heart transplant. It was not just about getting the organ, you have to take care of it and it was a big responsibility for someone so young. I was used to my parents doing a lot for me regarding my health care: if my mom didn't think it was a good idea, I didn't do it. Linda wanted me to be in charge of my own health and not always relying on my parents to make the decisions for me. (I completely understand this now as an adult. Later, Linda was a significant advocate for me and my family.) Better news came for me at the end of January at 8:00 a.m. On January 31, 1996, Dr. Coe called mom to say I was listed on the Western Canada transplant waiting list.

***

While I was waiting for my new heart, news about my medical situation was spreading quickly in Medicine Hat. The media thought it was a fascinating human-interest story. We started doing interviews with local television stations like CFCN and CHAT TV regarding my recent diagnosis. I kind of liked the attention but I didn't understand why my story was a big deal. I did use the opportunity to spread the word and educate people on organ donation.

I tried to keep up with my school work by doing correspondence and attending school when I felt well or didn't have appointments. I never went to class though, I went to the library instead to work on my correspondence courses. This was also a good opportunity for me to get one-on-one help with teachers if I was having trouble in specific subjects. Another bonus was I was able to visit with friends. They'd stop by the library to see me, which kept my social life alive.

Being a teenager usually means you get to be a bit more independent. Not me. My parents had to keep tabs on me at all times. After I went on the transplant list, we started carrying around a pager, which mom held onto. If the beeper went off, we were provided with strict instructions, which meant calling the U of A hospital immediately to see if a heart was available. The beeper could be set off by so many things, like airplanes or radioactive rays in the sky. There could be dry runs too that meant we could call Edmonton and if they confirmed they found a donor who was a match, we would have to start driving to Edmonton. We could get all the way there and not end up with a heart. Sometimes something happens during the transportation of the organ that prohibits the transplant from taking place. Thankfully, I never experienced any dry runs.

I tried not to worry about the beeper. The little black pager from AGT Mobility was deceiving because it was a small piece of ordinary plastic but it could actually save my life. From time-to-time I would look at it and think to myself, "Do I really want this to go off?"

"What will happen when it does?"

"Will I live or die?"

The doctors had told me that some people wait years for a heart transplant. Since this was now a subject close to my heart (pun intended), speaking out about organ donation became an outlet for me. Aunty Terry was a nurse at the hospital in Medicine Hat and she knew what sick people and their families went through. Together my Aunty Terry and I, with the help of mom, set up a booth at the Medicine Hat Mall to raise organ donation awareness. I was amazed at how many people walked by us or gave us dirty looks. Not many were interested in hearing about organ donation and I don't know why. Perhaps it's never talked about in polite society? Are people so afraid to die that we ignore the subject completely? The experience tarnished my world view slightly and I started to think that some people were ignorant and selfish. Here I was, 13 years old, and I had already faced death and stared it in the face a few times. I was not given any choice if I wanted to die or live and people were sauntering by me choosing to stay oblivious. They could have helped someone out of a tragic circumstance, yet they looked me in the face and ignored being educated about organ donation. It made me so angry but I knew I was once in their shoes. Before I was sick, I was ignorant too. I would like to think that if these people had a family member or a friend who needed an organ transplant, they would help. I never hated these people for their ignorance, I just wished they would open their minds a little more. You can't imagine how much you help when you donate your organs.

Blood work was part of my medical routine at home and I went to the cancer clinic at the Medicine Hat hospital. Another aunt worked there and it was nice to have a visit with her when we stopped in to get blood taken. Everybody knew us really well because we lived in a small town and my story had spread and touched many people. I loved going to the clinic to joke around with the medical staff and patients. The patients made me feel like all my problems were small and that I was okay. There were a lot of people at the clinic with cancer and I felt terrible for them because I had a treatment. I was just waiting to get it. These people didn't have that. I felt so bad and asked myself, "Why did God decide that I would have a disease that had a treatment, while these people fight for their lives against a disease that was so powerful and overwhelming."

For a few seconds, I was happy to be me, with my sick heart and all.

The doctors caring for me knew my time on earth was limited and that I was getting weaker. I think my parents knew it too. By this time I had developed a fairly solid relationship with God and I surrendered to whatever was going to happen was in his hands. I stayed humbled and tried to be thankful for every single moment I had with my family, my dog and my friends. A few weeks after being put on the transplant list, Dr. Giuffre had talked to my parents about double listing me in the United States to better my chances of receiving a heart. We had spoken with Dr. Coe about the situation and he felt that we should do what we thought best in our hearts. Dr. Giuffre helped us in the process to double list and spoke with the chairman of Alberta Health out-of-province assistance, Ian Bailes. Ian was the one in charge of such matters and assisted in our fight to double list.

I was now a celebrity across the province, making the front page of newspapers such as the Calgary Sun. My family didn't know what can of worms we were opening. I had only just been listed on the transplant list in Alberta for a few weeks and we wanted to double list. Dr. Giuffre felt strongly about this, as did my parents. Restrictive cardiomyopathy has a serious prognosis and sudden death is common with little or no warning.

Dr. Giuffre completed many hours of research regarding what centres we would be able to double list at in the States. We had looked at the possibility of double listing in California in Loma Linda, but unfortunately, that would require us moving to California. Regulations wouldn't allow us to stay in Medicine Hat while being on the list in California. Moving to California actually sounded exciting to me and I would be allowed to bring Tinker when we got his vaccinations up to date. A small part of me really wanted to move and I was thinking about all the people I would meet there. But only my parents would move with me and I would have to leave the rest of my close-knit extended family behind. We also found out that if we moved to California, we would be taken off the list in Edmonton. So moving to the sunny state defeated the purpose of being double listed.

Dr. Giuffre told us not to let our hopes crash as he was continuing to research other options. He had spoken to the Mayo Clinic in Rochester, Minnesota a few times (when they were trying to diagnose me earlier) and the clinic said it would allow me to be listed in Rochester and live in Medicine Hat. Great news! However, we faced another obstacle: funding for out-of-country care.

When there's care available in your own country, the government won't fund you to go elsewhere. However, we were limited in time: I might not live long enough to wait for an organ to become available in Canada. In February of 1996, good family friends, Art and Gwen, wrote to the premier of Alberta at the time, Ralph Klein, about my situation. They told him that the purpose of being double listed was to help defy the odds in getting a heart quicker. They wrote that my condition was incredibly rare and only Stanford University in California had treated children with the dual diagnosis of restrictive cardiomyopathy and lymphangiectasia. Disappointingly, nothing came out of the letter.

As the fight for my life continued, I pretended nothing was wrong and went to the movies with friends and chatted to them about school. I tried to be a normal teenager. Except everything in my life was completely the opposite of normal.

Medicine Hat, being a small city, really started to rally behind my fight against the government. With the help of Art, Gwen, Aunty Terry, Uncle Steve, and friends of the family, Nadine and Casey, we arranged an auction to raise money to help with the extra expenses of living in Edmonton or Rochester after the transplant. The auction was scheduled to be at the Seven Persons Community Hall on February 18, 1996. Double listing was still up in the air and the auction was in the midst of being planned when a much-loved figure was in the hospital fighting for her life.

My Great Aunt Estella Bray (Great Grandma Crockford's sister) was a wise and very sweet lady. She always had the answers to questions people hadn't even figured out to ask. She used a wheelchair and attended every family function since I could remember. It was odd to have someone who had been around me my entire life, not be there to give us her wisdom. Aunt Estella passed away on February 16, 1996, two days before my benefit auction. Great Grandma Crockford was never one to celebrate when someone passed away and unfortunately, my grandmother didn't come to my fundraiser. I understood. She was suffering too and very sad. Despite the sad circumstance, the auction turned out well. We called it a "Heart for Kristy" and everybody did such an amazing job. It was nice that people did all that work to help me. Items donated and auctioned off ranged from gift certificates to restaurants to a rug cleaner. The event lasted over eight hours and we raised approximately $40,000 dollars. The funds went into a trust fund to help my family wherever we ended up staying when I received the heart. It was also to help cover medication costs and some travelling expenses as well any other unexpected expenses. (One unexpected expense was the purchase of an adjustable reclining bed. When my lungs filled with fluid, having my chest elevated helped me to breathe.) It was great to see how many people turned out to the auction, even some of my close friends came. It was a lot of fun and one of my best days. I got up and thanked everyone for coming. I was humbled by my supportive community.

A week after the fundraiser, (February 26, 1996) I was planning on seeing a movie with my cousin Derrick and we left together from my house. Mom called to me as I was walking down the sidewalk. The hospital beeper had just gone off. I had to go back inside and wait.

I was numb. I had no feelings whatsoever. No panic, no fear, no tears. What was wrong with me? Why wasn't I reacting to this potentially joyful news? All I could really do was think about how the pager was ruining my life. How the stupid black box interrupted my chances of enjoying a movie with my cousin. The prospect that the beeper could be the harbinger of good health never crossed my mind. I really thought there was no hope.

Mom contacted Edmonton right away and we learned it was a false alarm. (The only other time the pager went off and it was a false alarm was a month later on March 29, 1996.) I was so relieved and I thanked God for the setback. Yes, I wanted to live but I was terrified of having my heart taken out…and someone else's put in. The other thought that never left me was someone had to die for me.

A HEART
FOR KRISTY
BENEFIT AUCTION

DATE:
FEBRUARY 18, 1996

TIME: 1:30 P.M.

PLACE: SEVEN PERSONS HALL

KRISTY PLOTSKY is a 13 year old grade 8 student at Seven Persons School. She lives on the outskirts of Medicine Hat with her brother Billy, Dad - Blaine and Mother - Margo.

In the past 7 months Kristy's life has changed dramatically. Kristy always enjoyed water-skiing, volleyball, downhill skiing and other activities with her family and friends. However through the early months of 1995 she started noticing that something was wrong. After many tests, 15 trips to Calgary, 2 major surgeries (1 open heart) and just about every test available, have found Kristy needs a new heart and a transplant is her only option. The words rare, never seen before, and no documented cases have come up many times.

A new heart for Kristy is an exciting option for her after the events of the past seven months. During this anxious time of waiting for a donor, Kristy has been very patient. Kristy's parents have also been patient but anxious. They are currently looking at a 3 - 6 month stay away from home when Kristy receives her new heart.

Many people have expressed their desire to help Kristy & her family. Along with practical encouragement to the family we can all help by supporting them financially while they are away from home. A benefit auction to raise funds to help with their stay away from home and the costs of medication not covered by Alberta health care is what this is all about.

You can help with the BENEFIT AUCTION by donating items or purchasing items at the auction. Hope to see you there.

FOR MORE INFORMATION CALL:
Gwen - 526-9692 or Nadine - 527-1863

Auction Services donated by Brent Schlenker of Schlenker Auction Service. Printing of flyers and posters donated by Prime Printing (1995) Ltd.

CHAPTER SIX

The double listing fight

We continued our fight for double listing as I stayed on the transplant list in Alberta. In the beginning, when I first knew I needed a heart transplant, I felt as though I would get my new heart in May. May was a special month to me, more so because it was my birthday month. I also thought May would be a good month because I would then have the summer to recover. I could spend some much needed time at home with my family and hopefully, return to school in September with my fellow classmates. I longed for that normalcy again, just to be like everyone else and not have my life on hold.

A few months into the waiting game seemed like forever. While waiting, I attended doctor visits, news conferences, did media interviews, watched TV and worked on school work. I tried to make it to school at least once a week. I also spent time going to church and it was a comfort to me. I had so many sleepless nights, lying awake thinking about my life. I was not certain anymore if I would live or die. When all you hear are the odds of what the disease does to you, you start to wonder and think about the reality of the situation. I tried not to let it get me down because I knew my parents were fighting to keep me alive. I wanted to tell them I accepted whatever would happen. God had a plan for me.

Mom and dad were not big religious folks but attended church on special occasions like Christmas and Easter. I think, deep down inside, they prayed and I was sure they were praying now more than ever. I have to admit that even though I was 13 years old, I wasn't afraid to die. You cannot stop the inevitable and sometimes things just don't work out the way you want them to.

I used Tinker as my emotional crutch. I believed he saved me so many times from falling into a deep depression because he listened. I could be completely honest with him about how scared I was. During all my sleepless nights I had someone to talk to. If I was to tell you that Tinker felt all the pain I was going through, you'd probably laugh and say, "He's a dog! How could he know?"

Yes, he was a dog but he was so much more. Every time I cried at night in my bed (so my parents wouldn't see), Tinker gracefully licked away each tear. He was telling me, "Kristy, you will get your heart and everything will be okay." He felt what I felt. I saw it in his eyes. I knew he cried when I cried.

With no reply from Ralph Klein and still fighting against time and fighting to save my life, Art and Gwen wrote a letter to the Alberta Minister of Health, Shirley McClellan. They stated the same things they had stated in the letter to Klein. This letter got a reply but it wasn't good news. McClellan turned our request for out-of-country care down. In her letter dated March 21, 1996, she wrote that my case had been submitted to the Out-of-Country Health Services Committee. (This committee was formerly the Out-of-Province Supplementary Assistance Committee.) They had reviewed my case and information in a letter that Dr. Giuffre had written on February 20, 1996. McClellan said given my age and my medical profile, the committee was confident that the priority of my condition would enable me to receive a heart transplant without delay in Alberta. McClellan also said that the committee couldn't find anything about the severity and terminal prognosis of restrictive cardiomyopathy and lymphangiectasia in the medical literature Dr. Giuffre had provided.

A further complication was that the committee couldn't find anything suggesting that lymphangiectasia increased my risk of death while waiting for a heart or after transplant. It was an obscure disease at the time. Doctors were unsure of what would happen before or during surgery.

Dr. Giuffre had written in his letter that: *from the medical literature, we know that children with the rare diagnosis of restrictive cardiomyopathy have a very high mortality rate. Eighty per cent of the children die within one year of the diagnosis being made. And most of the deaths are not from slow deterioration but, unfortunately, are sudden with few signs, if any signs, of impending death.*

I was too young to understand the complete ramifications of McClellan's letter and refusal to let me double list. I also didn't understand then how politics and the government work. I did know that I was shocked that someone had the ability to make decisions about me that dramatically impacted my health: this was truly a life and death matter. McClellan's letter only made my parents fight harder.

I was denied the right to live because politicians wouldn't allow me to double list to help my chances of a full life. In 1996, double listing was not common. Our appeal was among the first cases Alberta Health had ever dealt with. I think nowadays double listing isn't an issue because the boundaries have been expanded. Waitlists are different too. If an organ becomes available locally and no one from the area is able to take it, they'll look to other waitlists outside the region.

To lift my spirits in March, my family made a request to the Children's Wish Foundation. I would be granted a wish and that wish was to meet Reba McEntire, the country singer and actress. It was thanks to my close friend Nicole that I was a huge fan of Reba's. Before my restrictive cardiomyopathy diagnosis in 1995, Nicole's mom had bought some tickets to attend a Reba concert in Calgary at the Saddledome. I was invited to go along. Nicole was a big Reba fan and I became one too when I saw her live. My Reba experience was amazing, even though halfway through the concert I got sick.

I became extremely nauseated and Nicole was rushing me through the crowded Saddledome to get me to the bathroom. As we were dodging people and fighting our way to make it to the bathroom in time, we came to a flight of stairs. Sitting perfectly on the staircase ledge was someone's cup. It was meant to be mine.

I could no longer hold down what was about to come up. Nicole, as if reading my mind, grabbed the cup and, just in time, put it to my mouth.

"Here, throw up in this," she ordered.

I did what I was told.

With the cup filled with throw-up in my hand and Nicole's gentle but reassuring grip on my body, we slowly made our way to the Saddledome's sick room. I ended up missing most of the concert and

I was never sure why I was so sick that night.

My wish to meet Reba was granted. The Children's Wish Foundation would make arrangements for my family and me to meet the singer in Denison, Texas on her Texoma Ranch...after I had my life saving transplant. The foundation thought I wasn't healthy enough to go on a trip but I said I wanted to have my wish before my transplant. I really feared I wouldn't live long enough to receive a new heart. The foundation listened to me and I felt that they understood my reality. It was refreshing to know they were thinking realistically. It was also one less thing telling me I couldn't do something because of my health. In the end, the foundation made an exception for me and I would be able to have my wish before I received a transplant. (If I got a heart before the trip, my wish would be rescheduled.)

My trip was scheduled to begin on May 25, 1996 and my whole family was coming along: mom, dad and Billy. May was my special month and the wish was almost like a birthday present that we could all enjoy. The timing couldn't have been better and in the back of my mind, I thought this might be our last family vacation together.

I anxiously waited for the trip to start as all the details were being finalized. We would fly from Calgary to Dallas/Fort Worth where a rental car or a limo would whisk us to Denison (about a two hour drive from Fort Worth.) We also arranged to hire a rental car so we could do a little sightseeing in Texas. A Learjet would be on standby in case we had to rush back to Edmonton. I was so happy that my family had something positive to look forward to. A nice vacation was definitely something we all needed badly. Before we could get too excited though, we kept fighting for the chance to double list in the months ahead of the trip. The nurses at the Medicine Hat hospital petitioned Alberta Health to help my chances of being double listed. We gathered some 3,000 names from the Medicine Hat, Calgary and Edmonton area. The fight was still on.

CHAPTER SEVEN

Barriers to life

Dr. Giuffre was certain that my odds of survival were dependent on the Out-of-Country Health Services Committee's decision. Since they had turned the double listing down, mom and dad appealed the decision. During this time, we also met with the head of the heart transplant team in Edmonton, Dr. M. He was one of the best transplant surgeons (in 1985 he performed the first heart transplant in Western Canada) and had an abundance of knowledge. Dr. M was not impressed with our decision to double list or to fight the government and appeal the decision denying me to be double listed. We met with him on March 19, 1996 at 11:30 a.m. and he told us that if we proceeded in our fight against the committee's decision to deny double listing and funding, he would take my name off the list in Alberta. What a blow.

It all boiled down to politics and funding. If you want to know the specifics, you'll have to ask me in person. For now, all you need to know is the conversation made my parents angry because it made no sense. Why did doctors have the right to refuse care to a family because they're seeking to improve their daughter's chances of living? I can't imagine what doctors would do if it was their own child's life. Would they fight like my parents? Dr. M seemed so calm when he said he would take my name off the list. My parents pointedly told him that they would do what they had to do, which meant they would fight until the end, until I was healthy again. Dr. M had the power to do such a terrible thing. He was capable of lowering my odds of receiving a heart transplant. I was only 13 years old and I wanted to live. This doctor was going to stand in my way. I was hurt. We were going to have to fight even harder to be double listed. If we had to fight to stay on the list in Alberta, then so be it, we were ready. Dr. M never did go through with his threat.

Mom and dad found a politician to come along side us in the battle to be double listed: Alberta Liberal Health Critic Howard Sapers. Howard was the MLA for Edmonton-Glenora at the time and as he was the opposition to the Conservative government. Mom and dad had contacted him looking for answers and he brought our issue up during a session of the Legislative Assembly of Alberta on Wednesday, April 24, 1996. He addressed the matter directly to Premier Klein and the transcript is as follows:

Thank you, Mr. Speaker. Kristy Plotsky is a 13 year-old Medicine Hat girl with two rare heart ailments. Now, Kristy requires a lifesaving heart transplant and is currently on the waiting list at the University of Alberta Hospital. Her parents want to double Kristy's chances of receiving a heart transplant by placing her on a second list in the United States. The Alberta heart transplant program has said that they will take Kristy off their list if Kristy is placed on the United States list. My questions are for the premier. Given that there is absolutely no question about whether or not Kristy needs a heart transplant, will the premier please advise as to why she cannot be placed on both lists at the same time?

Premier Klein replied:

Well, again, Mr. Speaker, I'm only going on the advice of the minister of health, who advises me that the Out-of-Province Supplementary Committee, which I assume is a medical committee, reviews the capabilities of our medical programs and the specific needs of each individual patient. If an individual patient for some reason could not be served as effectively by our program, the committee certainly would recommend double listing. In this case, as I'm given to understand, the committee has recommended to the minister that indeed the facilities are available, particularly at the U of A here in Edmonton, are capable of serving the needs of this young lady.

Howard rebutted:

Thank you, Mr. Speaker. It's precisely that committee and those guidelines that I'm questioning. Given, Mr. Premier, that Kristy's doctor has said that she will die if she has to wait long for a heart in Alberta, doesn't the premier agree, based on what he just read, that it is consistent with government policy to have

Kristy placed on both lists?

Premier Klein replied:

Mr. Speaker, I'm certainly not familiar with all the details of the case, but you're asking me to question the advice and the recommendations of a very specialized committee that has been set up to examine precisely these kinds of situations. I will take the member's question under notice and discuss it with the minister upon her return.

Howard addressed the assembly again:

Thank you, and thank you for that commitment, Mr. Premier. Mr. Premier, while you're undergoing that review with the minister and the Out-of-Province Committee, would you please make a determination and then inform this assembly as to how long a wait a patient like Kristy must endure before this premier and his minister of health agree that Kristy or other patients in her circumstances can be placed on the United States list.

Premier Klein replied one final time:

It's a really good question, Mr. Speaker. I don't know what the answer is because I don't know precisely what the policy of the Out-of-Province Supplementary Assistance Committee is relative to the waiting time. That's one of the points I'll discuss with the minister upon her return.

My family was glad to have Howard speak out for us. The more people who were aware of my situation – the better. As the saying goes, the squeaky wheel gets the grease. It was really about awareness and the need for people to donate their organs.

Just under a week later, Howard returned a letter to our family. He sent his personal best wishes in regards to me getting a heart transplant in time. He wrote it was unjust for our family to deal with the barriers put up by the provincial government. He stated again that the matter was brought to the legislature by members of the Alberta Liberal Caucus. (It was brought to the Alberta Liberal Caucus on three separate occasions: April 24, May 9 and May 22.) Howard encouraged us to keep rallying against the government and said he hoped that every possibility to help me was left open. At this point, there was nothing Howard could do.

CHAPTER EIGHT

Change of heart

As time passed and we still hadn't heard from the provincial government about our funding for out-of-country care, we continued to use the media and petitions to garner support for me and organ donation. An independent film company had heard about my situation and wanted to use my story. It would be a documentary on families in waiting when a transplant is the only hope. We agreed to do the film to raise awareness about organ donation and transplants. The documentary was following other families at the same time too.

Life was getting more stressful for me at this point. I was in limbo and that, coupled with my deteriorating health, made me feel tired and anxious and not myself. Waiting to be healthy was a drain. My life was literally in the hands of a complete stranger and as you know, I constantly felt guilty over thinking about someone dying for me to live. The barriers put up by the government weighed on my mind as the days went by. My heart was a ticking time bomb and I didn't know how much time I had. These things added up and my family and I were starting to lose hope. However, we allowed the film maker to follow us around for a day at the end of April in 1996.

It was kind of different to have someone with you all day long, especially when you were supposed to act like he wasn't there, yet he was snapping all these candid photos. It was exciting and a little embarrassing at the same time. I never liked to be centre of attention, but I really had no choice. My friend Stephanie came along with us for the day, which put me a little more at ease.

We spent some portion of the morning at home where the film maker observed me taking my medication. Later, we went to Kmart and he followed us around while we were trying on silly hats and silly outfits. That part was really fun. People were staring and I knew they were wondering who I was or maybe they recognized me from news stories. I was glad when the day was over. When the sun set I was still Kristy, the girl waiting for a heart and not some TV reality star.

Photo of my mom and I taken by the Independent Film Company.

My cousin Leanne is a devout Christian and with her encouragement and support, we decided I should have someone lay hands on me and pray. My family started attending several Protestant churches and participating in prayer circles to help heal me. I understood God had powers and definitely could heal, but I wasn't sure if I believed that he would heal ME. I know some people might ask, "Why me?" I always asked, "Why not me?" I analyzed my situation and thought there are people going through far worse things than me – they are the ones who should be receiving God's healing powers. Then I met Billy Smith.

Billy Smith is a world renowned faith healer. He came to the First Assembly of God, a church in Medicine Hat, and laid hands on me. He prayed and then shouted, "You are healed!" and ordered me to run through the church aisles. I didn't believe what he said, especially to the degree that I wouldn't need a heart transplant. I have to admit though, when I ran down the stairs from the stage and ran around the church, it felt like something was lifting me up. Call me crazy, call me whatever you want, but I felt something so strong lifting me. I had had my doubts about God making me healthy but after this experience, I felt he was going to heal me in whatever way necessary. That included finding me a suitable heart in time. Whatever was going to happen, I realized God was going to take care of me.

I wanted to know more about God and so my cousin Leanne and I discussed faith a lot. She was taking Bible courses at the time and I asked her many questions since I didn't know much about religion. My Great Grandma and Great Grandpa Crockford went to church frequently and attended a smaller church in Medicine Hat called Heights Baptist Church and growing up we would go with them. I'm not going to lie, I hated church and was more or less made to go to Sunday school when I was younger. Sunday school was not too bad but sitting in the pews during services was boring. Facing a life threatening illness, though, changes your perspective on a lot of things and one was church. I found faith and it helped me through my struggles.

Having a belief that things happen for a reason, I started to pray and build a relationship with God. I asked Jesus Christ into my heart and asked him to teach me more about God. While I was sick, I could have a conversation with him anytime, anywhere. I talked to him about everything. Tinker and I had many sleepless nights talking to God and praying about everyone and everything. Often I prayed about my family and asked if he would guide them through this difficult time. I loved having a relationship with God and I stopped questioning my faith and completely surrendered to him.

I didn't talk to mom and dad about my relationship with Jesus. Not because they wouldn't listen but because they probably didn't want to hear about it. When you're faced with tragic circumstances in life, you aren't rational all the time. Your mind seems to go off the deep end and the last thing you want to hear is how God has everything in his hands, especially when it's regarding your own child. My parents kept fighting for me and I was fighting too but I also had my faith as an ally. I held onto it and the possibilities of what being a strong Christian might bring me. I started to believe there was a God and he had a mighty plan for me.

Other ways of coping with my health problems included seeing a counsellor at school. Mom and dad supported the idea and my counsellor Carol was easy to talk to. She helped me figure out many things about myself. I learned I cared more about how other people felt rather than my own feelings and how I didn't necessarily want to make things better for myself but rather for the people I loved.

Carol was someone I could share things with and let my feelings out instead of complaining to my family. I felt I could really tell her what was on my mind. I could tell her what I was stressing over and what my parents were stressing over. During one counselling session, Carol and I decided that I should make a worry box. My Great Grandma Crockford helped me cover a small, square cardboard box with some colourful fabric. When I brought the box to my session, Carol and I talked about what I would use it for. What kind of worries I was going to put into the box and how the worry box worked. Later that night, I wrote down different things that worried me on separate pieces of paper. Then I put the worries into the worry box. Each piece of paper that gracefully slipped from my fingers into the box was a worry gracefully falling away.

Most of the worries in the box were things that I had no control over like when I was going to get my new heart. I worried about my parents' financial situation and I didn't like that they were missing work on account of me. I worried about Tinker and how much he missed me while I was in the hospital. I worried about school and whether I would be able to continue. I also worried about death.

Dying was something I had to come to terms with and be okay with if I died a lot younger then I had ever imagined. To guide me through talking and thinking about death, Carol made arrangements for me to meet with University of Alberta Hospital child life specialist Judy Dahl. Judy was in Edmonton and extremely easy to talk to and super nice. She did so many neat things with all the kids at the hospital like crafts and sometimes even took them shopping. It was great seeing her every time I was in Edmonton meeting with my transplant team. She'd always check in to find out how I was feeling.

I had a good support system going with my family, Carol and Judy but Dr. Coe thought talking to more families who had experienced similar situations would be a good idea too. I had met one girl already and that was enough for me. I told Dr. Coe that I didn't want to talk to anyone else because everyone has different situations and different obstacles. My parents told me to stop being stubborn and start being open to speaking to other people who might have some insight into heart transplants.

I was being a little bit stubborn but I had good reasons: no one else knew what I was going through. There might be other young girls who received new hearts but that was the only thing we had in common. They were past needing a heart and were out and about enjoying life. Reluctantly, I agreed to meet with another family. Dr. Coe had one in mind and said that I would not regret meeting them.

I did meet with that family and other families and while I never regretted talking to any of them, I was really jealous. I wanted to be healthy and I wasn't. I was also a little frightened because one girl told me she had to live in Edmonton before a heart was available and then live in the city for six months after the transplant. I was scared that I would have to do the same and I didn't want to be away from home. One girl, Lucy*, finally got through to me and became my lifelong friend.

Meeting Lucy made me look at things differently. She was outspoken, spunky and full of life. She was so nice (as were the three other families we had met before my transplant) but my friend wasn't shy, which was good because I was. Lucy had been through a lot of illnesses prior to her heart transplant and her experiences were different than mine but never once did I look at her with any sort of jealousy. She made having a heart transplant look easy from the way she talked about it to how she took her medicine and handled the ongoing medical appointments. I looked up to her and we were close friends.

Lucy was the second real true friend I had made through my whole ordeal of being sick. The first was Annalies, who was one of my roommates at the Alberta Children's Hospital in Calgary. I had just found out I needed a new heart when I met Annalies. It was a scene right out of Lethal Weapon: she was showing me her scars and I was showing her my scars. Each scar told a story and we had lots of stories to tell. I have to admit, she had way more scars then I did as she had a very sick heart.

I soon learned that Annalies needed a heart double lung transplant. This meant she needed a suitable match for a heart and two lungs. This girl was in an epic battle for her life and even I couldn't grasp the reality of what it all entailed. What I did know was her struggle made me contemplate organ donation more than I had ever before. When I was sick, sometimes it felt like I was the only one who had ever needed a heart transplant, or for that matter, any kind of transplant. Annalies made me realize that I wasn't the only one suffering and there were many other people in the same situation, or worse, than me. She had such a good attitude and I needed to learn from her.

Annalies and I remained friends. She's currently waiting for a heart double lung. She has had many operations to keep her alive and is such an inspiration.

***

My life was getting more and more public and with my wish through the Children's Wish Foundation being granted, I was getting a lot of attention. Considering I was a small town girl meeting a huge country star, Reba McEntire, it was big news. My family was also using the media as a conduit to try to get the government to open us up for double listing. Dr. Giuffre was helpful enough to hold news conferences in his downtown Calgary office where we appealed to have me double listed. Time and my health were catching up to me and I had less than a year to find a heart. No amount of medication would stop or slow down the disease prognosis. We demanded action at the press conferences and prayed the government would react. The news people gathered around and rallied with us. We were in a bitter fight with the province and my parents didn't want to lose. In fact, losing was not an option because then it meant I might die.

Never in our wildest dreams did we think about the possibility of receiving negative feedback. Well, we got some. I guess it comes with being in the public eye.

It was an early morning and my brother told me that mom had some mail for me. Mom usually didn't check my mail (I don't recall a time when she opened anything of mine without my approval) and I wondered why she hadn't give me all my letters. What was Billy talking about? He made me promise not to tell a single soul if he told me about this particular letter. I was starting to wonder if I got mail that mom didn't show me. She could be forgetful at times.

Billy pulled out an envelope from a drawer in the computer room.

The envelope had an unrecognizable address. I had never heard of the person who had mailed the letter to me. I opened the envelope and pulled out a messy handwritten card.

I was shocked at what I read.

YOU ARE GOING TO DIE. YOUR PARENTS DO NOT CARE ABOUT YOU. I NEEDED A HEART TRANSPLANT TOO. MY PARENTS SOLD THEIR HOUSE TO BUY ME A HEART IN LONDON, ONTARIO. I'M HEALTHY NOW THANKS TO THEM. YOUR PARENTS DO NOT CARE ABOUT YOU BECAUSE THEY WILL NOT SELL THEIR HOUSE TO BUY YOU A HEART. IF YOU WERE MY DAUGHTER I WOULD SELL MY HOUSE TO BUY YOU A NEW HEART EVEN THOUGH YOU ARE KIND OF UGLY. YOU ARE GOING TO DIE.

I was shaking violently so my brother took the card back.

"What a messed up person, hey Kris?"

Billy told me not to believe what this person wrote. He or she was obviously jealous. I knew my brother didn't show me the card to scare me. I believe he cared about me a lot. Billy wanted me to realize that there were some people in the world that weren't nice and this is what happens when you are so public about something.

I think mom was too scared to show me the card and probably thought I might believe what the deranged person wrote. I think the only thing in the entire card that hurt my feelings was that they said I was ugly. The stuff about my parents was not at all true. Seriously, this felt like a scene from the movie *The Bodyguard*. I felt like I was Whitney Houston's character in the movie and somebody was trying to kill me – even though it was just a letter. No matter what, I knew my parents loved me. Besides, if we sold our house what would we come back to? This person probably didn't have a place to live. I have never understood why people talk badly about other people to make themselves feel better. Does it help? What does it prove? I never took the letter to heart but I couldn't imagine who would write and then send something that nasty to a 13 year old girl.

The more I thought about the note, the angrier it made me. I wanted to know who wrote it. Did they live nearby? What was he or she's contact with me or my family or friends? Had I met this person before? I assumed he or she must have seen me on the news and felt they needed to be rude and disturbing. Mom later turned the letter into the RMCP in Medicine Hat but we couldn't trace the address on the envelope. The person who supposedly wrote the letter, did not exist.

CHAPTER NINE

Doubling my chances

Every day that went by I was waiting, hoping and praying for life to change. I was getting excited to meet Reba and giving my parents a break from their push to have me double listed. They're private people and it was hard on them being in the public eye so often.

The month leading up to the trip, I was living at home. Every couple of weeks we'd travel to see doctors, mostly in Edmonton. When we drove home from seeing Dr. Coe in Edmonton, we stopped in Calgary to see Dr. Giuffre. My pediatrician in Medicine Hat, Dr. Hak, was still involved in my care and was kept up-to-date with my health by mom and my cardiac doctors.

When I was sick and I stayed home from school, I would stay with my Aunty Terry. Before my health problems, I was interested in cross stitching and now, during days when I wasn't too ill, she'd taught me more about patterns and embroidery. I had started a picture about a year before of a little bear praying on his bed. To be stitched along with the bear and bed was a colourful knitted afghan and a Raggedy Ann doll. At the top of the picture it said, "Don't Forget to Say Your Prayers." I was finally finished the picture and my aunt thought it would be neat if I gave it to Reba as a gift. I thought that was a lot of work to just give away, considering it took me over a year to make, but I decided it would be a nice keepsake for her. I made the picture out to Reba, Shelby (her son) and Narval (her husband at the time) and signed the bottom with my initials, KP. I thought she would love it and maybe even hang it in her house.

Cross-stitch picture I made for Reba.

On a day I was feeling not too bad, I got to attend my friend Megan's birthday party. It was early May 1996 and a bunch of us were at Megan's house including our friend, Tara, who had just got a miniature Chihuahua puppy named Mandy. Tara brought her over to Megan's so we could meet her. Mandy was so cute and no bigger than a newborn kitten.

It was fun playing with Mandy but talking about how we were getting older was difficult for me. My friends had completely different lives: they were thinking about the future and I was living one day at a time. We did talk a little about my birthday, that was in less than a week, and it was hard to think that maybe it would be my last one.

I did have an awesome time joking and laughing about boys (you know, girl talk) and how at 14 we could get our learner's permit for driving. We even talked about when I would get a new heart. My friends were always upbeat and positive about my transplant and we never talked about the alternative: me dying. They told me that after I had my (successful) surgery, we would all go camping, a favourite outdoor activity of mine. It was a good party and I was glad I had spent that time with my friends.

I celebrated my birthday a couple of days early with my family and Megan. On my real birthday, May 15, mom took me to get my learner's. I achieved 100 per cent on the written test! Remember I said I would get my heart in May? Well, May was flying by and I started to regret saying it was going to be my month. In some ways, I did really feel I would find a donor in May, but I tried to pretend I was in a different month, like September. I wanted May to be far away. I did have Reba to focus on and the trip to meet her was coming up. After my visit, it would be the end of May. There would be no time left in that month for a heart transplant. I wondered about my chances of being called for a new heart during my holiday in Texas but brushed that out of my mind. That was just not going to happen.

People say that waiting is the hardest part of the transplant process. Some receive an organ within as little as two months, while others have to wait years. I remember the months I spent waiting for my new heart: four months in total. The nights were the hardest because it was during this time that I was alone and I would go over my health and diagnosis and this and that over and over again. Some nights I wasn't sure if I would wake up the next morning so I used this time to pray.

Despite being double listed, there was no guarantee I would get a heart in time. Doctors told us that statistical research presented that 90 per cent of cases diagnosed with restrictive cardiomyopathy, die within one year of diagnosis. An article I read about my disease said there was an extremely poor outlook for children with my condition. It stated that 50 per cent of kids died within two years of diagnosis, usually of sudden death. Oh no. Did that mean my life was limited? I didn't even know how long I'd already lived with restrictive cardiomyopathy. No one knew the answer to that question because it had taken so long for doctors to find a diagnosis in the first place.

Things took a turn for the better on May 21, 1996. We received a letter that said our appeal to double list had been heard and we were now approved for out-of-country funding by the province. I was allowed to be on both the Canadian and the U.S. lists at the same time. I was double listed, which meant I was doubling my chances of getting a new heart. As soon as we returned from Texas, we would head off to Rochester to complete a U.S. transplant assessment at the Mayo Clinic. Then I would be put on the list there. There was nothing any Canadian doctor could do about removing me from being double listed. The long fight had paid off and we were relieved. The following is the letter we received from the Out-of-Country Health Services Committee:

I am pleased to inform you that your appeal of the former decision of the Out-of-Country Health Services Committee has been allowed. This means that your daughter, Kristy Plotsky, will be allowed to be double listed for a heart transplant. In making this decision, the committee reviewed, in great detail, the documentation available to it, which included the following:

The letter of support from Dr. Michael Giuffre, pediatric cardiologist at Alberta Children's Hospital.

The terms of reference of UNOS (United Network for Organ Sharing) provided by the Mayo Clinic.

The committee was aware that restrictive cardiomyopathy has a serious prognosis and sudden death is common. The guidelines state that full funding should be considered if a delay in obtaining a particular service in Canada might be significantly harmful to the patient. We feel Kristy would fit into this category. For these reasons, the committee felt it was reasonable to be double listed so as to increase the probability of obtaining a suitable organ match at the earliest possible time. The committee wishes Kristy the best of luck in obtaining a suitable organ match in a timely fashion.

The letter was signed by Martin H. Atkinson, MD, FRCPC, Out-of-Country Health Services Committee Appeal Panel.

With this good news, we all felt the stress lift. I was relieved at the possibility of doubling my chances for a heart. Now that that fight was over, it was back to the waiting game. While I was waiting for my new heart, I had the trip of a lifetime to look forward to. I was so excited about meeting Reba McEntire as well as making some stops along the way. My family and I were going to fly to Calgary and see some cousins. Cheryl (my dad's first cousin) and her husband Ken were going to meet us for lunch at the Calgary airport. As an aside, Cheryl and Ken have two sons, Stacie and Corey, and Corey was a goalie for the Vancouver Canucks. In April, Corey gave us tickets to see the Calgary Flames versus the Vancouver Canucks. Unfortunately, Vancouver lost but after the game we went to Earls Kitchen and Bar with Corey, Cheryl, Ken and a few members of the

Vancouver Canucks team including Trevor Linden, a player from Medicine Hat. It was a real treat. We loved going to NHL games and it took our minds off of all the medical stuff.

My family had agreed to meet Cheryl and Ken at the Calgary airport for lunch and then we would fly to Dallas/Fort Worth, Texas. My wish was coming true and it was only a day away. I was getting excited.

Corey, Billy and I at a Vancouver Canucks game April 1996.

CHAPTER TEN

If you only knew (It's a Reba McEntire song)

The day of my vacation arrived and I was like a little kid on Christmas. May 25, 1996 was finally here! We were scheduled to fly from the Medicine Hat airport at 9:00 a.m. to Calgary. This was our first ever airplane trip for our family and the plane taking off from Medicine Hat was tiny. It looked like a cylinder with wings. Dad almost hit his head when he stood up in the aircraft! The flight from Medicine Hat to Calgary was short – under an hour gate to gate. When we arrived in Calgary, we didn't have to worry about our luggage because it had been redirected to the Dallas/Fort Worth International Airport.

We arrived in Calgary on-time and met Cheryl and Ken for lunch. Our layover was about two hours, which gave us plenty of time to eat and have a nice visit. After lunch, we said our goodbyes and boarded our plane. I was over-the-moon excited and even a little nervous. There were butterflies in my stomach: the kind you get when you're on a scary ride and you know the drop is just ahead. I asked myself, "What am I going to say to Reba when I meet her? Would I be star-struck and not able to say a word?" I wondered what it would be like staying at her ranch and if we would be able to ride horses. I loved riding horses and at one time, thought I would be barrel racer when I grew up.

The plane taking us to Texas was a Boeing 747 and the biggest plane I had ever seen. (Keeping in mind the plane from Medicine Hat to Calgary was the first flight I had ever been on period.)

The 747 was so big that it had two separate aisles and lots and lots of seats. We sat on the left side of the aircraft, close to the window. (I love window seats. I love looking out and seeing where we are and what we are flying over.) Being on the plane was exciting but the flight was a lot longer than I thought it would be. I didn't get bored though, flying was all new to me and it also felt great to be away from my life and from all the doctors. Five hours in the air, we arrived at the Dallas/Fort Worth airport.

Circling over the city, I saw how big Dallas/Fort Worth was. Huge! After we landed and the cabin doors opened, I took my first steps outside. The hot Texas air swirled my hair around my face. Through the din of the engines, I heard the faint rustling of trees in the distance. It was all so beautiful and I forgot that I needed a heart transplant.

We all got off the airplane and tried to find the baggage claim area. The airport was enormous and there were people everywhere. You would hear someone yell, "Move over! Coming through!" and just as you turned your head to look, a man driving a golf cart would speed past you. I must admit, all the commotion and noise was a little scary and it kind of made me want to go back home. We kept searching for the baggage claim and found a sign that announced, "Luggage this way" but when we followed the sign we got to another sign that said, "NO EXIT. IF YOU PROCEED THROUGH THESE DOORS, NO ACCESS BACK TO AIRPORT."

Since we had no clue where to go, we ended up asking somebody for help. Guess what? When we asked where the baggage claim was, they said, "Follow the luggage signs."

We had now wasted an hour looking for our luggage.

A crazy two hours later, we finally found someone with a suitcase full of answers. We proceeded through the "NO EXIT" doors that we had previously avoided, and there stood our luggage. All by itself. Going around and around on the conveyer belt.

After we got our luggage, we headed to pick up the car we rented to drive to Denison. Reba was going to send a vehicle for us but we had said no. We were regretting the decision as we struggled to find the rental place. We asked for directions and found out we had to take an airport shuttle van to the budget rental center. We got our car and after a couple of hours stuck at the airport, we were free. We rolled out into the Texas traffic and were on our way. I was ecstatic. I wouldn't be meeting Reba until the evening of May 27, when I was scheduled to attend her Memorial Day Benefit Concert at Grayson County Airport. Reba was going to be singing along with special guest Billy Dean, a rising American country music singer and songwriter.

The weather in Dallas was very warm and the air was muggy. I found it hard to breathe, especially not being used to the heat. It was almost suffocating. Since it was hot, I started to sweat just by standing outside. The wind was strong, so strong that the palm trees leaned away from the gusts, but it didn't cool me off at all. It was tornado season and the forceful breeze scared me. All I needed was a tornado.

Before we had hit the road for the two and a half hour drive to Denison, we asked the rental staff for directions. It was late afternoon and I didn't like the idea of driving at night in a place we had never been before. Of course, my family cannot go anywhere without getting lost. Mom was driving with dad as her navigator in the front seat beside her. Billy and I were in the back seat. My brother was being an annoying back seat driver, like usual. He was an almost 17 year old boy and a relatively new driver, but he told mom what to do anyway. He knew all the road rules and was probably telling her that she didn't shoulder check properly or that she didn't come to a complete stop. Little things but annoying things. (Even though I was sick, some things just never change.) The sky was starting to get darker, signalling we were behind schedule. All because of that rigmarole finding the baggage claim.

BEEP... BEEP... BEEP.... BEEP.....BEEP!

The pager interrupted our frustrating drive. Edmonton was supposed to do a test page but the plan was for us to call them once we arrived in Denison. They must have gotten impatient and called us instead.

BEEP... BEEP... BEEP.... BEEP!

The pager blared again. After each beep, an angry buzz of vibration followed. It sounded terrifying, like there were wasps in the car with us.

"What are they doing?!" mom asked, annoyed with Edmonton. We had only been driving for about 15 minutes. I sat quietly in the back while my parents bickered about what we were going to do next. We were on the outskirts of Dallas, about approximately 70 miles (112 kilometres) away from Denison.

"Well, I don't know Margo," said dad. "We better stop and use a phone." (This was before the age of inexpensive cells phones.)

"I don't even know where we are," said mom, scanning the scenery for any sign of a payphone.

I still didn't say anything. I was both frightened and excited and it was like everybody was moving in slow motion except for me. I couldn't move at all: I was frozen in time. Sunset is my favourite part of the day and so I focused my eyes on outside. The sun was setting and the sky was illuminated by beautiful colours of pink, red and orange. The air was moist and soft on my cheek. It felt like I was dreaming. Everyone around me became a blur and turned into background noise, the kind a snowy TV channel makes.

Dad pointed out we had passed a Taco Bell a few minutes ago.

"Turn around or flip a shitter (make a U-turn)," he said.

The tone of their voices told me something was not right. My parents sounded stressed, maybe confused, maybe scared. I didn't really think the insistent call was to tell us that a suitable donor had been found. No, Edmonton was only testing the pager. But what if it was about a match? Everything was happening so slow or so fast, that I didn't want to speak and make this moment a reality.

Billy had to add his two cents. He told mom to drive over the middle curb and flip a shitter instead of waiting to find somewhere to turn around. Mom disagreed but Billy said if a cop was to stop her, she had a solid reason for making the U-turn.

"Your daughter might be getting a new heart to save her life tonight."

Mom, always a conscientious driver, whipped over that curb and flipped a shitter. I was blown away that mom had the guts to do something like that. (I guess she was getting better at standing up for herself. She was getting good at it considering how long we had been fighting the government and everything else we had gone through the past few years.) We sped towards the fast food restaurant, everyone except me, agitated by this point. Nobody was yelling yet, but it was almost at that point.

We arrived at the Taco Bell and there was a payphone. With someone already on it. Mom, as nicely as possible but slightly impatient, told the woman that we needed to use the phone. Right away. The woman replied, in a rather snotty and sarcastic voice, that she was using it and we would have to wait. That was the end of the line for mom; she was ready to blow.

"Listen up," said mom in a wickedly serious tone. "My daughter is waiting for a heart transplant and we just got a call from the U of A in Edmonton, telling us that a heart is available."

The woman took her time saying goodbye to the person on the other end and reluctantly gave up the phone. She had no sympathy and no regard for my life or any of us. The lady gave mom a "f-you" look and walked away.

Mom and dad were still smokers at the time and while mom was on the payphone trying to get through to Edmonton, she was puffing away on a smoke like a steam engine. Dad was right beside her, doing the same. That's when I knew something was up. They weren't big smokers and could go awhile without a cigarette. But here they were, acting like they had been deprived of nicotine for days. I was sitting in the car and waiting. Part of me hoped this was the test page we had talked about because I wanted to meet Reba.

Mom was on the phone for a little longer then I was comfortable with. How long does it take someone to say, "Okay, you're in Denison? Good. Have fun. Bye."

The conversation mom was having was long; long enough to talk about the possibility of a heart being available. Long enough to have a discussion about my health. Long enough to tell us that we needed to come home. Mom was pacing back and forth too, walking as far as the payphone cord would let her. Each time she felt a tug, she turned and repeated her walk in the other direction.

Billy and I sat in the back seat. Not a peep from both of us, which was weird because Billy was usually a chatterbox. I turned and looked at him at the same time he turned and looked at me. Without saying a word, he got out of the vehicle to see what was happening. It was like he knew exactly what I was thinking and he needed to go find out what was happening for me. I sat all by myself, with my hands folded neatly on my lap and stared out the back window. I saw people going on with their lives. Time hadn't stopped for them.

My mind was churning and I imagined the most drastic situations. What was the worst case scenario? Was it that a heart was available or was it that this was only a trial to see if the pager was working? I didn't even know what I wanted anymore. I hesitantly refocused my eyes on mom, dad and Billy and tried to read their lips. To this very day, I wonder sometimes why I didn't get out of the car to find out the news. This was big: it was about me living or dying. Getting a heart or not. I did care about the answer, of course I did, but the car was my protection from the truth.

Before this afternoon, every time someone had asked me how I was doing, I would tell them I was okay. When I wasn't okay at all. That was a lie to myself. I wasn't okay. I was not okay at all. I had to face reality. I needed a new heart and one might be available. Now.

CHAPTER ELEVEN

The call

The rental car that I sat in was the only thing keeping me from what was happening to my life. I could make my own reality in the vehicle and make believe something else in my young mind. I had created a bubble the whole time I had been sick. I ran away from every feeling, every fear I had ever had and I had to face it all, bang, right now. I tried so hard to feel happy about the possibility of receiving a new heart but negativity grabbed me again. I said to myself in both prayer and shock, "OH MY GOD!"

The brain is powerful and with all my critical thinking and analysis of everything, it made me go a bit crazy. When something happens, or you create a fictional situation for yourself and you put yourself in the "what if" position, you never know what you'll actually do until the time comes. I had tried for five very long months, the longest months of my life, to prepare myself for when I got the call. The call to tell me a heart was found.

The sky was turning black but I could make out dark blue clouds hanging in the distance. They were so graceful and at that particular moment, I started to question God and question the idea of heaven. I thought this might be the end of the road for me. Finding a heart was difficult but surviving the surgery was going to be a whole different level of stress. I didn't think I would survive with my own heart, let alone find a new one in time. It was the thought of removing my entire heart and putting another one into my body that was terrifying.

There were a lot of emotions coursing through me at the same time. I was scared, panicked, excited, humourless, shocked, paralyzed, sad, worried, and anxious. My body was experiencing sensations that had every single feeling attached to it. I had flashbacks of the past two years of my life and they surged into my head like a ravaging flash flood. The pain of my first surgery went through my mind as did spending last Christmas with my family. Finding out I needed a new heart surfaced in my memories as did cuddles with Tinker. I was allowing myself to feel these moments but not the one I was living.

I couldn't hear a word my parents and brother were saying to each other and my mind put words into their mouths. Then Billy walked over to the vehicle and opened the door so nonchalantly that it made me sigh with relief. It had only been a test page. Billy got in the car and closed the door. It was the two of us again.

Mom was still on the phone and she and dad were still puffing away on cigarettes. They both looked like they were definitely on a mission. Just then my shoulder felt heavy and I turned my head and noticed Billy had his arm around me.

"Well Kris..."

Silence.

"You got your new heart."

"WHAT?" I gasped. And the flood gates opened and tears fell down my face. At that moment, I found an insurmountable tidal wave of mixed emotions hit me. I was sad. Someone just died for that heart to be given to me. I was joyful. This might be the end of the waiting game. I was scared. Will I live through the surgery? Will I make it back to Canada in time?

My life was going to be saved. I was one of the lucky ones, who had found a suitable donor. But what about the family who just lost their loved one. I trembled while my tears fell, tears of joy and tears of sadness. For so long I had been strong for mom and dad. I felt that if I cried in front of them, I was vulnerable and weak. Every night I cried with Tinker at my side and now, all of a sudden, all my hard work of keeping my tears to myself, was gone. I had blown it.

Billy asked me why I was crying.

"Aren't you happy, Kris? You're getting your new heart."

My brother was good at comforting me and I can't believe how well he was acting with everything going on. I knew he was being strong for me. I should have been happy but I was terrified. I was scared to die if my body rejected the heart. Well, we could deny the heart and I secretly hoped that was what my parents would do. But no one in their right mind would do that. Maybe I wasn't in my right mind. All I could really think about was what I forgot to do before I left for Texas this morning. I forgot to say goodbye to Tinker. I thought I would only be gone a few days, now it turns out we were going to Edmonton for a heart transplant. I won't be able to meet Reba or stay at her ranch or go to the concert or sightsee with my family. What about the double listing? We had waged war to have me double listed and now all the time seemed wasted.

Since Edmonton had been trying desperately to contact us for a few hours, time was of the essence. A heart doesn't have a long shelf life. It has to be transplanted into the recipient once out of the donor. We needed to get to Denison to get on that Learjet and we needed to do it now. (The Learjet couldn't come to get us because it can't land with a full tank of fuel.) We needed to figure out how to get to Denison and we had no idea where to go. We were lost.

Mom and dad decided to call 911. Mom was still on the payphone outside so dad went into Taco Bell to use the restaurant's phone. The staff said they were too busy to dial 911 and wouldn't help us. There were Dallas/Fort Worth police officers in a cruiser across the street but they were too busy to help us too. What the heck was the deal with that? They did give dad directions to the airport but that's not what we needed. We needed someone to take us immediately to Denison to get on that Learjet. If the situation had been stressful a few minutes ago, it was tenfold now. Meanwhile, I was still crying while my parents frantically tried to come up with a plan.

We had no idea if we would even get to Edmonton in time for the heart to be a viable transplant for me. We were stuck in Dallas, completely on our own, with no help from the police. We would have to backtrack to Budget Car Rental at the Dallas/Fort Worth airport.

Budget was awesome and helped us. A clerk arranged for one of the employees to drive us back to the airport, where CareFlite, an air ambulance, would meet us and fly us to Denison. Before being loaded onto the helicopter at the Dallas/Fort Worth airport, I made some calls.

It was amazing how, at that moment waiting for the helicopter, that every single person who had ever been my enemy, I now considered a friend. I wanted to make amends with whomever I had ever been upset with in the past. I phoned my maternal grandmother and talked to her. We were not close and I had been standoffish with her but I told her I was sorry about that and I loved her. Then I talked to my Aunty Terry and my cousin Jen and they said they were going to drive to Edmonton that night. Aunty Terry promised me she would bring Tinker to me since I never said goodbye to him. I also talked to my paternal grandparents and told them I loved them and hoped everything would be okay.

It was like this was the last moment for me. All I had was the here and now. I was living like I was dying. If you were going to die tomorrow, what would you say to those you love, or those you were hurtful towards, or those who were mean to you? I wanted to tell everyone I loved them like I was never going to see them again.

I had never been on a helicopter before and this air ambulance was small. There was room for the two pilots, a nurse, a stretcher with me on it and a seat for mom. Unfortunately, this meant dad and Billy wouldn't be able to come with us to Denison. I wasn't too happy about this but we needed to go right away. I knew everything was being done for my benefit so I gave dad and my brother a hug and we said our goodbyes. They said they would get to Edmonton as quick as they could.

Mom and I went out the doors to the helipad and I was so sad that dad couldn't come with us. I cannot imagine what he was thinking. His daughter was going to have a lifesaving heart transplant and he couldn't come with us. I climbed into the helicopter and we were off. I had tears streaming down my face. I was scared, scared for everyone involved. I didn't know what would happen in the next six hours and how I wished for a crystal ball to show me the future.

CHAPTER TWELVE

Bless your new heart

The CareFlite was awesome and made me laugh and forget about all my stress and worries. The pilots had huge headphones on as did the CareFlite nurse. They had an extra set and gave them to me to wear. We were all laughing while trying to scout out the Texoma Ranch, where we were supposed to be staying. Mom had no clue what we were saying but I filled her in from time-to-time.

The pilots were super nice and we had a great conversation about where I was from. I told them I was from Medicine Hat and they didn't know where that was. They then asked if it was near Calgary because they had heard about the famous Calgary Stampede. I said it was.

We had an awesome chat, which took my mind off my situation. Being on the helicopter was like being on a ride at Disneyland. The trip from Dallas to Denison was about 40 minutes and then I would be put directly on the Learjet and flown to Edmonton. That flight would be just under three and a half hours.

We arrived in Denison and Reba's people were there to greet us. The country star's crew had even been paging the beeper to tell us a heart was available. They were so supportive of the situation and gave me a hat signed by Reba and a poster for the benefit concert I was supposed to attend in two days. Reba signed the poster, *To Kristy,*

Bless your New Heart, Luv, Reba McEntire. Sorry we missed you, but we're so happy for you. I thought that was kind of her people to meet us at the airport. They told me that they had other stuff for me as well but that they would mail it home for us.

Mom and I got on the Learjet (it was a nice plane complete with leather seats) and I thought "This is it. This is the only thing that stands before me getting my new heart."

We left for Edmonton at 11:00 p.m. I couldn't believe I still had three hours to go before we would reach Alberta. There was a huge tin bowl full of candies and chips in the cabin and the snacks looked tasty. The pilots had asked if I wanted anything and I wanted to dive into the cookies. What better way to ease stress than eat! However, because I was going in for surgery, I wasn't allowed to eat or drink anything, even if my mouth and body craved it.

The pilots were awesome and they told us to make ourselves at home and enjoy the flight. Mom and I didn't talk much during the trip. I tried to sleep most of the way and closed my eyes with my head on her lap. I was snapped awake a few times when I thought we were going to crash in a storm. The turbulence was terrible and the thunder and lightning was bad. In fact, there wasn't any turbulence or thunder and lightning. What felt like a storm was actually the speed at which the Learjet was travelling. It was fast but that flight was the longest three hours of my life. It seemed like 15 hours but that was because I wasn't looking forward to what was going to happen next. I also missed dad and Billy and was hoping Tinker would be at the hospital to meet me at the door.

I didn't have a choice in what I was going to do next. If I did have a choice, it would be really stupid to turn down the transplant. I wanted everything to be over and done with. I wished I could hop in a time machine and go back two days ago. But this day would still happen. It was inevitable. Wishing or hoping wouldn't change one thing.

I started thinking about the donor family and what they were going through. At this moment, two families were coming together to share a tragedy. A few hours later, one family would rejoice with the success of a heart transplant. While the other family would be left to grieve. Unbelievably, this lamenting family was donating the heart of their loved one to me. Who was wonderful enough to do such a thing? I didn't know who but I would soon have someone else's heart pumping inside me. A total stranger died and now I will take his or her heart and live. How did my donor, this loved one, die? I started to cry.

The three hours on the jet gave me lots of time to think. There were so many feelings going through my mind and I can't imagine what my parents or brother were experiencing. I was a little unsure that the donor heart would still be available for me when we arrived in Edmonton. They never gave us a time limit that night but had said at previous appointments that I had about four hours from receiving the pager call, to going in for surgery. Time was ticking. I was also scared we would arrive at the hospital and it would be a dry run. That would mean we came back to Canada for nothing. The problem is, you never knew until it happened. You can't predict the future. You're not supposed to.

At 1:34 a.m. on May 26, 1996, we arrived at the Edmonton airport. From there, mom and I took a pre-arranged taxi to the U of A facility. The cab driver dropped us off at the emergency doors and I walked myself into the ER while mom got her suitcase. My luggage was left behind in Texas because it wasn't like I would need any of my clothes anytime soon. (I must say, the outfits the hospital gives you leave little to be desired but after having a heart transplant, I didn't feel like wearing nice clothes and going out anyway.) A nurse met us in emergency and started the process of prepping me for my heart transplant. She was sweet and I knew she felt empathy for me. It made the process much easier. I hated when I got a mean nurse, or a nurse who didn't like his or her job. That was the last thing you want when you're going in for major surgery and this was major surgery. It wasn't like taking a motor out of a car and putting another one in its place.

It was 2:00 a.m., well past bedtime, but the team of doctors and nurses performed like this was another day at the office. Nothing new. I was amazed at how well and quickly they acted. It was nice. My nerves were in a bundle and I was shaking. I couldn't stop trembling while the nurses seemed so calm and collected. What was wrong with me? Oh yeah, this was life or death and the time was fast approaching for me to take the step into the OR (operating room).

A nurse asked me to get on the scale and took note of my weight and height. She asked me when the last time I had anything to eat or drink. I answered her questions through chattering teeth. Then I was told the heart was at the hospital and everything was looking good. My heart transplant would be a go.

I was getting a new heart. It was surreal. I couldn't believe it was happening. I felt nauseated for the family who was saying goodbye to their loved one. I wanted to know the donor's story and find out how the person died. Another part of me, a big part of me, didn't want to go through with the transplant because I was terrified.

I was given some details on what my body was going to be going through shortly. I would be on machines during the operation: connected to a heart-lung machine, which does the exact same job as what my lungs and heart do. The heart-lung machine provides a pumping action, replacing your own heart's pumping so the heart is still for the surgery. It also pumps in oxygen to the blood. Basically, the heart-lung machine carries blood from the upper-right chamber of the heart to a special reservoir called an oxygenator. Once the blood is inside the oxygenator, it pools with bubbles and reaches the red blood cells. The blood then turns from dark red (oxygen-poor) to bright red (oxygen-rich). A filter removes all the bubbles from the oxygen-rich blood and the blood travels through a plastic tube back into the body's main blood outlet – the aorta. From the aorta, the blood then is circulated throughout the rest of the body. That was a lot of medical talk and you can see why I was stressed about going under the knife.

My prepping was done. I had my gown on and a cool turban on my head (sarcasm here). On my feet, I had some slippers that were made out of a tissue-like material. Mom and the nurse started walked with me to the operating room where the transplant team was waiting. The nurse took a shortcut to the OR and I got to see how on-call resident doctors live. The resident doctors' staff room was disorganized but can you blame them? These people are busy night and day doing surgeries, being on-call and whatever the case may be. There were scrubs everywhere and an empty pizza box on the table. If I was a doctor, I would live the same way, if not worse.

Finally, there in front of me, were the operating room doors. The heavy metal doors were closed and seemed to glow (they were painted white): the portal to the rest of my life. Once I stepped foot through them, I would be put to sleep. I had one last thing to do before I went into the OR – talk to dad.

On the right hand side of the doors, there was a red phone

hanging on the wall. I called dad to say the last "I love you" before passing through the operating room doors. Dad was in Dallas waiting for the next flight to Edmonton. He told me he loved me and that when I woke up, he would be there with me. He said he knew everything would be okay. I wanted to cry for him. Mom was here but my poor father was sitting in an airport lounge, far away from his daughter who was about to go in for a heart transplant. I said goodbye and that I loved him and then I hung up the phone.

The moment we had all been waiting for arrived. With my sweaty hand clasped tightly in mom's sweaty hand, we walked through the operating doors that opened in unison. Everyone inside the OR said hello, like nothing big was going to happen. These people had been patiently waiting for me. They pointed to the operating table and told me to hop on up. I climbed onto the smooth table and sat while they took my arms out of my hospital gown and laid the garment flat over my chest. It was freezing cold in the OR and I shivered. Almost all the medical staff had their faces covered with surgical masks.

Things were speeding up and I started to cry as they took sandpaper slips and vigorously rubbed my shoulders with them. It felt like they rubbed my skin off but I knew it was to make the monitor stickers stay in place. The stickers measure everything in my body. They notify the doctors and nurses working on me about any sudden changes in my body temperature or blood pressure. The stickers were put on and I was given the okay to lie down. It was now 3:00 a.m.

A nurse had already started an IV for me when they prepped me so this team didn't need to start one right away. Mom was still in the operating room with me but now it was time for me to go to sleep. I looked up at her and questions spilled out, "Everything will be all right, right? Mom, it's just like everything else. I will be put to sleep and then I will wake up, right? I will be healthy after this, right? Mom, I'm going to be okay, right?"

The doctors started to put medicine through the IV in my arm to make me sleepy. I felt a tiredness take over my body and a sensation that I had peed my pants. My eyes were getting heavy but I fought the torpor. Once I was asleep, that was it. Dr. John Mullen, the surgeon, would prepare to take out my heart and no one could stop him.

What if I didn't wake up?

"Mom, I'm going to be all right, right? Right?"

I kept repeating the questions in my head, looking for reassurance and fighting hard to not fall asleep. Mom's voice lingered in my head and I heard her repeatedly say, "Yes, you'll be fine."

The sight of her eyes welling up with tears left me worried and weakened with the thoughts that it will not be okay. The soft palms of her hands rubbing my forehead calmed me and made it hard for me to fight the medication putting me to sleep. I could barely see the outline of mom's head. Her image faded in the distance along with her voice. I couldn't hear my mom anymore. The lamp above me shone right into my eyes and made me squint. With my eyes heavy with tears, the light resembled lights of heaven shining down on me. I wondered if I was still alive. The sounds of the operating room dimmed in my ears. The light from the lamp dissolved. I felt like I was falling, falling into a dream or falling into heaven. I fell asleep, deep asleep.

CHAPTER THIRTEEN

Somewhere, out there

I can barely open my eyes. I carefully squint with one eye half-open for a brief second. In that moment, I see a tree and a pig standing next to me. I have no idea where I am. It's too hard to keep my eyes open. I have to keep them closed. I hear voices. I open my eyes. It's too overwhelming to resist the heaviness of my eyes. I close them again.

Billy is here with cousin Jen. I tell Jen that I finally got my period. I needed an ice cream pail because I was bleeding buckets. I'm finally a woman.

Where did Billy and Jen go?

I don't feel well.

I must have been dreaming.

I didn't get my period and I wasn't bleeding buckets. I feel a little sad and ashamed that I really didn't get my period. I wonder where I am. I don't remember anything.

I hear whispering. I recognize that voice. It's my cousin Jody, whispering softly. Jody is with me, brushing my hair. We're on a Learjet on our way to Edmonton. I don't know the reason. I have no idea why we're going to Edmonton and I can't remember anything. I know there are no seats left so we are lying on our luggage. It feels like I have been flying on this Learjet for at least three days now.

I open my eyes and I'm awake for a few moments...

Jody is here, brushing my hair. We're not on a plane. I can't really make out where we are, where I am. I'm lying on something that is soft but my back is aching so badly. I can't really move anything. My arms are like steel rods and won't bend. My feet have no feeling. I don't know what's going on. In the distance I see mom and dad. I see Grandma Jackie and her boyfriend Ron. Did Billy and Jen leave?

I close my eyes and I see Billy. I see Billy running. I can't see what he's running from. Then I hear him yelling, "Kristy, hurry! We have to run from the dinosaurs and jump on the plane to get out of here. Kris, hurry up or else you won't make it."

I start running full speed and then my brother grabs me and lifts me up and through the open plane doors. I look behind us and see dinosaurs chasing us. I can't quite make out how many there are because they stirred up the dirt of the road so badly. I can't count the dinosaurs in the dusty air. The wind's so strong that it's blowing my hair everywhere. It doesn't help that we have the plane doors open and it feels like there's a storm inside the aircraft. We're flying too close to the ground: one more inch and the wheels of the plane will hit the dirt road under us. I look around to see if anything else is chasing us. That's when I notice the dinosaurs are gaining on us. I turn my head to tell Billy and I notice a black and white figure a few metres ahead of the plane. I open my eyes wider and notice it's Tinker. What's Tinker doing here?

"OH MY GOD!" I scream to Billy. He looks with concern, "What is it Kris?"

I point to Tinker and Billy makes the plane speed up, to catch Tinker. We desperately try to grab Tinker and save him but dirt fills the air and we lose track of him. I'm screaming and Billy is frantically looking for Tinker but no such luck. We can't save him.

I look back and notice the dinosaurs are still in full view of our plane and still gaining on us. For a few seconds the dirt clears and I see Tinker slowing down. He can't run anymore and is lagging behind the plane. We have to get out of here because the dinosaurs are just about touching the plane. Then to my horror, a dinosaur grabs Tinker.

Tinker is gone.

I can't believe he's gone. I'm heartbroken. How could this happen? I'm lying here helpless and somebody needs to do something. I try to tell someone to help Tinker but when I open my mouth, I realize I can't talk. I'm drenched in sweat. What's happening to me? Am I dead? I look around, everything's such a haze. I see light but only a pinprick. I close my eyes again and all I can think about is Tinker. I want to cry. I want to go home. I repeat it in my head, "go home, go home, go home."

***

"I hate to admit it," I tell Aunt Terry, "but I wish I had bigger boobs."

I've always felt like such a late bloomer. Well, we decided to go get breast implants. Mom was coming with us. The place we were going to get our implants had some kind of promotion: three for free. So there we were, mom, Aunty Terry and me, ready for our new racks.

I look in the mirror after the surgical procedure, which I must admit was much easier then I had anticipated, and voila: boobs. I was finally a woman and I was proud of myself. I didn't even have a huge scar from where they inserted the new boobs. Mom and my aunt had theirs done at the same time. When Aunty Terry came out to show off her new set, they were very big. Mom really didn't have much change in hers. I'm very content with mine. The three of us got a steal of a deal.

When my uncle comes to pick us up at the beauty salon where we got the implants, he's not happy at all with Aunty Terry's big breasts. He tells her if she doesn't get them taken out he'll divorce her. I'm appalled. I thought they looked fabulous. All of a sudden there's a huge noise and I open my eyes for a few seconds.

I hear Billy's voice. I can't make out exactly what he's saying but nevertheless, I hear his voice. Then I see something. It looks like the light of an airplane. I look a little harder and realize it's a fighter jet and my brother is the pilot. I had no idea he knew how to fly a plane like that. He motions for me to jump into the fighter jet with him. I do and then I ask him what he's doing. He tells me we're going to blow up Shirley McClellan's house. He tells me he stole the fighter jet from the army and that we have to be quick. The police probably already have a warrant out for our arrests.

We fly over Shirley McClellan's house and let a missile drop straight over her house. I look out the back window of the plane and I see bright red flames jump to the sky. The noise of the missile exploding goes straight through my head. It hurts. The fire is super bright. It hurts to look at it.

I hear the sirens of the fire trucks on their way. I hear the sirens of the police cars on their way. I wake up to the beeping of the IV machine.

I close my eyes once again.

I'm turning into someone I don't like. I would never, ever blow up someone's home. I'm ashamed. I feel so remorseful. The police must have caught me and that's why I can't move. This is my punishment. I know I'm in a hospital bed but I don't know if I'm dead or alive. Maybe when we dropped the missile from the fighter jet, we weren't far enough away and the residual blast made the plane crash.

I keep my eyes closed and I feel myself falling again. I'm falling through a dark tunnel. At the end of the tunnel I see a reddish yellow light. The light of a beautiful sunset or the light of an inferno?

I keep falling. I hear screaming and, finally, I feel the ground. The feeling of the ground touching my feet is amazing. I start feeling around with my fingers. I feel salt-like pebbles with the tips of my fingers. The texture's rough but I'm glad to be on the ground. I open my eyes, which feel a little sticky and are a bit blurry. I have no idea how long I've been lying here on my stomach. I rub my eyes with both hands and blink my eyelids a few times. Then I open them wide to see exactly where I am. I can't see Billy anywhere. I have no idea what happened.

I'm amazed to find that I'm on a beach. The tide is low and the water is far out down the beach. A sunset is gently caressing me. The sand sifting through my fingers feels amazing. I carefully move my legs and my arms to bring myself up into a sitting position. All of a sudden I feel exhausted. My arms feel heavy, like they're made of rocks. I have no idea what I have just been through but by the way my body is feeling, it must have been a lot. I turn my head to look around and get an idea of where I am. When I look behind me, I'm shocked to see the fighter jet that Billy and I were in, is now in pieces. The pilot seat is intact though but my brother is nowhere to be found. Maybe I'm dreaming. Maybe he didn't help me blow up Shirley McClellan's house. Nothing is making sense anymore.

I don't know how long I've been sitting on the beach when I hear other voices. Kids are running on the sand towards me. I look and notice to my amazement that Billy is with them. I wonder if he'll recognize me and say hi. He's only a few feet away from me. He runs past me. I don't get why he didn't stop.

I notice my body is severely bruised and it looks like I haven't showered in days. I hear a loud noise, like the sound of a gunshot or a bomb blast. I look towards the beach where the kids are playing with Billy and notice that everybody is standing still. Standing still and looking directly at me. I turn around to see if they're looking behind me. That's when I see it too. A huge fighter jet is headed directly for us. The plane starts dropping missiles on the beach and one is headed straight for us. I realize that I'm reliving what had happened previously.

I get to my feet and start screaming and running. I'm trying to tell everyone to run as fast as they can but nobody can hear me. Were they already hit? No. The missile hits the beach and all I can see is plastic arms and legs flying everywhere. I start to fall again. I fall into a tunnel and I see Tinker. I see him running for his life. I'm running right beside him. I want to save him because I know the dinosaurs are here. And there they are. In an instant, Tinker is grabbed by a dinosaur.

I hear Billy and Jen talking to me.

I see Jody brushing my hair.

Then everything is black.

I stop falling. All is silent, except for the sound of someone on a respirator. I open my eyes and I see a pig standing by a tree holding a pitchfork. He looks sinister and I'm terrified. What's going to happen now? Then, out of the corner of my eye, I catch it, a familiar face. Mom. Finally, I know everything's going to be okay. I try to tell her to come to me but I can't move.

***

It had all been a dream. I had been in ICU for about four days before I fully woke up. The more I was able to wake up to reality, the more I knew nothing I had dreamed was true. To my relief, Billy and I did not blow up Shirley McClellan's house and Tinker was safe and sound. My aunt and cousin had arrived at the hospital with him 20 minutes after I went into the OR. (Ironically, Tinker had been lost for a few hours a couple of days after my surgery.)

The dreams, nightmares, whatever you want to call them, were probably from all the stress I was under. I had been worked up before going into the OR. That, plus the large amount of medication I was on, didn't help my head. The evil pig with the pitchfork turned out to be part of a mural on the ceiling above my bed where I was recovering from surgery with my new heart.

CHAPTER FOURTEEN

A new heart for Kristy

My heart had been switched with the donor's heart at 6:30 a.m. My transplant operation was complete at 11:00 a.m. and the procedure had gone well. The heart started on the second jolt of defibrillation (an electric shock to the heart) but the doctors had to keep my chest open for several days. My new heart was enlarged and putting pressure on my lungs. Also, the right ventricle was not pumping properly. I had been sedated as well so I wouldn't move with my chest wide open. (That was the reason my arms felt like rocks.)

It had been a few days since my heart transplant.

The surgery to close my chest was on Tuesday, May 28 at 3:00 p.m. and I came out of the operating room at 4:30 p.m. That night I was kept heavily sedated and paralyzed and that was when I started the week of strange and eerie dreams that had felt so real.

I was feeling worse after the transplant then I did before it. I had had this assumption that I would feel better immediately after surgery. This wasn't the case. I knew I would be in pediatric ICU for about two weeks and I hoped in due time I would get better and get my strength up.

The first time I sat up, I talked to Grandma and Grandpa Crockford on the phone. The media was also wondering how I was doing and I said it was okay to let them come in and talk to me. Actually, I don't know if I really had a say. I was still clearly out of it at that point. I kept the news clip of the reporters interviewing me and I see I have an IV in my neck on both sides and my hair unkempt and matted. You can see that I was very high on something. I told the media that I wanted to get out of the hospital and go waterskiing. It's right there on the tape. I can't believe I made it through the meeting.

I had a long road of healing ahead of me but I had my family to support and help me on my way to recovery. The roughest time was over. The waiting was done and my heart transplant was a success. I was going to survive. On Wednesday, May 29, 1996, the Edmonton Sun wrote a column in the newspaper with the headline: Tragedy Eased by Life Saved. The column talked about a man not knowing for sure if his daughter's heart saved a Southern Alberta girl. The father said he found comfort in the thought that it did. The man's daughter was Dawn Marie Tremblay and she had died Saturday, May 25, 1996 after a car accident near Rimbey, Alberta. She passed away one day short of her twenty-third birthday.

Dawn's father said he had read about a 14 year old girl, who had received a lifesaving heart transplant only hours after Dawn's death. The article also pointed out that Dawn had donated all her organs: her heart, her lungs, both kidneys and a part of her liver. Her fiancé, who was in the vehicle with her, was hurt in the crash. He was mourning the loss of his loved one as was Dawn's family.

As for my old heart, I didn't give it much thought. Deep down, I was glad it was out. I wished I could have seen it but the doctors wouldn't let me. (I recently discovered that my old heart is somewhere in Calgary.) I was mostly thinking about my new heart and was kind of in shock that I had someone else's heart beating inside me. It was weird but in a good way.

As each day at the U of A hospital passed, the nurses encouraged me to build my strength a little at a time. The doctors wanted me to keep my lungs clear and so physiotherapists came into ICU and I practiced breathing with a clear plastic contraption that had three balls in it. The harder I blew, the higher the balls went. Each day Judy Dahl, the child life specialist, came to see me to see how I was feeling and to lift my spirits. I was still on a number of different medications and still had a number of IVs in my body from my neck, to my hands, to my feet, pumping drugs into me. I was not well enough to eat without throwing up yet, which meant my meals were given to me intravenously as well. Some days, I seemed to feel total despair because I was tired and regretted the transplant. Other days, I seemed to feel brighter. Lucy, my friend who had already been through the transplant process, came into ICU to see me a few times when she had a checkup at the U of A. I was jealous of visitors because I wanted to get out of bed and walk around like everyone else. I had been in the hospital for a few weeks (it felt like months) and my back was starting to hurt and I could feel bedsores starting to form. The nurses were great helping me with everything as were my parents. They rented a place across from the hospital called the Campus Tower Suite Hotel. Tinker was staying with them and I longed for the time when I could get out on a day pass and see him.

I had strength problems because I was lying down for days. I couldn't move my feet up and down. This is what is called foot drop and the physiotherapists recognized it right away. (Sometimes people have foot drop so badly that it can't be corrected and so they will drag their feet on the ground.) Thank God I was one of the lucky ones. The physiotherapists worked with my feet so that I was able to move them.

I also had a problem with my arms. They both had been bent at 90 degree angles at my elbows. I couldn't straighten my arms but the physio would come every day and work with me until I was able to go down to physio by wheelchair.

I lost all sense of time in the hospital. I had no idea what day it was but I was looking forward to getting out of ICU. While I was there, I was thankful for the littlest of things like the nurse washing and doing my hair. When she brushed it, it gave me fuzzy feelings all over my body. I had been in intensive care for about two weeks when she noticed there was a bed sore on the back of my head. I hadn't even known it was there but it was definitely tender to touch. We took note of it but never gave it much thought after that.

My Aunt Terry had bought me a book so we could chronicle the days after my heart transplant. Every person who came to see me wrote in the journal. I'm grateful for the book today as I was tired a lot right after my surgery and it's amazing to look back at everything that happened, especially since I wasn't cognitively aware of most things.

Leanne wrote me a poem and tied it in with our "favourite things" joke.

Verse # 1 ♥
Kisses from Kristy - Talks from the Heart
Bright blue eyes shining - laughter and farts
Blonde hair and freckles your sweetness and spunk
These are a few of our favourite things

When you're drooling
When you can't talk to us
When we're feeling sad....
We simply remember our favourite things
And then we don't feel sooooo bad!!!!!!

(Not to mention one of my most favourite things: my sweet little
cousin with the green turban.)

The following are pages from the journal. (Every time I call out for Tinker, I imagine it was because of what I was dreaming.

May 25/96

Medicine Hat → Calgary → Dallas → Dennison → Edmonton. Took the Jetsons 16 hrs!!!
A heart is available for Kristy!!!!
What an unbelievable day.
Dad & Billy have to wait in Dallas.

The phone lines in Medicine Hat are buzzing.
Jen, Auntie Terry left for Edmonton @ 9:30 pm
Oh forgot - most important - Tinker is coming to be with you.
Leanne & Rob on their way to Edmonton from Calgary.
EVERYBODY IS PRAYING!!!

GRAMMA CROCKFORD IS CRYING!!!

Kristy your causing quite a stir. Everyone loves you!!!

First journal entry in the book my Aunt Terry started for me.

Very hard afternoon for Auntie Terry — trying to not talk to you all the time so you can rest.

Tube feed — 10 cc/hr. NG — in. Temp 39³ — Tylenol. Every morsel of spit that runs down I wipe off immediately as I'm supposed too!!! They talked of closing chest today but decided not to. May be tomorrow.

Keeping you very sedated. We got your new home rented in Campus Tower (right across from hospital.

Auntie Terry, Mom & Dad went & slept @ the new pad. Will be back in a.m.

Journal entry from May 27, 1996.

Mom + Dad here at 8:00 pm
Very confused + talking constantly
about Tinker + just everything.
Very Cold. Air bed arrived about
10:30 pm. A lot more comfortable
+ warm.

Journal entry May 29, 1996.

May 31
Dad sat with you until
4:00 AM. You kept him pretty
busy. Waking up off + on
You were getting more lively
as the night went on. Mom
came at 4:00 + sat with you
until 11:00 am You were awake
more off + on through the
night. Took respirator tube
out around 8:30 am Did well.
speech was very slurred.

Journal entry May 31, 1996.

Every day I thanked God I had received a heart. I was utterly exhausted but I was seeing positive changes in my health. Prior to my transplant, doctors couldn't feel a pulse in my feet. Now they could. As time passed, I started improving and regaining my strength with physio playing a major role. On June 5, I had a special visit from two U of A Golden Bears football players. They gave me a notebook and wrote:

Kristy, don't let any boys break your new heart.
Kristy, good luck and I love your attitude. Best of luck.

I was moved to a private room in ICU and on June 6, all my IV's were disconnected except for one in my hand. (It was a precautionary measure. I had bad veins and they wanted to make sure they had quick access if they needed it.) Then I was moved to the ward and into a private room on Level 4 (4D2.) I remember looking around and thinking that the puke-green walls were ugly and needed more colour. It was in this dreary room that I went through my routine of looking at my scar. It wasn't new as I had a scar in the same spot from a previous surgery. I did have staples and I was anxious about getting them removed.

I had been cooped up for a while and I begged for the chance to go outside, like a puppy dog asking for a walk. The doctors said yes and for the first time since my surgery, I could go outside! I went out in a wheelchair and it was great to be in the fresh air. Dad got Tinker from the apartment next door so I could see him.

I was excited to see Tinker although I couldn't hold him like I usually did because I was still very sore. I knew he knew something was going on but he was thrilled to see me too. On June 7, I wrote in the book by myself, which was really hard. My writing was squiggly and shaky because my hand was hurting from the IV and I was on a lot of medication.

I had to start learning about the drugs I was taking. The transplant clinic tested my knowledge of my medication and if I didn't know my dosage and the reason why I was taking it, they wouldn't discharge me. Memorizing the list wasn't bad…it was taking the pills. I especially struggled with cyclosporine (used to prevent the rejection of transplants).

One morning at breakfast I had to take the cyclosporine: an enormous capsule that reeked of skunk and sewage. I slowly lifted the pill to my mouth, coaxing myself to take this awful excrement-infested capsule, and opened my lips just enough to push the giant pill through. I took some water and forced myself to swallow. My mind was racing with thoughts telling me I wouldn't be able to take the medication.

"No matter how hard you try, Kristy, this pill is too big to swallow," my brain told me.

I rejected the negative thoughts and swished the drug down with a gulp loud enough that people walking by my room could hear it. I swallowed and swallowed and swallowed, trying to reaffirm that the pill went down and I had won the battle. I felt a knot forming in my throat; the walls around my room seemed much smaller than seconds ago. I was in a fight. Who was going to win: me or that pill?

I swallowed, hard, several more times before I realized the pill was stuck. It was not going to budge. I tried drinking more water but no luck. My eyes started to burn and pressure formed behind them as tears threatened to break free. I was alone in my room, battling the medication that was going to keep me alive. I needed to master this and I wasn't giving up but by now, I had giant crocodile tears sliding down each of my cheeks. My nose had started to drip and I could barely breathe.

"This is it," I thought to myself, and the knot in my throat slowly moved, inch by inch, upwards, helped along by nausea. I could still smell that pill, the skunk smell lingered. Perhaps it had rubbed off on my fingers. I regret making myself push that stupid oversized skunk-smelling capsule of a thing called anti-rejection medication into my mouth. I heard the disappointing voices of the nurses telling me this is life or death. Take the pill or die.

I bowed my head and prayed to God. I was done. I couldn't fight it anymore. That was when all the contents of my breakfast came cascading out like a waterfall and ended up on my tray of hospital food.

There was the pill.

Yep, that giant skunk capsule was smackdab in the middle of the vomit. It was staring at me, grimacing at me, daring me to take it again.

"You're going to lose," it taunted. "Give it up."

A nurse came in and provided a much needed interruption between that capsule and me. Unfortunately, I had to take the cyclosporine via drip.

Cyclosporine capsule, you may have won that one but I had plenty more tricks up my sleeve.

On June 8, I was able to go out on a pass for a few hours to visit my parents' hotel. That was when my good friend Nicole from

Medicine Hat came to see me. She provided some much desired companionship and I got to catch up on what everyone was doing back home. Nicole filled me in on the boys we liked, how school was going and who was getting into trouble. When I took a nap, having her beside me was soothing. I was only able to leave the hospital for a short time but it was a relief to see someone other than medical staff and something other than hospital walls.

The saddest part of that day was going back to the hospital. However, the next day I was given consent by my doctors to spend the night at the hotel. Just to sleep somewhere other than the hospital was extremely exciting and comforting. I say comforting because it was the first time I had slept somewhere else other than the hospital since my transplant. It was a step towards going home. I was thankful for the overnight pass but my thoughts were tinged with regret. Here I was, enjoying an evening with my family, while another family was in the midst of grieving their daughter.

The morning of June 10, after I spent the evening away from the hospital, I was sick and throwing up. I always knew there was a significant chance of rejection. Doctors had told me that it was very high within the first three months of transplant but decreased after about a year. We knew if rejection was going to happen, it was going to be early. I prayed that what I was experiencing wasn't my body rebelling against my new heart. I didn't want this heart to get damaged and have the donor family feel like I had wasted it. I was severely worried.

My parents took me to emergency and the doctors said that I may be experiencing a mild rejection. They decided to give me a dose of steroids and after a couple of days, I started to feel better. To my relief, the steroids had helped.

Besides the scar that was the daily reminder of my lifesaving heart transplant, I also had a scar on the left side of my groin area because I was on dialysis during my transplant. The doctors were concerned about my kidneys since I had gone into slight renal failure during surgery. I started taking immunosuppressive medication too and was in a private room because I was at an increased risk for infection. It was nice to have a room to myself. I didn't have the noise or intrusion from another patient and it meant decreasing the risk of contracting a bug from the hospital. I was also able to escape to my parents' hotel from time-to-time.

I was exhausted easily and there was no way I could walk the distance to the Campus Towers hotel. Mom would push me in the wheelchair to their room and then push me back to the U of A hospital. Those wheelchair outings were probably giving her one heck of a work out. I, on the other hand, spent a lot of time reflecting and, sometimes, even wishing that I hadn't had a heart transplant at all. I was spent all the time and didn't have any energy to do anything. Just getting dressed was tiresome. I think it was my body adjusting but I was impatient. I wanted to feel better, now! I wasn't even sure that I would feel any better in a couple of months. It made me think that the doctors must have made a huge mistake about me being ill. I had felt way better prior to the heart transplant. I was starting to regret having it. It was making me feel super crappy.

The transplant co-ordinator, Linda Buzzell, told me that it's something you have to get used to. It was a big surgery and my body needed time to heal. I couldn't understand why I felt terrible and weak. I kept hoping and praying for the day when I would feel fantastic, or at least okay.

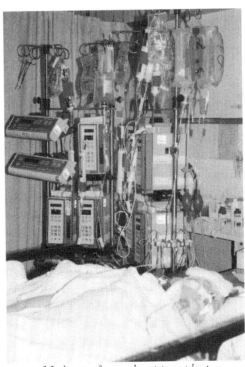

Me hours after my heart transplant.

Donor's family happy for Kristy

Article from Medicine Hat News.
Printed with permission from the Medicine Hat News.

Me with Dr. Coe during a clinic visit after my heart transplant.

CHAPTER FIFTEEN

Alive and well

I started noticing that Aunt Terry wasn't visiting me. I thought maybe my aunt and uncle were busy working. Besides, Edmonton is an over five hour drive from Medicine Hat. I had asked mom if everything was okay and she kind of changed the subject. I got the feeling that something had happened when I was in dreamland. I wondered if the family was fighting but, of course, nobody told me anything.

On June 10, 1996 I was finally discharged from the U of A. I had to remain in Edmonton, close to the hospital, so I moved into the Campus Towers Suite Hotel with mom and dad. I still spent a lot of time at the U of A having my blood taken, attending physio and heading up to the pediatric cardiology department to see Dr. Coe. (Sometimes I might be sent to get an x-ray if my blood work was wonky.) These appointments were scheduled for three times a week.

The day after I was discharged, June 11, 1996, I was starting my daily routine when I met up with my dear friend Annalies. She was at the hospital starting her physio routine before being put on the list for a heart double lung transplant. It was really nice to see Annalies again. Unfortunately, she wasn't going to be in Edmonton long but it was good to catch up in the short time we had together. We were both going through so much and had become close. I looked up to her and she gave me strength. At times, we used each other for support. I knew what it was like to have a heart transplant but I was numb to the thought of needing two lung transplants as well. This girl was an angel.

Me and Annalies in Edmonton at U of A hospital

I had to get up early in the morning to get my blood work done as my blood had to be taken before I took my medication at 8:00 a.m. The other thing was, if you wanted to get your blood work done quickly, it was better to be at the lab early. I have to admit, getting up early and all the appointments was hard. The payoff was that even though I didn't have much energy, it was nice to have the latter half of the day open.

Dad had gone back to Medicine Hat to work and make sure Billy was okay and so it was just me and mom in Edmonton. We were usually free by 1:30 p.m. after I had an echocardiogram (like an ultrasound but it uses sound waves to produce images of the heart and measure blood circulation) and was seen by Dr. Coe. If the results of the echo were good, meaning my heart was functioning properly, mom and I would visit Lucy (my friend who also had a heart transplant) in a town just outside Edmonton. We might also visit with Bev and Jim at their house for a little bit too.

I got weekends off from the U of A: no appointments, no doctors, no needles! It was nice not to have to go to the hospital. I had seen enough of it in the last few years. It was also great to have a couple of days to myself and not be scheduled to be somewhere.

Dad had to work on Father's Day, June 16, and was in Medicine Hat so mom and I went to Bev and Jim's for the day. The weather was beautiful. The sun was strong and I began to feel like I was a normal person spending time with loved ones. I was sad that dad couldn't be with me but mom and I tried to make the best of it. Mom and Jody (Bev and Jim's adult daughter) had had a few too many that night and instead of going back to our apartment, we stayed at Bev and Jim's. When it was time to get up, mom was feeling very under the weather (as you can imagine) so she drove me to the U of A and told me she would park the car and come in and meet me in physio. I said I would be fine alone and I would call her once I was done physio and my appointment with Dr. Coe.

When I saw Dr. Coe, I told him how mom had a terrible headache. (I didn't tell him exactly why she had a headache.) Of course, being such an awesome doctor, he called her to make sure she was okay. He then sent some Tylenol home with me to give to her.

After the appointment, I called mom to come get me. It was amazing how well I was doing: health wise and being on my own. I was getting around the U of A without a wheelchair and I was finally feeling fantastic. I had waited a long time to feel this great. This was an important milestone for me too because it was the first day I attended all my appointments without mom or dad. When I got back to the apartment, I did something for mom: I did some of the dishes. I washed them slowly but I did them. I had waited a long time to be able to do a mundane chore like this and it was such a great moment that I wrote about it in my book.

On June 21 we tried to persuade Dr. Coe into letting me go home for the weekend. Grandma Crockford was turning 80 and the whole family was meeting at Grandma Jackie's home for the big birthday. It would be my first time seeing my entire family since my heart transplant. I wanted to go home so badly and sleep in my own bed. I wanted to rub my feet on our luxurious green carpet.

Dr. Coe didn't have good news for me. He didn't approve of my plan to go to Medicine Hat for the weekend. He felt that I was not well enough to travel. My lungs were full of fluid and an echocardiogram was done. It showed that one of my new heart valves wasn't pumping blood properly. I was devastated because I wanted to go home. It was hard for me to come to terms with certain things that pertained to recovery. I wanted things to go back to normal. I wanted to go home. I knew eventually there would come a time and I would go home for the weekend but I didn't want to wait for that time. I wanted to go home ASAP. I must admit, I was a tad bit jealous that everyone was in Medicine Hat celebrating grandma's birthday and I was stuck in Edmonton.

We used the time we stayed in Edmonton to our advantage. Mom and I had to become pros at my medication. I was taking twelve different types of drugs and the dosages varied. It was a lot of medication and it became extremely confusing. Mom is brilliant and thought of the greatest idea ever. She decided to colour code all my medication with stickers. We had a colour coding key that we wrote up in case we forgot the colour of a medication. We bought packages of white reinforcement stickers and then coloured the inside circle of each sticker to correspond with the colour we had chosen for each drug. Each colour meant a different medication.

Green was for diltiazem. (Novo-Diltiazem is a brand name. It's used for high blood pressure among other things.) I was taking 30mg of diltiazem - twice a day.

Yellow was for acetylsalicylic acid (Aspirin is a brand name. It's used to treat pain, fever, and inflammation among other things.) I was taking 81mg a day.

Maroon was for apo-furosemide (Lasix is a brand name. It's used as a diuretic among other things.) I took Lasix to get rid of extra fluid in my lungs. The dosage of Lasix always varied depending on my blood work.

Purple was for ranitidine (Zantac is a brand name. It's used to treat acid reflux among other things.) I was taking 5mg of Zantac - twice a day.

Peach was for prednisone (an immunosuppressant drug). My dosage of this medication varied as well but I would have to take it for at least a year. (It was one of four important drugs I had to take.) Prednisone came in pill and liquid form but since I wasn't a big fan of liquid medication (it left a bad taste in my mouth and could lead to ulcer-type sores), I took the pill. The pill was very small, smaller then a baby Aspirin pill or like the size of a little Nerds candy. At times, I was taking 18mg of prednisone, which meant at one time, for one drug, I was taking three 5mg pills with three 1mg pills to get 18 mg. That is six little tiny pills of the same drug. With prednisone, you can't just stop taking it. You have to be weaned off of it slowly because it's a steroid.

Azathioprine (Imuran is a brand name. It's categorized as a rejection drug) was another medication I was taking, we used the color yellow. There were two yellows- Imuran was a brighter yellow. Aspirin was orangey-yellow I was taking 50mg of Imuran - twice a day to keep my body from rejecting my new heart. The drug lowered my immune system so it wouldn't fight off the foreign thing (someone else's heart) in my body.

Rust was for iron, which I took to bump up my iron levels. I was taking 300mg of iron - once a day.

Blue was for acyclovir. (Avirax is a brand name. It's an antiviral drug.) I took 800mg (one tablet) - four times a day. This drug was one of the most expensive (about $450 CAD for about a three month supply) and was not covered by our drug plan. I needed this medication to prevent cancer: a big worry after you've had a heart transplant. (Long-term use of immunosuppressive medication can increase the risk for certain cancers such as skin cancer.) My family and I used to joke about Avirax and said that it was "boobs in a jar" because one of the side effects was that your boobs got larger. I have to be honest, I didn't mind taking this drug one bit although it never worked in my boob department.

Dark blue was for cyclosporine. (Neoral is a brand name. It's categorized as a rejection drug, one of the most important of the rejection drugs.) My dosage varied. I took Neoral in the liquid form but not by choice. I couldn't keep the pills down because they were huge and as soon as I unwrapped a pill, this awful smell came out. The odour was so bad it made me want to vomit on the spot. (It was this pill that I fought with in the previous chapter.) The smell that lingered from the drug was similar to the smell a skunk gives off, but unfortunately, you had to put this in your mouth. Sometimes I tried different techniques to take the pill like plugging my nose as I put the pill in my mouth. However, I already knew that it was gross and it was difficult to pretend that it didn't have a nasty smell or wasn't gargantuan.

The liquid form was gross too and couldn't be mixed in with certain juices. Water wouldn't be able to hide the bad taste either. I had to be very careful with the Neoral because it would be absorbed into whatever it touched. For instance, I couldn't pour it into a Styrofoam cup because it would be absorbed by the Styrofoam. The easiest way to take it was to draw it in a syringe, then put the syringe in chocolate milk and draw some chocolate milk. I would shoot the concoction in my mouth as fast as I could, making a million different funny faces at one time. Then I picked up the rest of the chocolate milk and guzzled it as fast as I could without choking. (I couldn't drink chocolate milk for about two years after because it reminded me of the gross taste of the medicine.) I would once and while switch it up and have some good old orange juice instead of the chocolate milk.

Pink was for magnesium. (A mineral for the heart and bones.) I took 11/2 tablespoons -once a day.

Brown was for Potassium. (Slow-K is a brand name. It's an electrolyte replacement.) The dose always varied depending on my blood results.

Last but not least, black was for septra. (Novo-Trimel is a brand name. It's an antibacterial agent.) I took 2 teaspoons daily. All heart transplant patients were put on Novo-Trimel because our immune systems were weak.

It took me a while to remember all the medication I was on but I knew the most important medication was the Neoral, the cyclosporine. I knew all the medications I was taking were important and I knew why they were important. I had to know them. It was a big deal at the U of A to understand your medication and the side effects. Dr. Coe expected me to answer immediately when he asked me what drugs I was on and how much I was taking.

Right after my surgery it was tough to remember everything because I was still in the early stages of having a heart transplant and my medication was always changing. However, with the colour coded system, it wasn't long and I became a whiz at my own medication and the side effects. Speaking of side effects, I did notice some. The cyclosporine caused my cheeks to puff out like a chipmunk. My arms and back became hairy and I had hair growth on my face. My eyebrows, once blonde and perfectly shaped, were merging into a long and dark unibrow. I wouldn't necessarily have to be on all these medications for life but a lot of them I would be. It was the end of June and I was looking forward to the day I could get a pass to go home to Medicine Hat. I know Tinker was looking forward to going home too. He had stayed with me the entire time I was in Edmonton. I knew he needed to get back home but he had helped me through many tough times. Deep down, he felt exactly what I was going through and knew everything was going to be okay. He was such a big inspiration in my life and seemed to always know just what I needed. Despite his love, there were moments I got down on myself about life in general.

My cousin Leanne and her husband Rob were great to visit me but other family members seemed to forget I was in Edmonton. I couldn't grasp what could come in-between people you supposedly loved but something had. I didn't know the full story but the gist was there was an issue over money. I felt guilty about that. It was all my fault. If I hadn't been sick, then all this fighting about money would have been avoided. My parents never gave me any of the details or talked much about the entire situation and I never really pushed it. I'm sure they thought I had bigger things to worry about and that I was too young to understand it all anyways. The guilt, plus the shame, plus the fact I wanted to go home already, was starting to make me irritable.

When Canada Day weekend arrived, I was given the green light to go home. I had to be back in Edmonton for my Tuesday morning appointments but that didn't dampen my thrill of heading home. I was so happy to be able to sleep in my own bed and wake up in my own room. I could turn on my own light or take a bath in my own bathroom. These little things are some of the things I missed the most. Oh, to be in my own bathtub! My hospital room had a shower but no bathtub so taking a bath was great for my emotional well-being. I could soak in the tub and be in the moment, thankful to be alive, and I could take time to pray about the family who was responsible for me living. Precious moments. I was also ecstatic just to have a family supper with Billy, dad and mom. I didn't care what I had for supper, I would even eat turnips (which I hate) because I was eating them in my own house. The Medicine Hat News was excited as well to have me home. On the day I left for home, Friday, June 28, 1996, it printed an article with the headline *Guess Who's Coming to Dinner?* Yes, it was me and it was news to talk about.

I was flying back, travelling from Edmonton to Calgary and then from Calgary on to Medicine Hat. I left Friday evening at around 6:30 p.m. Because I was immunosuppressed, there was one stipulation I had to abide by in order to leave the hospital: I had to wear a face mask in the airport and on the airplane. You can imagine how that felt. I was embarrassed and I thought people would stare at me or, worse, think I was contagious and be scared of me. I wanted to feel normal too but nothing about my situation was normal and now I had to wear a facemask, very not normal. It made me feel like I didn't fit in, like I didn't belong. I felt a little like the celebrity Michael Jackson, who, on several occasions, was photographed wearing a mask over his nose and mouth for no apparent reason. I think people looked at me and wondered why I was wearing the facemask but being polite, didn't ask.

Our plane was late arriving into Calgary from Edmonton but thankfully, they held the connecting flight. Since our plane had to wait for us, everyone was joking that our luggage wouldn't make it onboard. Tinker was in the baggage hold and I was anxious that he'd miss the plane. I was so relieved to hear him yelping mid-flight. Poor Tinker had never been on a plane before so this was a ride of lifetime for him. I could hear him barking the whole way to Medicine Hat. He was terrified and I felt bad for him. Everybody on the plane heard him and joked about making sure the dog got on the plane but not the rest of the luggage.

The media was waiting for me to arrive at the Medicine Hat airport. They took some lovely photos of me walking off the plane with my chic doctor's mask. I didn't mind that people were sticking around the airport for me, it made me feel like everyone had been battling along with me. I knew I had so much support.

I have to admit, when I stepped out of the airplane and into the beautiful warmth of the prairie wind, the smell of Medicine Hat carried on it, I felt free. I felt free to be home and free of disease and I felt like I was finally okay. I could breathe and I was happy for the first time in a long time, happy to be me. For so long I had hated myself because of what I had to go through but now I felt like I was going to be all right. I felt like someone had lifted a million tonnes off of my shoulders. I took the longest, deepest breath I had ever taken in my entire life and let it out in relief. I was alive and well

Guess who's coming to dinner?

MEDICINE HAT NEWS

HEALTH

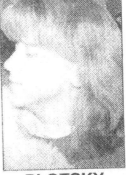

PLOTSKY

Kristy Plotsky is coming home to Medicine Hat tonight.

The 14-year-old heart patient arrives in the Hat at 6:30 p.m. at the municipal airport for a three-day visit. Plotsky heads back to Edmonton Monday night.

"We just found out that the doctors are letting her come back to the Hat," mom Margo Plotsky said this morning. "Kristy is thrilled. We all are."

An earlier trip to the Hat for Kristy's grandmother's birthday was cancelled because doctors at University of Alberta Hospital were wary about letting her travel outside Edmonton.

Margo says doctors told her Kristy's health is good enough to let her go.

Kristy received a new heart three months ago.

Margo says Kristy plans to visit family and friends while she's in the city.

Reprinted with permission from the Medicine Hat News.

Happy to be home

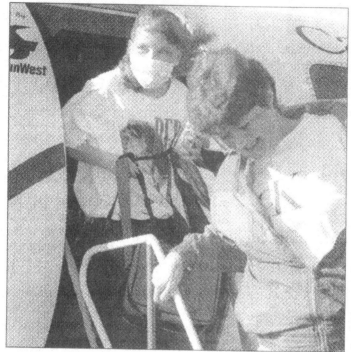

Kristy Plotsky and mother Margo arrive at Medicine Hat airport Friday evening. Doctors in Edmonton decided Kristy, 14, was well enough to spend the holiday weekend at home in Medicine Hat. Kristy received a new heart three months ago.

Reprinted with permission from the Medicine Hat News.

I walked into the airport to meet up with my family, who had been patiently waiting my safe return. Dad and Billy were first in line with big hugs and kisses. We took Tinker out of his kennel and I knelt down to pet him. That's when I noticed he was missing his two front teeth. I wondered if he had been gnawing at the door of his kennel and that was when his teeth came out. (He looked just as cute.)

Tinker's kennel was full of poop too (the flight actually scared the poop right out of him.) I got down on my knees and I gave him the biggest hug ever and whispered in his ear, "We are home, buddy."

I went to get back up and I fell over. I mean, I fell right over. I didn't have enough strength in my legs and knees to push myself back up and onto my feet. I also didn't have any balance and that's why I toppled. I was a little embarrassed and hoped no one from the news had witnessed my crash. A family member had noticed and didn't delay jumping into action and helping me back on my feet.

I'm lucky that mom is such a smart lady because without her, I would have missed taking my medication. She was obviously thinking and packed my drugs in our carry-on bag. Thank God she did because I had pills to take at 8:30 p.m. and our luggage wouldn't arrive on the carousel until about 9:30 p.m. Then it was home sweet home.

CHAPTER SIXTEEN

Seeing tomorrow

My first night back in my own bed, Friday, June 28, 1996, I laid awake looking at the ceiling. It was difficult to think that only a few months ago, I had been lying here, praying for some kind of miracle and not knowing what would happen day-to-day. Now I was here in the same bed, the same room, praising the Lord that I received my miracle. I knew I was going to be okay but I felt sad. Tears prickled my eyes when I thought about the family, the family of the woman whose heart I had in me right now, who allowed me to be in my bedroom again. I was able to see tomorrow. I was alive because my donor family signed a donor card and talked about organ donation. I was able to keep breathing and keep living because of them. My parents were able to see me grow and mature and maybe, one day, see me get married. How do you thank someone for such a precious gift: the gift of life?

Although we had an idea of whose heart I might have received, I wanted to know what kind of person she was. I knew her name and that she had been engaged. I wondered if I really had her heart. Could it be possible that through all this, I'll actually meet her family one day? As usual, I had conflicting feelings. Hope and hopelessness. Joy and grief. Guilt and relief.

It was weird to think about how two families, who have never met, can collide in life. That's when I let the tears go. I cried for the girl who had passed away. I had never known her but I cried for her as if she was one of my own family members. I was here with her heart, alive and well, pumping in my body, letting me take each breath and giving me life. At the same time, her family was in mourning and in so much pain and disbelief. If the tables were turned, I could have been the one giving her life.

It was at this moment that I realized the gift of life is the most precious gift that another human can give. Dawn was my angel, my guardian angel, and she was going to take care of me.

***

When I woke up that beautiful Saturday morning on June 29, I looked outside to see the brightest, most spectacular blue sky ever. It was like someone had draped a bright blue sheet over my window. There was not one cloud in sight and it was glorious. It gave me a feeling of optimism and I knew that while there would always be bad days, no matter what we can rely on the sun being in the sky. It might be the cloudiest day ever but every morning the sun will rise, even if you can't see it. It'll always be shining above the clouds.

We set our eyes on what we see, not on what we cannot see
What we see will last only a short time, what we cannot see
Will last forever.
2 Corinthians 4:18 (My favourite quote.)

I had had a solid sleep in my own bed. In the hospital, it was tough to get a full night's rest because of all the distractions like the lab coming in and poking me at 4:00 a.m. (Definitely annoying.) Today was going to be busy but I didn't want to feel rushed. I wanted my weekend to be as relaxing as possible so I didn't jump right out of bed like I might have done before my transplant. Back then, I was in a hurry because I didn't know how much time I had left on earth. Now that I had a new heart, I took things slowly: savouring each moment.

I was only in town until Monday and I had a lot to do. I had a lot of people to see and places to go. I needed help with some of little things like putting my socks on and climbing into the truck since I didn't have my full strength back. Otherwise, I had a full weekend planned with family.

I think I subconsciously avoided my friends. I didn't meet up with any of them. They didn't seem like a priority at the time and I was scared about what they might think of me. I had changed a lot, not in terms of my personality but in regards to my appearance. Like I've said before, I was experiencing some side effects from the numerous medications I was on. The prednisone gave me chipmunk cheeks. The cyclosporine was making me grow hair on my face, arms and back. I was tired and looked drawn. I also wanted to use this time to spend with my family. Although many people wanted to see me, I wanted to sit around at home. (As well, I thought that if anyone wanted to see me, they could come over to my house.)

I was feeling a little under the weather but the time would eventually come that I would have to make my way back to Edmonton. I wanted to make the best of being home. I had some visitors, like mom's photographer friend who snapped some candid pictures of my family. I also walked the dogs by our garden on the acreage. Of course, the Medicine Hat News stopped by to get an interview. My first supper at home since the transplant was low key: quiet but perfect. At the end of the day, I was exhausted physically and didn't have much strength in my body. I slept well.

Sunday morning I went to church. I wanted to have a nap after the service but people really wanted to see me. I was excited to visit Aunty Terry and Uncle Steve because they had a baby ostrich born the same day I had my heart transplant (May 26). Fittingly, they had named the ostrich Kristy. During the visit with my relatives there was no mention of any past conflicts. That was fine by me. We were all family after all.

Uncle Steve and I with the Ostrich born May 26, 1996.

I never wanted Monday to come but it was inevitable. However, I knew the next time I came home, it would be for good. Each day I was gaining back a little more strength and I really felt that things would only get better from here on in.

On Canada Day, Monday, July 1, the day I had dreaded all weekend, arrived. It was a quiet day as we were getting ready to fly back to Edmonton. I wasn't looking forward to the trip but I knew that the worst was over and I was on a healing path now: not sick and waiting. Tinker would stay in Medicine Hat so I said my goodbyes to him and my family and then mom and I returned to our "home away from home."

Edmonton had become a familiar place: the doctors were familiar to me and I knew my way around the hospital. (I still would have rather been home.) The next day, I had my regular blood tests done and everything seemed to be going well. I was already looking forward to the weekend ahead because Leanne and Rob were driving from Calgary to see me. It was always so nice when people visited. Mom and I love each other dearly but we also needed breaks from each other. We got along most of the time but there were days when I was moody and not in good spirits. I was also a teenager (that should explain it all). Having company gave us a buffer.

The week, of course, dragged on as always but I was happy I was feeling better. I had more energy and I started to feel like my heart and my body were becoming one. I was me again.

On Friday, July 5 I had my usual routine morning of blood tests, a Dr. Coe appointment and physio. All the tests turned out good and finally, it was the weekend. Leanne and Rob arrived on Saturday and we went for a drive and did a little shopping. We came home to the Campus Tower Suite Hotel, made supper and then played The Farming Game all night long. The Farming Game is a board game where you pretend that you're a farmer and you buy fields, grow different crops and sell them for money. It's pretty intense and one of my favourite games. We all took The Farming Game seriously and were addicted to it. Rob was the funniest person to play the board game with. If he was losing and then all of a sudden, he hit good luck, he would shout out, "I'm back in the saddle! OOOOOHHHH WHOOO!" As soon as I heard that line, I knew my land was in trouble and I could bet that Rob was going to win the game.

On Sunday, we got up late and had breakfast. We left for the

Edmonton Valley Zoo around noon and spent a few hours there. The zoo was so much fun and the weather in Edmonton was fantastic: a bright blue sky with a radiant sun. Leanne and Rob left in the early evening and mom and I headed to Bev and Jim's. Another week was gone and another one was on the way. I couldn't believe that it had already been seven days since I had been home. Time was passing quickly and with each day, I could feel that I was getting stronger. Oh sure, I still had really bad days. Sometimes I was nauseous from taking copious amounts of pills or felt tired and sore from my incision. In these moments I would ask God, "Why me? Why did I have to get sick? Why wasn't it someone else?" I never had anyone in mind to take my place but, sometimes, I felt sorry for myself. I tried to push the self-pity away because I knew how lucky I was to be alive and have people around who cared about me.

Monday came and my routine kicked in again. You know it by now. After physio, I spent the rest of the day with Judy Dahl. She showed us the LRT (Light Rail Transit) in Edmonton and we took it downtown. The three of us had lunch out and I enjoyed it. Later that night, mom and I took a load of our stuff over to Jim and Bev's since we were going to be checking out of the hotel the next day. The place was expensive due to the location (across the street from the hospital) and we didn't know how much longer we would have to stay in Edmonton. Since we didn't know a lot of people in the city, we decided to stay at Bev and Jim's until I could go home for good. (On our last day at the hotel, we found out the room we had been staying in the entire time was an allergy room, meaning no pets allowed. Oops. We had Tinker with us for a good month and we never knew we weren't supposed to.)

Moving out of the hotel was like starting a new chapter. I was excited to go to Bev and Jim's but also a little apprehensive. Living with them meant I'd have to get up earlier to get to my appointments. I'm not much of a morning person although it's my favourite time of day. Campus Tower was so close to the U of A that meant I could sleep in. That would no longer be the case. Living with Bev and Jim did mean I was one step closer to Medicine Hat.

Check out day was Tuesday, July 9. First, we went to the hospital and I had to get an echo plus an EKG (also known as an ECG. An electrocardiogram is a test that measures the electrical activity of the heart. It spits out a paper with line tracings of the heart's electrical activity.) and an x-ray and see Dr. Coe as well go to physio. After we saw Dr. Coe, we checked out of the Campus Towers Suite Hotel and headed over to the mall where Bev was working at Kmart. The store had this huge cardboard cut-out of Reba McEntire holding a bag of Fritos Scoops (a new kind of chip then) and she was standing in front of a blue Ford truck. Bev knew how much I loved Reba so she gave me the flat version of the singer. With Reba in hand, we headed to Bev and Jim's house where we would be staying until I was given the okay to go home.

Wednesday, July 10 was a laid back day and I got out of the hospital earlier than usual. I did my physio at 10:30 a.m. and talked to Dr. Coe and then picked up some more prescriptions that I needed. Mom and I later wasted away part of the day by going to West Edmonton Mall. It's the biggest mall in Alberta and besides lots of shops, it has a water park and carnival rides. We walked around for a little bit and returned a bag mom had purchased for my medication. (We decided it wasn't going to work.) We later met Bev for supper at the mall where she worked and then headed to her home.

Thursday was pretty much the same thing and then it was Friday. I hung out with Bev and Jim's daughter Jody and her husband Bruce for a while. I loved seeing them. Jody looked like the country music superstar Mindy McCready and Bruce looked exactly like actor Bruce Willis. It was nice when people stopped in at Bev and Jim's; it really took my mind off of things.

The weekend was here and we spent the day with Jody and her best friend at Allan Lake, near Edmonton. It was a gorgeous afternoon. I had to sit in the shade the entire time because the medication I was on increased my risk of skin cancer (also, being a redhead, I don't tan very well) but I had a blast anyway. It was great to relax and not stress about anything but I was missing dad and I was sure mom did as well. I knew spending time with Jody was good for mom too. She needed a way to destress from all the recent events.

With the weekend over, it was time for my hospital check-in. We got up early on Monday, July 15 to get my blood work done. In order to get a true reading of my cyclosporine (rejection drug) levels, they had to take my blood before my scheduled dose at 8:30 a.m. Most of the time, the outpatient laboratory was extremely busy and that meant there was always a significant wait: at least an hour. It didn't bother me though. I had become a pro at this waiting game and would dive into the celebrity magazines in the waiting room.

We usually arrived at blood work about 7:00 a.m. and waited to see a technician. As soon as we were done, we hurried to the cafeteria to grab something quick to eat, like toast and chocolate milk for my meds. Mom couldn't live without her Diet Coke back then so she grabbed one of those. When we were done breakfast, we headed straight up to the transplant cardiology department to Dr. Coe's office. I would need to have an EKG done as well as an echocardiogram. After the echo, we saw Dr. Coe and he read us what the EKG and echo showed. The results were that my heart was functioning perfectly and there weren't any concerns although I had a bit of a temperature, which had already lasted for a couple of days. It was a little concerning and the doctor thought I might have an infection. Infections are tough to fight when you are immune suppressed. I got some antibiotics and was told to take it easy.

Besides Dr. Coe, I had to see another physician that day about my right elbow. Even after physio, my elbow wouldn't straighten. The doctor took a look at my arm and said not to worry. The elbow was stiff from surgery and would straighten out as time went on. (I was never that stressed about it.) The bed sore on my head never healed and it was itchy and bothering me the most but at least I was on my way to a healthy life with next-to-no hospital visits.

CHAPTER SEVENTEEN

On my way

Dr. Coe spoke the words I had been praying to hear for so long on Tuesday, July 16, 1996. "Everything is good. You can go home."

I can't explain how happy I was to hear those words. I felt like I could do anything: run and jump and spin. I felt like I could fly. I could go home! It was amazing how some things just worked out. Mom was overjoyed too. Now I wanted to get out of the hospital as soon as possible.

Sometimes, when things were going well, I got worried about how fast it could all be taken away. Things change in a blink of an eye and it might not be on purpose, but it creates obstacles and challenges. I was worried that Dr. Coe would change his mind all of a sudden. If we were still at the U of A, he could make us stay easily. The quicker we got out of Edmonton, the harder it would be for us to come back. I don't know why I had this thought process in my head. I think when you spend a lot of time in the hospital, you worry about things like that. Mom, on the other hand, seemed to find a whole bunch of things to do before we left. She took her time packing our stuff, getting gas and calling people. She also had to find some time in there for her Diet Coke pick up and a puff on a cigarette before we did anything associated with leaving the U of A.

Before we left, I did make some time for a friend I had met prior to my heart transplant. Susanne* was another one of Dr. Coe's heart transplant patients. She was one of the people I talked to before I had my surgery and we had met up about a half-a-dozen times. Susanne was just like Lucy and I envied her too. The more I talked with Susanne, the more I realized that even though we had different heart problems, we were both dealing with the same emotions of having a new heart and our own being damaged goods. Susanne was also like Lucy in the same way in which she handled the situation: confidently and without fear. Maybe they thought about me like that, I don't know, but every time I talked to either of them, they seemed to have this charismatic charm. I swear if you didn't know them, you would never have known what they lived through. Susanne and Lucy were my real life heroes.

The afternoon I left, I gave Susanne a hug. We wished each other good luck with everything. After my short visit with my friend, mom and I got into the car and left the hospital and the city in the dust. We were on our way home, back to Medicine Hat.

Before returning to the 'Hat, we stopped in Calgary and had supper with Leanne and Rob. After that, we made our way home and met dad at Great Grandma and Grandpa Crockford's house. It was a quiet homecoming and the news was not involved this time, which made me happy. Tinker was also happy for me to be home.

I'd have to adjust to life at home after my transplant. I was still really weak and needed some time to relax. The next week would be a busy one as I settled into a routine. I also had to count on doing things myself much more. For the last few months, I had had someone around me pretty much all the time. It could get a little nerve wracking not getting a break for some me-time. Someone had always been watching me and making sure I was breathing. All of a sudden: I was completely alone…and I was looking forward to it.

The next morning was beautiful and not just because of the weather. The most beautiful part was waking up in my own bed, in my own room, in my own home and knowing I wasn't leaving. I couldn't waste too much time revelling in the comfort of my bed though, there was a busy day ahead. I had an appointment with Dr. Hak, my pediatric doctor, at the Medicine Hat hospital and a dermatologist appointment to look at the sore on my head. I had physio too. Even though I was out of Edmonton, I had to keep up with the physio.

My first two appointments went well. I went to physio at the hospital. I was a little annoyed about it since it was time consuming. I could be outside doing other things instead of inside on the treadmill. I had to do a five minute warmup walk, 10 minute speed walk and then a five minute cool down. I did some stretches as well. After physio, we stayed at the hospital to visit my Great Uncle Bill Crockford, who had been admitted recently.

Uncle Bill wasn't doing so well but I knew he would be happy to see me. From experience, I had found out that having a visitor while in the hospital was exciting and showed you people cared. Uncle Bill congratulated me on my accomplishment of receiving a new heart. He had tears in his eyes when he gave me a big hug. He said that I was very strong and that he was very proud of me.

My Uncle Bill had been through a lot. He lost both his legs from hardening of the arteries, (which caused gangrene) and he had troubles with his heart as well. Maybe that was why he was proud of me. He knew what it was like to have a heart problem and to overcome it was a big accomplishment. I left his hospital room that day with tears in my eyes. He wasn't going to live much longer but I still wished for a miracle for him. I was tired of being sick myself, but on the other hand, I was more tired of seeing people sick and suffering. (I had seen a lot of that while I was in the hospital and I also thought about my donor family.) Uncle Bill always had the best sense of humour about his health. If I could get through my health obstacles like he did, I would be doing well. He always laughed and I needed to laugh more too.

After seeing Uncle Bill, we stopped at the Medicine Hat hospital cancer clinic. I had come to know the staff at the cancer clinic well. My Aunt Irene worked there and, post heart transplant, I started getting my blood taken there too. A technician named Liz was a wizard at getting my blood in the first poke. Not many people could do that and so we kept going back. Liz was also nice, which was a bonus. I loved going to the clinic and visiting and catching up with Liz, Aunty Irene and other staff. (Even some of the patients got to know me.) Since I had been in Edmonton for so long, we had a lot of catching up to do. I had more appointments the next day, including physio. I saw Liz again at the cancer clinic and she gave me some stuff to clean the sore on my head. I was doing really well and had come far. Mom kept in touch regularly with Dr. Coe and I would have to go back to Edmonton in a week and a half. It was dad's birthday and there wasn't anything special planned for his big day.

It was a low key event. We didn't have a cake but we were all glad to be together in the same city to celebrate. Dad didn't look any different from 40 to 41 but there was a big difference from last year to this year. His birthday this time marked a high stress period for our family. There was a whole different level of anxiety that came with post-transplant.

The last year had morphed from us being an everyday regular family, to me fighting for my life. I went from being diagnosed, to having my first major surgery and then the open heart surgery and my transplant. The first year is crucial. I had a new heart, not the heart I was born with, and rejection was a possibility. We were stressed because we didn't know if my body was going to say to the heart, "Nope, you don't belong here. Get out."

My healing journey was continuing and I was excited to go back to school in Severn Persons. Some nervousness did creep under my skin. What were the kids going to say and think about me? I looked different for sure with my chubby steroid cheeks and my eyebrows that had gone from white-blonde to dark. I called some of my friends from school and they said they were excited I was home and, more importantly, that I got my new heart. My friend Megan lived right across the highway from me and I could ride my bike to her place. Her parents and mine also knew each other so every time I went over to their home, mom felt I was safe.

I spent the night there a few times and I never felt weird taking my medication in front of Megan. Mom did worry that I might sleep in and miss taking my drugs so she always called me at 8:30 a.m. on the dot to make sure I was awake and had taken my meds.

Summer was rushing by and it was hard to believe that I had received my new heart almost two months ago. I spent a lot of July golfing with dad. I drove the golf cart for him and watched from the sidelines. I never played. I was learning the game, plus regaining my strength. (I wanted to practice my driving too so that was why I drove the cart.) I kept up with my regular physio appointments, which still took an hour out of every day. In spite of the mandatory physio, I was becoming a "normal" teenager again.

On Thursday, July 25, we received the terrible news that Uncle Bill had passed away. I went to physio at the hospital and all I could think about was the visit I had had with him the week before. I knew

Great Grandma Crockford was upset at losing her son and although we knew Uncle Bill was going to die, it wasn't anything you could ever fully prepare yourself for. The last thing he had said to me was that he was proud of me. I had wished for a miracle that day and maybe this was it: the miracle of no more suffering. He had left a place of pain for a place of peace: heaven. I had shared a spiritual connection with my uncle that day in his hospital room. He knew I would be okay.

When someone you love dies, you are left with the grief that you will never see them again on earth. Death is incomprehensible and inevitable. It's something we can't fight and we never know when it's going to happen. I had thought I was going to die but I had cheated death. My donor hadn't. How many times could I cheat death before it caught up with me?

Uncle Bill's funeral was held on the morning of Monday, July 29, 1996. That same day, mom, dad and I left for Edmonton. The drive to Edmonton would become routine as I'd have to go to the U of A hospital twice a month for check-ups. We drove to Calgary and stopped for supper at Ken and Cheryl's house. We visited for a while and Ken gave me an autographed picture of Corey in his goalie equipment. He sent Billy a hockey stick. After saying goodbye, we made tracks to Edmonton and arrived at Bev and Jim's house a little before midnight.

The next day I had to see an adult transplant cardiologist, Dr. Burton, because Dr. Coe was on a (much deserved) holiday. I have never met anyone in my life as busy as Dr. Coe. Oh my gosh, it was strange being back at the U of A hospital since my transplant. However, it was back to my same old unremarkable appointments: blood work, ECG, echo, x-ray and check-up.

Before I knew it, my family was back on the road. The one-night trip to Edmonton was over without any blips on my health radar. We took Bev with us and along the way, picked up my cousin Chantal in Calgary. She would be staying with us for a while. We got home late that night.

After settling in that same night, mom went to get the mail. We picked up our mail at the downtown post office in Medicine Hat. Chantal and I stayed home and watched a movie while mom was out. When she returned, she had a letter for me and passed me the envelope with my name on it. When we opened the envelope, there was another envelope enclosed. This one had been sent to the U of A hospital:

Ms. Kristy Plotsky
C/O Heart Transplant Unit
University Hospital
Edmonton, Alta.

The return address was from the Winnipeg Blue Bombers. I wasn't a huge football fan but I did know who the Winnipeg Blue Bombers were. The letter was dated July 20, 1996 and was from Cal Murphy, the Winnipeg Blue Bombers head coach. His friend Graham Kelly, a Medicine Hat sports columnist and alderman, sent Cal the Medicine Hat News during football season. That was where Cal read about my heart transplant. Cal had received a heart four years before my transplant and wanted to congratulate me on my recovery. The coach said if I wanted to attend a football game when the Blue Bombers were playing in Calgary or Edmonton, I would be able to meet him. I thought this was really neat: to meet someone who had a heart transplant and who was in a high profile career as a coach for a CFL (Canadian Football League) team. I was honoured Cal requested to meet me.

Dad and mom called Cal's secretary the next day to set up a time to meet. I was excited to meet Cal and find out how he was dealing with his lifesaving heart transplant. His letter inspired me. It wasn't only me battling this; I had support from many different people, in many different areas. When you have a transplant of any kind and you meet someone who needs one or who has also had one, you get chills down your spine. Transplants, in general, were still fairly new back then: not like nowadays. Organ donation was rare and people didn't talk about it as much as they do currently. We transplant recipients have a lot in common, such as the side effects of medications and the lifelong battle to be healthy. Getting a transplant doesn't mean you're cured, it's lifelong treatment. When Cal wrote me, I felt that connection. We were both heart transplant survivors and we shared a unique bond: borrowed hearts.

BLUE BOMBERS

WINNIPEG ⬤ **FOOTBALL CLUB**   1465 MAROONS RD., WINNIPEG, MANITOBA, CANADA R3G 0L6

PHONE (204) 784-2583
FAX (204) 783-5222

July 20, 1996

Ms. Krysty Plotsky
c/o Heart Transplant Unit
University Hospital
Edmonton, Alta.

Dear Krysty

My friend, sports columnist Graham Kelly, sends me the Medicine Hat News during the football season. It was here that I read about your receiving your new heart on May 26.

As a heart transplant recipient myself four years ago, I just wanted to congratulate you and encourage you in your recovery. People will still ask, "How's the ticker?" not realizing that you no longer have a diseased but a healthy heart. To be given such a new lease on life is one of the greatest gifts, an unselfish donation by the donor family at a time of great sorrow for them. It is truly one of God's miracles.

A successful transplant returns the recipient to a fully active and productive lifestyle. I wish you every success. Best wishes also to your family who have been and will be your greatest support.

Sincerely

Cal Murphy

Cal Murphy
Head Coach & Director of Football Operations

/jm

P.S. If you are a football fan and would like to attend a game when the BLUE BOMBERS are playing either in Calgary or Edmonton, I would be happy to meet you. Just drop me a line, or phone my secretary at 204-784-2565.

A COMMUNITY SPONSORED NON-PROFIT ORGANIZATION

Meeting Cal murphy after the game.

Not only did Cal write me, I had letters from lots of other people sending their support. People told me how happy they were that I got my new heart and told me they hoped I would feel better and be back in Medicine Hat really soon. The letters were from different kids who went to my school at Seven Persons. Some of them I hadn't even met before. It was inspirational getting the messages and pictures knowing that many folks were rooting for me. The cards and drawings always put the biggest smile on my face. I loved reading all of them:

Envelopes full of cards and pictures and more cards and more pictures came in the mail, either to my home or sent on from the hospital. Some messages were for me before my heart transplant but most were from after. Unfortunately, I didn't get the mail until I returned home but it was nice to see and feel all the support. I had a hard time realizing the girl the letters were for, was me. I was the Kristy they were all fighting and praying for.

One letter I received stood out from all the rest. It was from Christina, a girl who lived near me. She went to a different school but I had met her because she was Megan's neighbour. She wrote me a kind letter that I opened in the car while waiting for mom to get groceries. Here are Christina's words.

May 4, 1996

Dear Kristy,

I just want to let you know that I am thinking of you and that you and your family are in my prayers every day. I wrote a poem about you and, of course, everything that is written in the poem comes from my heart. I wrote this poem as an assignment at school. I hope you don't mind me writing about you. I figured that since this poem is about you, I should give it to you. I was asked to read it in front of my class and I think everyone liked it. I hope you like it too.

All my family, friends, teachers and people at my school (Medicine Hat Christian School) are all praying that you might receive a new heart and that your body won't reject it. I think you are so strong by the way you act, cheerful and friendly, and I admire you. When I saw you at the benefit auction with your friends, you looked great. I was kind of tongue-tied, I didn't know what to do or say in front of everyone. Usually that isn't a problem for me; usually I get in trouble for saying too much! I'm sorry that I couldn't talk with you longer. I had to go and I wasn't sure what to talk about.

I still remember when you came over with Megan. We played with my puppy, Max. I don't know where you are now. Edmonton, Calgary or here in Medicine Hat? But if you are ever in Medicine Hat or somewhere close by, I wouldn't mind seeing you. I'd like too, really. Or else call me if you are bored and we could talk, even write me a letter or a note if you want. I'll give you my address and phone number on the bottom of this page just in case.

If you like to read books as I do, one of my favourite authors is Lurlene McDaniel. She writes books about teenagers and children who have serious health problems. I don't know if you would like to read books like that but I did enjoy most of her books. I found out about becoming a volunteer from one of her books at the back page. I would like it if you wrote me back or called me sometime to tell me what's happening and how you are feeling. I can understand it if you don't want to or can't, but just remember that you're always in my prayers and thoughts and many others too, I'm sure.

Your Friend,

Christina

Enclosed with the letter was the poem Christina had written about me.

Also enclosed was a beautiful ring wrapped in a piece of loose leaf. On the paper it said:

Kristy,

I hope the ring fits, it's too small for me and I hope you like it. It is two hands holding a heart with a crown on top. I hope it means something special to you.

The letter was dated May 4, 1996 but I received the treasures late July. Although I had already had my heart transplant, reading the letter gave me chills. Here was this girl, a girl I had only met a few times, writing me a letter and telling me how I inspired her. After reading her letter, I questioned whether it was really about me. It was hard to hear good things about myself, especially when I didn't see myself the way other people did. I didn't feel like I deserved the attention and that I was special in anyway.

I sat in the car, all by myself, with the letter in my right hand and the ring in my left. I never knew the reason why Christina gave me the ring but it was a special present. To me, it represented the sacredness of the heart. The heart is not only a vital organ in your body but also a symbol of love. The heart is something that can be broken, not physically but emotionally, and this ring symbolized how protective you should be of your heart and how lucky I was to have two hearts in my life. My new heart was the most precious gift of all. My heart was protected, protected by my love and by Dawn's love. (Later, I found out that Christina's gift was a Claddagh ring, a traditional Irish ring representing love, loyalty and friendship. I never wore the ring because I was scared I'd lose it. I still have it today.)

Sitting in the vehicle I cried happy tears. I cried for several minutes and thanked God for all the blessings in my life, particularly for giving me a second chance, a second chance at life. I kept Christina's letter tucked safely away and one day, we would go to the same high school together. I don't know if she even remembered writing me. I never told her how much her words meant to me until now. Many more cards arrived telling me how people prayed for me and how happy they were to hear my operation was successful. The letters of support were incredible and helped me feel better, especially when I was down. Twenty years later, I still have them all and read them every now and then.

PRECIOUS LIFE

SHE IS TOO YOUNG
TO GO THROUGH THIS
ONCE FREE
NOW HELD CAPTIVE
TO HER OWN BODY.

SHE CRIES OUT,
"WHY ME?"
AND THE SILENCE
TERRIFIES HER.

WE WATCH
WE HEAR
SHE FIGHTS
SHE'S TOUGH

NEVER KNOWING
WHEN THE BEEPER
WILL GO OFF.

WAITING.
THE PATIENT FAITH
TIME KEEPS TICKING
THE WORLD GOES ON;

ONE GIRL
WHO'S LIFE IS THREATENED
STRUGGLES TO HOLD ON.

PATIENTLY WAITING - Kristy Plotsky waits patiently by the phone with mom Margo and pet Tinker. The 13-year-old needs a heart transplant and waits to hear from the hospital. A benefit auction in honor of Kristy Feb. 18 at the Seven Persons Community Hall.

Poem Christina sent me.

CHAPTER EIGHTEEN

Echo, echo, echo

Summer break was dwindling down in days. It was mid-August and life was hectic for mom and dad. They were getting caught up with work, getting caught up with stuff at home, as well as taking me to my continuous doctor appointments, blood tests and physio. Physio was super boring but I really liked my physiotherapist, Sharla. We always had such a fun time joking around with each other. However, she never let me slack off: not once. She always timed my warm-up, cardio and cool-down and pushed me to gain strength in my body.

I wasn't going to physio as often now. I only had to go a couple of days a week now, instead of three times a week. Making time to go to physio was still demanding as I had to be driven to and from the hospital.

Gwen and Aunt Terry thought it would be a great idea to buy a treadmill for me with the money from my trust fund, the money we had raised at the auction. I could do physio at home and it would save on trips to the hospital. We priced out treadmills and I bought one. It certainly cut down on the weekly physio trips and saved time for my parents and me.

School was on the horizon. I had been moved on to Grade Nine and this would be my last year at Seven Persons School. Before heading back to class, I wanted a few things done. On top of my to-do list was getting rid of my unibrow and the thin layer of peach fuzz on my face. The extra body hair and my bulging cheeks from the medication were weighing down my self-esteem. By having my face waxed and my eyebrows shaped, I would look much better and give myself a boost in the confidence department.

Mom took me to a makeup and aesthetics salon called 2nd Look on August 21 after my physio. For $21.40, I had my face waxed and my eyebrows professionally shaped. As the saying goes, it hurts to be beautiful and whoever said that was right. It hurt like a lot and I should know, I was a pain expert. The waxing was a different type of pain from surgery pain. There was a big difference between the pain I put myself through to look good, and the pain where I didn't have any choice. Thank God I didn't get my face waxed right before school because that day and the next, my face was as red as a tomato. At least the waxing wasn't expensive.

Dad, mom and I left for my Edmonton appointment on August 22, 1996, a week before school began. We drove to the city the night before and the next day we saw Dr. Coe and he gave us fantastic news: everything was good. My tests and blood work showed that everything was in working order. We had supper with Lucy and her family. My friend was happy everything was going well for me. Then we left for Sylvan Lake where we saw my Uncle Dale and Aunty Irene for a short visit. After that, it was on to Calgary to spend the night at Leanne and Rob's house. It was nice to be able to break up the five hour drive. The other reason we stayed in Calgary was because we had been invited to a picnic the next day.

The Children's Wish Foundation held an annual picnic in Bragg Creek, west of Calgary. It was an event for kids, who had wishes granted, and their families. The day turned out to be sunny and warm. Billy came for it and we went on a trail ride, which was fantastic because I loved horses (and still do). Then we all went for a wagon ride. It was a day to remember.

Back home in Medicine Hat, the countdown for Grade Nine was on...and I was getting stressed. My long awaited return to class was approaching quickly and I was extremely nervous and anxious. I didn't know what people would say when they saw me since I looked like a chipmunk storing food in my cheeks. That last week and a half of summer also brought some terrible news. I found out Lucy had a *1B rejection. (The higher the number, the increase in risk. 0 is no rejection.) After two years, her body was rejecting her new heart. This was exceedingly bad news. A rejection could mean a second heart transplant or even death for Lucy. Hearing the word *rejection* and Lucy's name in the same sentence came as a complete shock to me. I prayed for her and asked God to give her strength.

School was in three days. I was becoming more and more frightened with each thought about what kids would say to me or if they would treat me differently. Would I even have friends? All these questions flooded my mind and all I could do was think about walking into school on the first day and everybody staring at me: not because I had a heart transplant but because of how I looked. The spa treatments hadn't unpuffed my face. As a teenager, the way you look is important. Yet, I looked horrible and on top of that, everyone was going to be looking at me because I was the sick girl from the news. I had a new heart and my friends might have thought I changed too because my heart changed.

The morning of the dreaded day was here: Thursday, August 30, 1996. I was scared. Actually, being scared was a significant understatement. I was terrified. One of the things I was worried about was seeing so many people after having my heart transplant. I might get overwhelmed answering a lot of questions.

Thank goodness mom was nice enough to drive me so I didn't have to take the bus. My cousin Derrick, who was in my grade, came along with us. It was comforting having someone to walk into school with me. To my relief, the day turned out well. People were considerate of how I looked and tried not to stare at me too much. There were a few times when I walked by some people in the hallway and I knew they were talking about me. I didn't hear exactly what they said but I definitely knew they were talking about me because I caught them staring. Ashamed, they quickly ducked their heads or turned away. I had been gone for about six months in total and people start to gossip when you've been away that long. I knew people gossiped about me. They gossiped about things that were true and things that weren't true. I knew people said good things and bad. At the end of the day, I was just happy the first day had come and gone.

I did have trouble getting up the next morning for school, the first day had tuckered me out, but it was Friday and I was looking forward to class. Not much had really changed while I was gone; everybody looked the same, everybody except me. I had remained friends with my girlfriends and they knew I was still Kristy. No matter what had happened to me, I could relate to the teenage angst and drama over boys and friends. I was glad to be back in class and school gave me a sense of how things used to be. It gave me hope that I could be normal again.

When I got home from school that second day, I had to meet with a journalist from the Bow Island Commentator, a newspaper for small communities in southern Alberta. A reporter talked to me and took some pictures. Being interviewed by the media was old hat. Sometimes it was annoying and other times I didn't mind it much. With my story being in the news a lot, I didn't have much privacy but if people were willing to read about me, I wanted to use the exposure for good: advocating organ and tissue donation. Talking with the Commentator, I encouraged people to sign their donor cards and talk to their families about organ donation. It saved my life and could save countless others.

I rested during the weekend to get ready for a full week of school. On Monday, I had a bit of a runny nose but I went to school and I was fine. On Tuesday, I had an upset stomach but again, I went to school. I had to watch how much school I missed because there were going to be lots of missed days coming up when I'd have to travel to Edmonton for appointments. I wanted to not miss any more days than I had too. This was going to be a hard task, not only because I hadn't been attending school full-time for the last year and a half, but also because of how I was feeling. I was still recovering and had a long road ahead. I was nowhere near being clear for rejection. I thought about Lucy going through her rejection and hoped she was okay.

Mom and dad had decided that because of all the transitions, it would be a good idea to have Linda Buzzell, the transplant coordinator, speak to the junior high students at my school. She had done it for Lucy after her transplant. Linda could talk directly to my peers about the risks of having a heart transplant and also inform them that they needed to be extra-careful around me. Since I didn't have the nerve from my heart to my brain saying, "Hey heart, speed up," kids had to know not to play pranks on me. They also had to avoid me if they were ill. Linda's presentation would give students a better understanding of my situation and, hopefully, impart to them that just because I had someone else's heart, it didn't mean I was a different person. Linda flew in from Edmonton that Wednesday around lunchtime to talk with about 100 students about my situation. The presentation was going to be aired on T.V. and Amy Stalker from CHAT TV Medicine Hat was there to take in the event at Seven Persons School. My parents were there too, as well as my counsellor Carol. It was awkward sitting amongst all the students while someone was up at the front of the gymnasium talking about me. It was weird and awkward at the same time but yet a relief. My fellow students would have a better understanding and some insight into what I had gone through over the last few months. Linda was a great speaker and explained the transplant process a lot better than I would have. Her presentation also showcased the need and importance of organ donation. If anything, I hoped students would bring up the topic of donation at the dinner table that night. The more people talked about organ donation, the more it put the subject out there.

Over all, Linda's talk was well put-together and the students seemed to listen. I was impressed by her and there were even a lot of questions asked by different students. She answered them thoughtfully as I sat amongst my friends. I didn't have to go up to the front and talk, which was fine by me. I'd rather speak in front of thousands of people I don't know, than five I do know.

We brought Linda back to our house and had a short visit with her before mom took her back to the airport. Later, my family went over to Grandma Jackie's house to watch Chat T.V. There I was: on T.V. again. The news segment talked about the importance of organ donation and how I was helping students become more aware of the risks involved after a heart transplant, or any transplant for that matter. It was a good story but I was left thinking about how chubby my cheeks looked on screen. I looked different from last year and it was a huge change even for me. I think it would take some time for people to get used to the new me. I also had to grow up a little faster than most teens my age. While I didn't feel exactly more mature than my peers, I definitely had a different perspective on things like life and death.

The second week of September, mom and I had to return to Edmonton. On September 8, we started the long drive towards the U of A hospital. We always went the day before my appointments because they were early in the morning. We had supper Sunday night at Lucy's house near Edmonton. My friend was okay but still having routine tests for rejection. My mom and her mom got along well and shared a unique connection, like Lucy and I. It helped that whenever I was around Lucy, I felt like I wasn't being judged or stared at. I could be me. If I was sad about something, Lucy understood because she had been through it. She was kind of my mentor. She seemed to handle things with such great ease and always seemed happy. I admired her for that.

The next day, we went to see Dr. Coe and have the regular ECG and echo. Everything was good: my heart was functioning properly. I did have my stool tested because I was having stomach problems. The stool came back positive for a bug. I was given yet another prescription for an antibiotic. We left Edmonton in the early afternoon and headed to Calgary where we stopped in at the children's hospital to see Michael, a boy from Lethbridge, Alberta. He was close to my age and we had met before. He had had a heart transplant around the same time as me. He was doing very well on his road to recovery.

Back in Medicine Hat on Wednesday, mom talked to Lucy's mom, who said that her daughter had rejection of *3.5. This was not good. Her body was continuing to reject her heart. I felt so bad. I had just received my heart and was doing fine, while my good friend was dealing with rejection. I thought Lucy would get through it but the complications were getting worse. All I could do was pray for her and her family.

That Thursday, September 12, I wasn't feeling very well. My stomach was upset but I had to go to the cancer clinic in Medicine Hat that morning to get blood work done. Then mom drove me to school. While still feeling crummy, I was good at pretending that I was okay and toughed it out for class. When I got home though, mom drove me straight to emergency. They took an x-ray, blood and did an ECG. We didn't find out much in emergency but we knew that it wasn't my heart causing the stomach ache. That was good news! I went home happy.

After supper Janice Walters, Reba McEntire's good friend, called mom. Janice told her to tell me to watch the Country Music Association Awards in about four weeks. Reba would be performing and there would be a surprise. I was excited and couldn't wait for the show.

On Friday, mom ordered CMT (Country Music Television

Canada) and TNN (The Nashville Network) so we could watch the show on October 2. We also received a call from the Children's Wish Foundation about going to see Reba in Vancouver that upcoming December. Although it was all talk at that time, I had never been to Vancouver and I thought it would be so much fun.

Saturday was mom's 40 birthday. I had arranged to have a party for her at Grandma Jackie's house. Jody came all the way from Edmonton for the event, which was very nice of her. The milestone birthday party was low key and even Aunty Terry made it for the evening.

If I had written my story several years ago, I may have included all the skeletons in my family's closet. I'm a completely different person than I was back then and more importantly, we have all made amends. Because the past is the past, I don't feel it's necessary to hash out every detail of why my parents and my aunt stopped speaking for many years. That's over and done with and they're closer than ever.

***

Dr. Coe had asked me to share my transplant story with others about to go through the process and on Friday, September 20, mom and I met with a family from Tilley, Alberta. Their 11 year old daughter needed a heart and lung transplant. We met with them more so to talk from the heart transplant point of view but it was very informative for all of us. When I meet a family who is going through something similar to me, I feel for them. It's rough. The family wishes so badly that they're you; that they've already been through the surgery and the recovery and the threat of rejection. I know what they're thinking because I was in their shoes.

It's like there's a river between you. I'm on one side and they're on the other. I see things differently than they do. There's no bridge but there are rocks in the water and they have to try and cross the river by stepping on these rocks. The hardest part is sometimes the river's current is swift and keeps you from getting across, while other rivers are slower. The one thing to remember is, just because you crossed the river, it does not mean you won't fall back in. In no way are you safe. You always have to be careful to not fall back in the water. I was still on the bank of the river. We left for Edmonton on Sunday,

September 22, at 10:30 a.m. I drove from Medicine Hat to Gleichen, about two hours away. That was a big deal for me as it was probably the furthest I had driven since I got my learner's. You'd think September would be snow free but this was Alberta. There was a squall and since I didn't have enough experience to drive in the snow, mom took over and got us to Edmonton.

That Monday, I had my regular tests and everything showed that I was doing well: no problems. Lucy was at the U of A for a heart biopsy (cardiac cath) to check for rejection and we all had our fingers crossed there would be nothing but good news for her to report. We visited with Lucy after her biopsy (she had to lie flat for four hours) and then stopped to see Michael. Since his doctor was also Dr. Coe, Michael was at the hospital for his check-up. He was doing well.

We left Edmonton that afternoon and headed towards Calgary where we had supper with Jody. We got home around 9:30 p.m. and got a phone call from Dr. Coe. He told mom that my cyclosporine was a little high; it was in the high 200. My level should have been slightly lower, approximately 150. The result didn't worry me; I would have been scared if my level was too low. Cyclosporine prevents rejection and a low level would mean my body was at an increased risk for rejection. On the other hand, a level too high can cause toxicity and then I would have no immune system and be put at risk. This was another lesson about the importance of taking my medication and going for blood work. Even though it was a hassle, my life was still being finely balanced and required continuous monitoring. I thought about Lucy and what she was going through. I went to bed that night and said a prayer for her and hoped her biopsy would be clear of rejection.

The next day, Lucy's mother phoned to tell my mom that Lucy's biopsy showed no rejection. Wow! What a relief. I was sure it was a huge weight lifted off of Lucy's and her family's shoulders. Now Lucy needed to take care of herself and feel better.

Billy and his girlfriend were in a car accident the next day. Thankfully, neither of them were hurt. It wasn't his fault, some lady had run into him, but his truck was totalled. My brother was into boxing and after the collision he wanted to get checked to make sure he didn't have whiplash. He also needed a physical for boxing (it was mandatory in order to start training) and went to our family doctor in Medicine Hat, Dr. Jeraj. Dr. Jeraj ordered blood tests and an ECG and was a little alarmed to find that Billy had a heart murmur. It's not unusual for people to have heart murmurs but when you have never had one in your life and all of a sudden you have one, there are questions. With my history of heart problems, Dr. Jeraj took Billy's murmur seriously. He said my brother should have an echo done immediately.

My parents made an appointment for Billy to see Dr. Hak the next morning at 8 a.m. Dr. Hak did more blood work and another ECG. The blood tests came back with good results: there was no indication of anything wrong or abnormal. However, the doctor was still concerned about the murmur and booked an appointment with Dr. Giuffre in Calgary for October, 2, 1996. That was the same day as Reba's surprise. I hoped we would be home in time to watch the music awards. (I think we made arrangements for grandma to record it in case we didn't get back in time.)

Billy never confided in me about the heart murmur. My brother and I got along but sometimes we were in different worlds. We both had to grow up quickly in very different ways. He had to learn how to take care of himself, without a parent or someone always being around. (I'm pretty sure he liked that bit though, lots of freedom.) I had to grow up because I was sick. Sometimes, these differences pulled us together and sometimes they pulled us apart. In this case, I had insider knowledge gained from my many doctor and hospital visits. I thought Billy might want to ask me questions and lean on me for support. It was kind of nice to know something that he didn't. As an older brother, he always had a protect-my-sister and know-more-than-you attitude. Now I knew stuff about things he didn't and I could help calm his fears. But Billy never showed any kind of sign that he was scared. Mind you, he's a boy and if he had been frightened, he probably would have kept it to himself. It's weird how some guys don't show emotion.

Finally, October, 2 arrived and we all drove up to Calgary that morning. When we got to the Alberta Children's Hospital, I paid close attention to Billy but I never asked him what he was thinking. I should have. I was there for him if he needed me but I didn't reach out. In any order, I felt terrible for him but deep inside, I didn't think anything was wrong. It was difficult to fathom that my big brother was sick when he was healthy and active. He was boxing and worked out a lot and cared about his health. He hadn't been sick or struggling to even open his eyes like I had.

After Billy had his echo, my parents, brother and I sat quietly waiting in the doctor's office. You've heard me say, the waiting is the hardest part of all. I really think you spend more time in life waiting then you do sleeping, maybe it was just my life. Here we were again, waiting, except this time it wasn't about me. This time my parents were in this waiting room about to receive news of whether their son had restrictive cardiomyopathy. I can't imagine seeing your daughter go through her diagnosis and experiences and then think your son might have to go through it as well.

The room was silent. There were no jokes being told and Billy didn't have anything smart to say. Everyone was quiet. What do you say in a moment like this anyway? Of course, your inner dialogue is debating, "good news or bad?" As the saying goes, no news is good news.

There was a knock on the door and Dr. Giuffre entered. He greeted everyone before he spoke. At that particular moment, I had a glimpse of my past flash in my head. For a moment, I wasn't present with my family in that room.

Kristy, you need a heart transplant. Kristy, you need a heart transplant. Kristy, you have restricted cardiomyopathy.

"Billy, you have *restricted cardiomyopathy*."

What did I just hear Dr. Giuffre say?

I heard it again.

"Billy, you have the same disease that your sister had," said Dr. Giuffre. "You have the beginning of restrictive cardiomyopathy."

I told myself not to cry, repeating a mantra in my mind:

Don't cry. Don't cry. You can't cry. Be strong. Be strong for mom and dad and Billy.

Oh God, how could this happen again? What are we going to do? Why us? Why us? WHY? Don't cry, Kristy. Be strong. Your family needs you. You will give Billy the hope and faith he needs if he needs a heart transplant. Oh shit, this is my fault. All the times I was sick in the hospital, all the times I fought with Billy I wished he was the one who was sick and I was the one who was healthy. Oh crap, this is my fault. I wished for it and I got exactly what I wanted. How am I ever going to explain myself to everyone?

I tried hard to listen carefully to every word Dr. Giuffre was saying but I kept falling in and out of the past and the present. A flash here, a flash there. I went back to when my family was fighting the government. I went back to when I was waiting for my heart, then getting my heart. I went back to when I wished I wasn't sick when I was angry at Billy and wished it was him instead of me.

I was in a fog and when it cleared, I looked at the person who was receiving all the bad news right now: Billy.

My brother wasn't crying and probably wouldn't cry in front of us. Dad wasn't saying a word and neither was mom. Dr. Giuffre was silent as well. Everyone in the room had already been through so much. Here we were, about to go again. When would it ever stop?

CHAPTER NINETEEN

Waiting again

Dr. Giuffre had told us that Billy had the beginning of restrictive cardiomyopathy. The doctor said he wanted my brother to have a biopsy done at the Foothills hospital. A biopsy, or cardiac catheter, would give doctors a better diagnosis of the disease. Dr. Giuffre's nurse booked the appointment for us and we left. I think my parents needed to get outside as soon as possible so they could absorb the shock with a cigarette. I don't know why people think that smoking relieves stress, but my parents definitely believed it did. We left Calgary that day with heavy hearts.

During the drive home, I asked myself what was worse now: the waiting or the knowing. I never said anything to Billy on the way back to Medicine Hat. I felt like he might hate me deep inside for giving him the disease. I don't think he suspected that I wished him to be sick but it's human nature to blame someone else for putting you in that situation. I think the reason we do that is because it's easier to come to terms with certain issues if we think it was someone else's fault. I tried to look at the positives like restrictive cardiomyopathy has a treatment option. I was living proof that a heart transplant could work. However hard I tried to put a good spin on it, I felt drained. I knew once this news hit home, it would spread like wild fire. The media would be all over it. (They would find out in a couple of months. The Medicine Hat News printed the article

Plotsky Family Copes with New Challenge on Thursday, December 5, 1996.) The only thing we could do now was to wait, some more, until the biopsy was done. Wait, hope and pray. I prayed for a miracle, a miracle that my brother wasn't sick and the test was inaccurate. We were waiting again.

We arrived home after the long day trip. Because of the present ordeal, Reba's surprise didn't register high on my priority list. Watching the Country Music Awards did give my mind something to think about other than negative stuff. When Reba got on stage, I was shocked to see she had cut off her hair. Reba was known for her long, bright red hair but it was no longer long. She had chopped it off. She looked good but it was hard to care after hearing the heartbreaking news about Billy. My brother was pretending like nothing had happened; that everything was normal. I think he was in denial. Of course, after something like this, you would be. After I found out I had a heart problem and needed a heart transplant, I was in denial. I knew from experience though that we had to keep looking on the bright side. However, what was the bright side of Billy having this blasted disease? The disease I gave him. I wasn't going to tell anyone about my secret wish and now all I wished for, more than anything, was to take it back.

***

Four days later, I was in Edmonton once more. This time it wasn't for a check-up, it was to see my cousin Corey play in an NHL game. (It was nice to be in the city and not have to go to the hospital. Actually, it was weird.) Dad, mom and I, plus Ken and Cheryl, saw Corey's team, the Vancouver Canucks, take on the Edmonton Oilers. Normally, I would be cheering for the Alberta team but not when my cousin was playing for the other side. Edmonton won 2-0. Billy didn't come on the trip. We had more questions than answers about his condition at this point. Basically, all we knew was his heart had the early stages of restrictive cardiomyopathy. He wasn't on any medication yet and was fine being home alone.

A week later, I learned that Lucy's biopsy came back and it showed no rejection. That was relieving news for everyone, especially her family, but she was scheduled for another appointment in three weeks for yet another check-up. There was no news in regards to

Billy's health and the doctors were monitoring him. Heart transplants and doctor appointments seemed to be in both our futures.

A month before Christmas, mom somehow found the courage to phone my donor family. We knew Dawn's family was from Elk Point, Alberta. Mom searched the internet for her parents, Coral and Remi Tremblay. She found them.

Mom called Coral and Remi on November 21, 1996. I lay quietly on the bed next to her as she dialed the number to talk to the mother whose daughter's heart beat inside me. Coral answered the phone and mom introduced herself as the mother of a heart transplant recipient from Medicine Hat.

"Oh my gosh!" said Coral. "I am so glad you called"

The mothers talked about their daughters. I can't imagine calling a parent who has just lost their child. I'm sure my mom probably had a million thoughts running through her mind like what do you say and how do you thank someone for saving your daughter? I'm sure my mom also thought about the possibility that Coral and Remi may not be happy to hear from her. Fortunately, calling Coral was the best decision that mom has ever made because it opened the door for a new beginning for us and for the Tremblay family. (We later learned from Coral and Remi that the HOPE program had provided them with a list of where Dawn's organs were sent. Dawn's heart went to a young girl in southern Alberta. Also, mom had read the OR report that said I received my heart from a female in her early 20's who had died as a result of a car accident.) Mom and Coral agreed to keep in touch to update them on my health as time passed. They were part of our family now.

December was upon us in no time. On December 4th mom, dad and I were on a show in Lethbridge called *Elisha*. *Elisha* was a daytime talk show hosted by broadcaster Elisha Rasmussen. The program aired on CFCN. We attended the show and she interviewed me about what it was like to have a heart transplant. The segment I was featured on was called "The Gift of Life" and it was being recorded to air on Christmas Day. The interview went well but we had to pretend it was actually Christmas Day. That was kind of strange.

On December 9, 1996, I found out I was going to meet Reba at last. My family was invited to see her sing in Vancouver in the middle of the month. On December 14, mom, dad, Billy and I left for the coast in the afternoon. The concert was the next day and it was everything I had dreamt about. We were only given two passes and so just mom and I met her. Reba was really beautiful in person. She didn't remember who I was but I forgave her for that. She was in a wheelchair because she had broken her leg in a skiing accident. Doesn't that say something about her? A country singer who doesn't let anything stand in her way. My family had a blast in Vancouver. Dad, Billy and I had never been to the city before. (Mom had been a couple of times before to see her grandpa who had lived there.) We had a lot of fun and it was a great trip.

Me and mom backstage at the Reba concert in Vancouver.

Christmas was fast approaching and I took a couple of days before the holiday to remember what my life was like a year before. I thought about the different things I had been doing back then; what I had been worrying about and what my perspective on life had looked like. There had been a big change from then to now. Now I was always thinking about the family who donated Dawn's heart. This would be their first Christmas without their daughter. That made me feel horrible. The "firsts" are tough and here it was: the "first"

Christmas without her. My family was celebrating the "first" Christmas with me and my new heart. I wondered what kind of traditions Dawn's family had and if we shared any. Maybe they didn't even celebrate Christmas. I knew nothing about them other than I got my heart on Dawn's birthday and that she died the day before she turned 23.

I reached a personal milestone on December 22, 1996. That was when I made the decision to share with my church that I had asked Jesus Christ into my heart. I was baptized at Heights Baptist Church in Medicine Hat with Aunty Terry and Uncle Steve. I cannot begin to tell you how much being baptized meant to me. It actually means even more to me now that I'm an adult with children of my own. I made the commitment to follow God's word and become more like Jesus with each passing day of my life. There were times when I may have seemed far from Jesus, and even times when I completely turned my back on him, but in the end, I always return to God and Jesus. For that, I'm forever grateful.

Christmas Day marked exactly a year since the Medicine Hat headline announced, *Christmas in Hospital for Hat Girl*. I felt two ways about it: time had flown by but it also stood still. I felt relief and sadness. I couldn't believe how far I had come and what we had gone through as a family. We had supper that night at Aunt Terry's and I was grateful to be able to spend Christmas with family and be full of hope that hospital stays for me were going to be in the past. Things may just work out in the end.

There are certain things in life that you can't control and, sometimes, you need to let it be and hope for the best. You had to hold on and enjoy the ride. Billy was going through this and I knew I would be there for him, like he was for me. I never asked him if he thought I was the reason he was sick. Being a young teenager, I took the blame for his illness. Plus, it's part of my personality to think I was culpable. I know today I wasn't at fault.

While trying to stay upbeat about life, there were times after my heart transplant that I felt sick and weak and unable to go on. I remember those feelings and they haunt me every day. Even now the smell of hand sanitizer and other hospital odours reminds me of what I went through. Accidently hitting the top of my hand makes me nauseous because it prompts me to recall the nurse tapping on my hand to pop out my veins to start an IV. Then I remember how lucky

I am to have been able to get a heart in time and have the support of my family.

The year 1996 came to a close and 1997 sprouted fresh dreams. It was this year that everything changed and those dreams began to dim. At the end of January, Billy had appointments at Children's in Calgary. Dr. Giuffre said that the upper chambers of Billy's heart were the same size as his lower chambers and the pressure was the same. That was not the way the heart should be working. The bottom chambers should be bigger and exert more pressure than the top chambers. We were all in shock and once more, went away with plenty more questions than answers. Billy wasn't added to a transplant waiting list because the doctors didn't know a lot about the restrictive cardiomyopathy disease as it was rare. He also wasn't symptomatic: he didn't feel any differently than before the discovery of the murmur. He probably would have continued on with life if our family doctor hadn't uncovered the problem.

There was a bright spot in the cold and blah month of January: I met my best friend Janine. We became buddies that January when she came to Seven Persons School. She would be beside me through thick and thin and I never dreamed that in later years, she would be my saving grace. Janine is my Oprah and I am her Gail. Our years ahead would bring fights, tears and pain, trust betrayed and some backstabbing, but in the end, we would always apologize and be there for one another.

As the days rolled away from my heart transplant date, the more normal I started to feel. Other than the constant blood work appointments and medication, my life looked pretty much like a regular teenager's. My parents started to let me have a bit more freedom with my friends. They let me go on overnights more often and gave me more space. Early that spring, March 22, I attended the Moonlight Run in Lethbridge. The event raises money for charity and I got to be a part of it. I wasn't strong enough to run yet so I walked the five kilometre run. And finished! Later that night, race officials presented me with the Participant of the Year award. I felt like I was doing something good with my life.

Me and some friends at the Moonlight Run 1997.

CHAPTER TWENTY

I hate everything

School was going well but I was having a hard time dealing with some issues in my past and the constant threat to my future. Billy's diagnosis was weighing on me and I was also having a hard time adjusting to my life as a teen who had had a heart transplant. My life was a whirlwind and I felt out of control of everything. I think this was the start of experiencing depression. I might have also had some seasonal depression (the after Christmas blues) but mix that in with the responsibilities of having a heart transplant and then feeling like an outsider, it was a lot of pressure for a 14 year old. Lots of people take medication to soothe a sore back or head but who takes medication to help keep them from dying? Me. I would be on medication for the rest of my life. I talked to my counsellor Carol at school regularly about these kind of things and it relieved some bitterness but the only other thing that helped me feel better was writing down my feelings.

In English class our assignment was to write an essay about a relationship in our lives that had terminated before it became a good relationship. I struggled with this task for some time until writing the essay *Why*. My piece was about a relationship that was negative and then turned positive. I received a good grade on the assignment and I thought I'd send it to Shania Twain. I was a big fan of the Canadian country singer and knew she had struggled in her childhood. I received a letter from her in the mail a couple of months later on April 1, 1997. She wanted to know if she could send a quote from my story to a teacher in Springfield, Ohio, U.S. The teacher had asked Shania for some words of wisdom for his class and she thought of my story. I was absolutely thrilled she wanted to use my words and I didn't hesitate to say yes.

Shania Twain

April 1, 1997

Kristy Plotsky
Box 1291
Medicine Hat, AB T1A 7N1

Dear Kristy:

Thank you for your letter and your most incredible and inspiring story "Why?".

I'm so glad to hear the great news about the success with your new heart. There are not too many people that can say they celebrate two birthdays in one year. You're truly a special person who has found the true purpose and meaning of life through your own suffering and hardship.

That meaning is very clear in your very spiritually mature story "Why?". I'm so impressed and moved by your story that, with your permission, I would like to share it with others. Tony Mendenhall, a teacher in Springfield, Ohio, has requested a quotable of wisdom from me for his teenage students, and after reading your letter, there is just nothing I can think of that would be more suitable for that purpose than your story. I believe that "Why?" would inspire and encourage other people your age to search deep inside and find the true purpose of love, friendship and life. Could you please write or call Kim, my assistant, at (518) 856-0004, and let her know whether or not you mind if we allowed the school to use your story?

Please give my regards to your brother. I was saddened to hear of his news, but with a sister like you, he is sure to get through it.

Love,

Shania

TWAIN ZONE INC.
P.O. Box 269   St. Regis Falls, NY 12980
518-856-0004   fax 518-856-0034

JON LANDAU MANAGEMENT
40 West Elm Street, Suite 1J   Greenwich, CT 06830
203-862-8670   fax 203-625-6502

In May of 1997, Lucy was added to the transplant list. She needed a new heart as her heart was damaged by the rejection. That same month, I got my first paying job at the A&W Restaurant on Dunmore Road in Medicine Hat. There was an important anniversary to mark on May 26, it had been one year since I had my heart transplant. CHAT TV interviewed me. I had a party at home and lots of people came, even Annelies and her mom. Annelies was still on the waiting list for a heart and double lung transplant. I hoped she would have an anniversary like mine one day.

Billy was managing life fine but he was no longer able to box. Doctors wouldn't clear him for the sport due to his heart. This was probably the hardest thing for him because boxing was his life. He loved it.

I graduated Grade Nine and received the Girlfriend Award because I was nice to everyone and always happy in the hallways. I was leaving my small town country school, which I had attended for 10 years. It was sad and exciting. High school began for me in the fall of 1997. I was going to a new school too – Medicine Hat High School. Some of my other friends from Seven Persons went to a different school called Eagle Butte. (You were divided into schools depending on where you lived.) Grade 10 was ho-hum. I went to school mainly for the socialization aspect rather than the learning. I hate to say it but I didn't have great grades. Most days I woke up wishing I was a dog (specifically Tinker) so I could lie around and do nothing.

My Grandma Jackie and her boyfriend Ron got into a terrible car accident and grandma was rushed to emergency at the Medicine Hat Regional Hospital. Grandma had been thrown from the truck and since she laughed at everything, it was in her nature to joke that she flew out the window so fast that she left her shoes behind in the vehicle. Grandma had to have surgery on the tendons in her hand but the damage had been done. She was a hairdresser and had trouble cutting hair because her finger dangled in the way. She soldiered on and all of us grandchildren helped out as much as we could, washing hair, taking the curlers out of customers' hair and cleaning the beauty salon. In June, grandma still wasn't feeling well and went to the doctor. After numerous appointments and blood tests, she was diagnosed with cancer.

The next few months were hard on her. She endured

chemotherapy, losing all her hair, and work became impossible. I couldn't imagine life without grandma. She was glue for our family, dad's only living parent. Without Grandma Jackie, how would we all survive? How would the family go on? Could we go on? I believed grandma would beat the cancer. She was a strong woman, a fighter, but I hadn't realized how serious her illness was. As the summer months passed, things got worse for her.

Chemotherapy and radiation didn't help and eventually, getting out of bed became a chore for grandma. On October 16, mom and I were at the local Boylan Pharmasave getting medication filled. As I backed out of the parking lot, I heard sirens in the distance. I paused and looked at mom. Being the new driver, I waited patiently to find out which direction the sirens were coming from; I didn't want to get in the way of the emergency vehicle. An ambulance zoomed past us and then I proceeded, with caution, to back out. Mom hadn't missed a beat.

"The ambulance is headed in the direction of home," she murmured.

We left the drugmart, not thinking how the next few hours would change our lives forever. I drove home but before pulling into the driveway, mom saw the ambulance parked next door at grandma's house.

"Drive over there," said mom.

My heart was pounding and I couldn't catch my breath, which made my heart pound even more. I saw the blue Oldsmobile Cutlass that Great Grandma and Great Grandpa Crockford drove in the driveway and I knew something terrible was happening. I half jumped out of the car, forgetting to put it into park. Mom yelled at me to stop and I climbed back into the vehicle and put the brakes on. I parked, got out and then rushed up the cement stairs and was greeted by Roper, grandma's German shepherd. The paramedics were in grandma's room...

Great Grandma and Great Grandpa Crockford were sitting at the table. Grandma Crockford was crying and grandpa was resting his arm behind her. I saw it in their eyes; I knew Grandma Jackie was gone before anyone said anything. They had just lost their daughter to cancer. My heart broke. My eyes started to sting. I couldn't believe what was happening.

I was given the choice that day to see grandma in her room. The image, to this day, sticks with me. When I close my eyes, I see the same house, the same situation, and grandma on the floor. Not breathing. She had tubes in her mouth from the paramedics trying to revive her. They had tried to resuscitate her but as she was terminally ill and the family was there, they told the paramedics to stop. I didn't stay in the room long with grandma, but long enough to pray for the family to find strength, especially dad, his siblings and Great Grandma Crockford.

Grandma's funeral was on Monday, October 20, 1997. It was uplifting and the music, scripture readings and hymns were a perfect fit for her. She was buried exactly 10 years to the day that her husband, my grandpa, had passed away. Amazingly, they had both died at home, in the same house. My grandma's service included her favourite song, *One Day at a Time,* and my cousin Jennifer and I read some of grandma's favourite Bible verses. We, as a family, all pulled together. Aunt Terry, grandma's only daughter, broke down as the family was being led out of the church. Great Grandma Crockford was also devastated over her daughter's death and so was dad. He no longer had any living parents. Seeing my family broke like this was agonizing. Although I knew grandma was in a better place, it was difficult to look out my window at home, and see her house. Soon her home would be occupied by new residents and no longer be my grandmother's house. There would no longer be any tissues with red lipstick stains on them, evidence of her frequent touch-ups (something she taught me to do). There would no longer be any more coffee cups rimmed with the same bright shade. There would no longer be anymore sleepovers at her place, no more cuddles, no more goodies and no more family suppers prepared by her. Grandma was gone.

As you know, life goes on. It was unfair though. Unfair that I had lost loved ones so soon. I continued going to school while missing grandma every day. I didn't take time off and I didn't feel great. Being post-transplant was work. There was always somewhere to be, somewhere to go. Blood work here, holter monitoring there (a 24 hour continuous tape recording of a patient's heart rhythm) and more bloodwork and echoes and EKG's. I thought that after my transplant, stuff would slow down but it didn't. Your whole life is changed after a heart transplant.

November 9, 1997 we got a call to meet Shania Twain at the

Southcentre Mall in Calgary. She reached out to me because of the essay I had written and shared with her. Exciting! I needed some good news in my life. My parents asked a good friend of theirs if he wanted to come too. Darrell was a huge Shania Twain fan and he jumped at the chance to see her. We all drove up to Calgary together and met Shania in a private backstage area. There were lots of other people there like reporters and a three year old child the singer was also greeting. The toddler had been in a coma after a house fire and woke up thanks to Shania's music.

It was awesome meeting Shania and I was surprised to find out how short she was in real life. I had always thought she was taller than me. (I'm 5'7" and Shania was around 5'2".) She was just as beautiful as I imagined though. Her personality was sparkling and I couldn't believe that she remembered who I was. She asked about Billy too (he couldn't be there because of work conflicts) and I told her Billy was doing well. There were no changes to tell her of and no answers either. The Plotsky family stumped doctors with our restrictive cardiomyopathy.

I was blessed to have been able to meet Shania. It was a memorable experience. We took pictures with her and she signed covers of the CD's we brought. It was a great day: one that I sorely needed.

Meeting Shania Twain in Calgary, Alberta.

My second Christmas since the Medicine Hat News headline was different. It was our "first" Christmas without Grandma Jackie. Her house had been the family headquarters for holidays and now she wasn't there. Her home had been sold to strangers. It was a quiet Christmas, one tinged with tears.

I was going to Edmonton now once every two months instead of twice a month…unless something unusual came up in my weekly blood tests. In-between cardiologist check-ups in Edmonton, I was followed by my pediatrician, Dr. Hak, in Medicine Hat. I saw him for the small, simple worries like colds and sore throats. Biopsies were less frequent, twice a year. My chipmunk cheeks deflated but I'd never be rid of the bushy eyebrows. (If I don't wax regularly, I have a unibrow.) I learned to accept my hairy arms. I did shave them once but quickly realized that wasn't a great idea. The stubble was more annoying than the amount of hair. My face wasn't too hairy and it was definitely less noticeable than a couple of years ago.

In late January 1998, my world came crashing down again. I had slept over at a friend's house and learned the next morning that our dog Chuck had been hit on the highway. He was dead. I was upset and secretly blamed dad for Chuck's death. Dad was the one who let him out and he left the yard. (Chuck did roam but we lived on an acreage so he had room to wander.) I told dad I would go look for our dog but dad said not to bother, he would come back.

Chuck's death was horrible and my parents paid money to have him buried in a pet cemetery. I was sad and Tinker was too. The days started to get more and more depressing for me and I felt angry about life. I hated everything (but not everyone.) I was moody and quickly agitated by friends and family. I cried often and thought it must be connected to my heart transplant. I carried the weight of the world on my shoulders every day and I didn't want people to know that I hurt inside. I felt down half the time I was awake. I didn't know anything about depression and I don't think anyone talked about mental health issues then like they do today. I didn't know how to cope emotionally with my changes and I hid my sorrows. I felt that nobody would understand and that people already had their own problems to deal with and wouldn't want to hear about mine. Because of my blueness and the need to be surrounded by close friends to keep me busy, my friend Joy and I decided to switch schools for Grade 11. We would move to Eagle Butte in September where a good portion of my other friends were already going.

I was spiraling into a deep depression and was treated for a week with Prozac (fluoxetine: a prescription drug used to treat depression.) I had assumed that my depression was the result of all the rough situations that were happening in my life. I lost my grandma and my dog. I was dealing with a heart transplant and my brother being ill. Billy was still being seen by Dr. Giuffre but because of his age, soon to be 18 and an adult in the medical world, he would need to be referred to an adult cardiologist. On January 29, 1998, Billy saw Dr. Giuffre for the last time. Arrangements were made for an adult cardiologist to phone mom and dad with an appointment for Billy in the summer.

Dad got sick that January and mom had to rush him to the emergency department. He was feeling faint and his breathing was short. In the end, he was okay but it scared me. On top of it all, I wasn't doing well in school. Studying didn't come easy for me; I had to really work hard at it. I never had full weeks were I felt well and I missed classes, which made me fall further behind. I didn't know what I wanted to do with my life. I was then referred to a psychiatrist in Medicine Hat. I was glad to have someone to talk to but I couldn't shrug off the shroud of misery.

Meanwhile, just after Valentine's Day in 1998, my parents and I looked at a car that a good friend of theirs was selling. It was a blue, two-door Pontiac Grand Am in really good shape and it was perfect for me. The seller only wanted $2,500 for the vehicle. Mom and dad paid for it and Billy chipped in too as it was a birthday present for his favourite sister. (Haha, I'm his only sister.) I was excited about getting my very own car. How cool was that! I didn't have my driver's license yet but that would be coming in May when I turned 16. While I was getting my new car, Lucy was waiting for a new heart. She had been on the transplant list for several months already.

***

One August night, I was sleeping over at a friend's house. The next morning, August 20, 1998, I received a call from home. Mom told me that Great Grandpa Jack Crockford had passed away. I cried and cried. I felt horrible for my great grandmother, Anita. She lost her son, daughter and now her husband in a short period of time.

The Crockfords were salt-of-the-earth people. I was lucky that they were my grandparents. They took care of each other and had a solid partnership. They had been married for 63 years and were as in love as the day they first met. When I pictured a healthy relationship, I saw Jack and Anita. Great Grandpa was such a gentleman and if more men were like him in this world, it would be a great one. He was truly an amazing person and I'm not just saying that because he was my grandpa. He always forgave people and never held grudges. His smile was mesmerizing and he had an awesome sense of humour. He never complained about anything, even his severe arthritis. Grandpa would be missed and I still think about him all the time.

Exactly a week later, I was staying over at my friend's house again and I got a call from home; mom told me that Great Grandpa Michael Plotsky had passed away. It was another blow for our family. I lost two great grandfathers within a week apart. We just had the funeral for Great Grandpa Crockford and now we had to plan a funeral for Great Grandpa Plotsky.

Great Grandma Hilda Plotsky said that they arrived home, after visiting with Great Grandma Crockford helping her cope with the loss of her husband, when they came into the house. Great Grandma Plotsky said great grandpa went to use the bathroom. After a while, grandma said, "Boy, Michael's taking a long time."

She knocked on the door and he didn't answer. She knocked again and finally after three times and no answer, she barged in... only to find great grandpa slumped over the toilet. He must have had a heart attack minutes before. Miraculously, he didn't have it while driving.

This was the first time in my entire life that I had ever seen or heard dad cry. (I'm sure dad cried when I was sick but never in front of me. He thought he had to be strong for his daughter during that time.) My Great Aunt Lynn, Grandpa Plotsky's daughter and dad's aunt wanted dad to be a pallbearer but he broke down a few days before the funeral and couldn't do it. I remember sitting outside on the steps of Aunt Lynn's house, thinking to myself how horrible and how sad this time in our lives was.

My Great Grandma Plotsky generously asked me to write the eulogy for Grandpa Plotsky. I felt honoured and privileged to do so. On August 27, I gave the eulogy with tears in my eyes but I was able to get through it without breaking down completely. I didn't like to cry in front of people then. (When I was younger, I felt that crying was a sign of weakness. Now I have a totally different view on crying and see it as a good thing. I encourage my daughters to have a cry if they are feeling down.)

The summer of 1998, a bunch of us went camping. It was my family, plus some friends of mom and dad's, my cousin Jen and my friend Joy. We went to Tie Lake, near Fernie, British Columbia, for a week. It was one of the best weeks of my life. We rented a place on the lake and went turtle hunting, boating and waterskiing. The weather was fantastic, warm and sunny, and we were in the mountains. There was nothing better and I wished it could have lasted forever. When we got back home, summer was almost over and before I knew it, September was there. I was 16 and starting a new school. I couldn't imagine what the year ahead would have in store for me.

Eagle Butte High School was much smaller than Medicine Hat High School. It was a country school, which I was familiar with as my elementary school was rural. Eagle Butte was further away from home but I could take the back roads so it didn't take too long to get there. I definitely couldn't skip school here and go to the mall or anything as it was in the country. I liked the new place and got reacquainted with some old friends. Classes were fine. My grades were about average and English was probably my best subject. I had a knack with words but my punctuation and sentence structure left much to be desired. (The content was good though.) I hated math. My depression was there and pushing in more and more, like four walls slowly closing in on me. So slow that I could ignore it on some days and push it aside and get on with life.

CHAPTER TWENTY ONE

Things change

It was in early 1999 that the depression hit me the hardest. I didn't want to get out of bed and go to school. When I was at school, I felt like a levee, ready to burst any moment. I couldn't seem to feel good about anything and things just didn't seem right. I wanted to fit in at school but I always felt like I didn't. I was the weirdo who had to take medication, get blood work done, watch what I ate, be mindful of who had illnesses...things most teenagers don't have to deal with. I wanted to be normal and be without health problems, medication and a squad of doctors. But I wasn't normal. I was different. I wanted to worry about things other people worried about like boyfriends and bad hair days. I didn't have an identity. For a long time, my life had been on hold. Now things were moving forward and I was growing up but I didn't know who I was. Who was the real me? The person before my transplant or after? I was falling deeper into depression.

I wouldn't say I felt ugly and gross but I felt awkward. My scars were definitely something I was insecure about and wearing a bathing suit was hard for me. All my friends were in relationships. Love was something I craved but I didn't know if I would find it. I was experiencing low self-esteem and thought a relationship might raise my confidence. I liked some boys at school but nobody seemed interested in me. I needed to date someone who didn't know any of my medical history.

I found someone who didn't know my backstory. I was in a relationship with a boy I met online and he lived in eastern Canada, a few thousand kilometres from Medicine Hat. Being in a long distance relationship wasn't ideal but I was able to see various parts of my large country. I even went to Prince Edward Island with him and his grandparents. That relationship didn't last as it was too long distance; it was too hard to make it work.

While I was off travelling Canada that summer of 1999, my friends were living their lives. Janine had met a boy and fell in love. Joy had met a boy and fell in love. Nicole was the only single friend I had. I felt like I had missed out on lots being away though as I hadn't been part of their group. That same year is the year that the only friend who truly knew what I was going through, ended up getting the news she had rejection again. Lucy was fighting for her life once more.

Lucy was never doubled listed. I'm happy my parents doubled my chances at receiving a heart and got me double listed but it was a fight that some families didn't have the strength to take on. After my transplant, I didn't have to think about any kind of transplant list again. Until Lucy's rejection. My friend didn't make it. A heart was not available in time and she died in February of 1999.

Her passing hit home for me. It made me think about death and I wondered if death was in my not-so-distant future. I didn't go to Lucy's funeral and I regret not attending. I think about her all the time and wonder what life would be like with her here today. Even though I had only known Lucy for a few years, she was a dear friend and I loved her very much.

Things took a turn for the worse for our family in early 2000. We received the news that dad had the same heart condition as Billy and I. Dad had another episode where he was feeling faint and short of breath and had to be rushed to emergency. (In 1998 he had been sent home.) This time, there was some concern about his heart and given my history and Billy's diagnosis, dad was sent to Edmonton. That was where he found out that he too, had restrictive cardiomyopathy.

How much more could our family take? How many more pieces of bad news could we bear? I was beyond upset and to make myself feel better, I took my credit card out shopping. I ran up a bill of

$1,000 with no concern of how I was going to pay it off. I wasn't working at the A&W anymore. By this time, I had a job at a group home for mentally handicapped children and I wasn't making the best money.

In 2000, our family was yet again shrinking. Great Grandma Crockford passed away May 21, 2000 and I thought I might have no grandparents left soon. I couldn't believe how I could go from having full sets of grandparents and great grandparents, to having none in only a matter of years. Christmas of 2000 was not a cheerful one as our family was getting smaller and smaller. It was probably the only Christmas that my immediate family spent the holiday just the four of us. No one else. I guess the only guarantee in life is that things change.

My depression hadn't cleared. It was a dark cloud following me around. Some days were better than others. I never abandoned the feeling that I didn't fit in but my friends made me feel like I belonged... a little at least. I even had a serious relationship, a guy who was a good friend of Janine's boyfriend. It was perfect! Janine and I were besties and our boyfriends were too. It couldn't have been any better. However, my romance didn't last and we went our separate ways.

I was in Grade 11 and I finally had my driver's license. I was driving the Grand Am around and I have many fond memories of cruising the streets and going to the drive-in theatre in Medicine Hat with Janine and our boyfriends. After my relationship ended, it was difficult to hang out with Janine and her boyfriend considering my ex was good friends with her boyfriend. It became too hard and it took a big toll on my relationship with Janine. It's funny to think how a relationship ending was so significant back then. Having a new heart didn't stop me from feeling the heartbreak over the end of those two relationships: a boyfriend and a friend. While being rejected by love, three years after my heart transplant, rejection by my new heart wasn't weighing on my mind like it used to. The possibility of my body expelling the organ wasn't over but Dawn's heart and I were becoming one. Billy's condition hadn't changed and since he never had any symptoms of restrictive cardiomyopathy, he continued with life as if nothing was wrong. (Other than he couldn't box, which was a big bummer for him.) By this time, my brother had completed electrical school and was a journeyman electrician.

I had already been through so much and I couldn't imagine what else God had in store for me. The year 2001 was a bad time in my life. After my previous relationship ended in late 2000 and Janine and I drifted apart, I started hanging out with a new crowd. They weren't a good influence on met but I didn't care. I wanted be accepted by them so badly that all I cared about was fitting in. I was in a lot of pain from depression and being one of the in-crowd chased it away.

I had been dealing with depression for a few years and the hurt was adding up. My grandparents had passed away. Lucy had passed away. Then Susanne passed away from transplant complications. I was feuding with Janine. I was lost. I didn't have any clue what I was going to do with my life. I didn't have a passion or a talent or the money to go to university or... the grades. The only thing that mattered to me, an 18 year old, was normalcy. How do teens be normal? By keeping up with their peers at the bar.

That's what I did. I went to the bar.

I put on tight and revealing clothing, clothing that showed my belly and figure, and headed out. The legal drinking age in Alberta is 18 so I was legal to partake in alcoholic beverages. My friends and I usually went to the same bar in Medicine Hat called Crabby Mikes. I could get a jug of whiskey and coke for $2 on Highball Thursdays. Sometimes we would go to a country bar called Kickers Saloon. I never drove drunk and I never had one night stands – ever. I was a flirt but I respected myself enough to never do anything that would put me in jeopardy. Most of us at 18 think we know all about life and everything that goes along with it. I was always right, especially when arguing with my parents. The harder they tried to parent me, the further I pushed them away. They always gave me the riot act about not drinking and driving. We never talked about sex.

I was trying to find my independence. It was like I was freed into the wild after years of captivity. I had been sheltered when I was sick. I didn't have those young "teenage angst years" and the opportunity to get into trouble. I needed mom and dad so much during that time. Now I was being let into a world that I didn't know existed. I only knew hospitals, doctors, needles, tests, etc. I knew about all the non-normative life events that most people don't have to experience until later years. Don't get me wrong, my parents were trying to do what they thought was best for me, mom especially, and she was holding on tight. I talked about moving out and putting space between us. It was difficult for my parents too because they were used to being included in every event of my life. But I didn't want to be their little girl anymore, you know, the sick girl, the girl with the heart thing, the girl with the scars, the girl with the transplant, the girl who had to be careful. I wanted to be free. Free meant not listening to my parents and God. I wasn't going to church at all. I still believed in God and Jesus but they weren't a priority. I wanted to do what my friends were doing. Partying.

In reality, I was running from myself. I was running away from my heart transplant and needles and so on, but in reality: that was who I was. I was looking for acceptance from everyone else when I needed to gain acceptance from myself. I needed to work on liking myself. Not having the cool crowd like me. I know that today but back then, it was a different story.

With my rebellious attitude and new sense of the world, I was vulnerable and emotionally naive. I let people take of advantage of me because I wanted to believe what they promised in both friendship and love. Then it all happened, so quickly it left me spinning.

My girlfriend Tara, who I've known since we were five, was part of the in-group. She was the one who introduced me to everyone in that crew. I was hanging with them and that was when I met him – Josh. We had both gone to Seven Persons School around the same time. He moved away in Grade Five. The next time I saw him was at the bar with Tara in December 2000.

Josh was two years older than me and I had never dated anyone more than a year older. Josh pursued me and pursued me, continuously asking me out. I would say no but he never gave up. He was definitely determined to woo me. When we were at the bar he always asked me to dance. He knew how to pester me until I started breaking down. Sure, he was fun to hang out with, doing what most older teenagers do: drink. He was a good two-stepping partner but I knew Josh had a past, a past that I didn't want to get involved with. I didn't want to judge him for it, but I couldn't help myself. Josh's past consisted of cheating on his girlfriends. He also drank – a lot. Josh was part of my new group of friends and all I cared about was being a part of that group. I saw the ways he was a gentleman like when he opened the car door for me. Girls liked having his attention and here he was, focusing on me. Having him want to include me in the group made me feel good. I liked the attention but I knew, deep down, it wasn't right. I knew he'd repeat his past mistakes and he'd cheat on me though he promised he never would if I dated him.

I was in a period of upheaval. Dad was sick and my best friend and I were no longer speaking. I was in the midst of changing from Dr. Coe, my pediatric cardiologist, to Dr. Isaac, an adult cardiologist in Calgary. My group of friends was the one consistent: consistently caring only about sex and drinking. I was a part of that crowd.

I was shedding my image as the sick kid. I didn't want to be known as part of the "Heart Family" anymore. The media still did updates on every anniversary of my transplant and checked up with our family to see how Billy and I were doing. My relationship with my parents was far from good. I fought with mom constantly and we never saw eye-to-eye on anything. I loved my parents dearly but I felt controlled and defeated by them every day. They were used to making all my decisions and giving up that control was difficult, for them and for me. I grew up so fast but yet, in so many ways I was immature. It didn't help that I felt responsible for every financial hardship mom and dad had endured and were enduring. I felt responsible for the family feuds. I felt responsible for being sick. I couldn't imagine life getting any more difficult. Well, boy oh boy, was I in for a surprise.

CHAPTER TWENTY TWO

Positive

In the end, I decided to give Josh a chance and date him. That was January 2001. I can't say mom didn't warn me. She told me from the beginning she didn't think it was a good idea. She didn't know him all that much but she didn't agree with certain things he did like going to the bar. (Even though I went to the bar too.) She did know he had cheated on his previous girlfriends but people can change and so I decided to give Josh the benefit of the doubt.

Josh and I weren't together two months when I made the choice to have sex with him. I didn't say no because I was worried what he would think and say to people. I wanted him to think I was cool. Unfortunately, being the Supreme-Miss-Know-Everything, I thought I was invincible. I had unprotected sex.

I remember being told that I couldn't have kids. The doctors told me from the time I was 14 years old, that pregnancy wasn't in my future. I was okay with that: childbirth scared me. I thought, one day, I would meet a gentleman who would be my Prince Charming. He would accept my medical history and the insecurities that go along with it and we would adopt as many children as we could together. Then we would all live happily ever after. The end.

Yeah right. That only happens in the movies.

Josh and I didn't use condoms. That was fine since I couldn't have kids anyway. Pregnancy was a worry I didn't have. Sexually transmitted infections (known as STIs today. Formerly STDs) didn't factor into my decision either. If Josh had something, I'd be able to see it. Right? It's amazing what girls will do just because they are scared to say anything different. For some reason, some girls can't tell a guy, "glove or no love." I'm ashamed to say I was that girl. At 18 years old I had experienced a lot in my life and I was the girl who couldn't stand up for herself.

You might think that having a transplant would make me stronger and it did to some extent. It was like I could only defend myself to doctors. I found it difficult to advocate for myself with peers, people I knew in a different context. I ended up being the girl who let the guy use the age-old excuse that he was allergic to condoms. (I'm sure many girls have heard that before and many will continue to hear it.) I can't believe I threw away all my values and my promise not to have sex until I was married to make someone else feel better. I lost myself.

At the beginning of February, dad was admitted to the U of A for almost a month. My parents were living in Edmonton and with them away, they couldn't stop me from dating Josh. Billy didn't have a say about it. He had met a girl from Calgary and was talking about moving there. Dating Josh and going out with our friends made me feel normal and accepted. This group of friends was the closest thing to normalcy I could find. When my parents came home, they accepted that I was in a relationship.

After about two months of dating, I felt off for a few days. My stomach was bloated and I felt different, something wasn't right. Perhaps I was pregnant? No, that wasn't possible. I never thought I was having a heart rejection because I was bloated. My period was coming soon so I chalked it up to hormones. A few days later, I was freaking out about everything that I could possibly freak out about. It was unusual for sure and I decided I needed to go to the doctor, preferably one who didn't know who I was and didn't know my situation in case I was pregnant.

Can you imagine growing up in a small town where your heart transplant status is splashed all over the news and medical journals? How was I going to find a doctor who wasn't attached to me or my family's story? It was a long shot. First, I decided to confirm if I was pregnant myself. I made Josh buy me a pregnancy test and he bought the test without any fight. I had told him I hadn't been feeling well and he was anxious to know what was happening.

I told Josh to go for a drive while I took the test alone one weekend. I peed on the stick and then sat and stared at it. Seconds seemed like hours. I couldn't even blink in case the results started to form. Then I noticed the pink line... in the window that says, "positive." Was there really a line? Was it a figment of my imagination? The line was faded but, yes, definitely it was there.

Wait...

No, there wasn't a line. Huh? I wasn't sure. Was it there or wasn't it there? I looked at that pregnancy test from all sides for at least an hour, trying to make out the results. I called my girlfriend Tara and told her. She said my best option was to take another test tomorrow. I did exactly that. The second pregnancy test confirmed what I had been dreading – "positive."

Monday, I went to a walk-in clinic where I didn't think anyone would recognize me. I scoped out the waiting room and then called Tara.

"It's clear," I said to her. "There are no signs of anybody I know here. I'm clear. Now what do I do?"

She told me to go to the front desk. I acted like a child who had never been to a doctor's office before. I snuck up to the counter and the receptionist greeted me, "How may I help you?"

"I need to see the doctor," I whispered.

Dr. Clugston was on. I had picked this particular clinic because of him. His dad was a doctor who had seen me as a child and that was about 10 years ago. I didn't think Dr. Clugston Junior would know my story. He was young and hadn't been a doctor long enough to know my history.

I hadn't told mom and dad about my pregnancy yet. Besides, maybe I wasn't pregnant. The only proof so far was a grocery store pregnancy test. I did tell Josh about the pink positive stick and he knew I was going to the doctor to find out the result for sure.

I called Tara again. In fact, I called her every minute to tell her my exact whereabouts in the clinic. Seriously, I know calling her every minute might seem a little drastic but it was like I was on a mission and had just been deployed into terrifying territory. I was in battle and the clinic was a war zone and I was letting my captain know where I was and what position I was holding. The mission impossible music was ringing in my head the whole time. I was trying to stay low, duck and cover, hoping nobody (family, friends and strangers) saw me at the clinic. The last thing I wanted was someone to notice me. I wanted to be invisible and hoped no one would ask why I was there and force me to spill my guts: that I was an 18 year old carrying the biggest secret of her life. I could only imagine what the headlines of the news would be if reporters uncovered what had happened to me.

Transplant Patient Pregnant!

Transplant Patient Irresponsible!

I sat in the waiting room all alone, thinking over and over again: what if I am pregnant? What am I going to do? I also wondered about the powerful anti-rejection medication I was taking and how it would affect the baby inside of me. I pretended to look confident on the outside but inside, I was dying. I called my girlfriend and gave an update on my location and status, "My name's on the waiting list."

Then I was called.

"Kristy Plotsky?"

I shuddered and looked around in a panic to see if anyone recognized my name. I felt like Britney Spears, waiting for the paparazzi to jump out or some crazy fan to say, "Hey, I know you. You're that girl who had that heart thing… that heart surgery."

I would kindly reply, "Yes, I am that girl who had the heart transplant."

Then, that would be it. Everyone would know what I had done.

Phew. Not one person flinched or fidgeted when my name rang out. Actually, to my amazement, not one person in the room suspected anything. The only thing suspicious was how I was acting. I hung up my cell phone and walked into the doctor's office where the nurse asked, "What are you here to see the doctor about?"

A tidal wave of nausea hit me hard as I gulped and struggled to keep the vomit down while telling the nurse the reason for my visit.

"I think I may be pregnant."

"Oh well, in that case you can pee in this container," she said and handed me a signature pee container with an orange lid. I went to the bathroom and did as instructed by the nurse. I left the container on the counter and returned back to the office.

I waited patiently and silently, trying not to let tears fill my eyes. I couldn't believe after all the things I had been through; this is what I had done. I prayed to God for courage and strength. If there were any miracles in life, I hoped he would provide one and have the doctor say that I wasn't pregnant, that the results were negative.

I couldn't imagine raising a child; I was just a child myself. I didn't even know myself and I sure didn't know Josh that well either. I thought about my entire life in that doctor's office and everything my parents had done for me. I couldn't bear the thought of how they would take this news and how disappointed they would be with my choices.

"They're going to kill me," I thought. I mulled over my options: abortion, adoption and, perhaps, keeping the baby... Lost in thought, the door swung open, startling me. Dr. Clugston walked in.

"Plotsky... Kristy, right?"

"Yes, that's me," I said.

"Hi, I'm Dr. Clugston. Nice to meet you. Are you by any chance related to a Bill Plotsky?"

OH MY GOSH.... ARE YOU FREAKING KIDDING ME????

Seriously, what do I say? At this point, I want to bury myself in the deepest darkest hole and never come out.

"Um," I hesitated, "yeah. Why?"

"Oh, I know Bill and I recognized the last name."

Really, after all my fretting and freaking out about someone noticing me in the waiting room and the doctor knows my brother. Ugh, as if this couldn't get any worse...

Dr. Clugston had the results of my test with him. He held the key to my life.

"So am I pregnant?" I asked.

"Yep, you're pregnant."

You're pregnant.

I was pregnant. I was PREGNANT.

"Are you sure?" I asked. "Could there be a possibility that there was an error in the test or perhaps you may even have someone else's pee?"

"I'm sure you're pregnant. I tested your pee and it shows that you are pregnant."

I sat there. Stunned.

"Is this not a good thing?" Dr. Clugston asked, with a look of surprise on his face.

"No. It's not a good thing. It is actually a very bad thing. I had a heart transplant."

"Oh…uhhum…. Well, in that case you will probably want to speak with your cardiologist and try to determine what the best options are for you and the baby. There are plenty of options, you know that, right?"

"What… options? What kind?"

"Well, abortion is free and legal here in Alberta. If you decide not to go through with an abortion, there is adoption. Or you could…keep it."

Keep the baby? My family doesn't believe in having children out of wedlock. That was not what you do. I was raised to believe that you have kids when you're married. I was scared and felt like I had disappointed a lot of people: my parents, my family… my donor family. What would they think?

"Oh, my parents are going to kill me," I told the doctor. "Bill Plotsky, he is my brother."

"Your parents are going to kill you? I'd be more scared of your brother than your parents. Your brother will kill your boyfriend."

I choked up a half laugh and half snort because I had begun to cry by this time. Dr. Clugston had a point. I was so worried about my parents I had forgotten about my brother. What would Billy think? What would he say? All the information and worry and unknowns were making me want to puke.

"Here, take these pamphlets," said Dr. Clugston as he handed me some brochures. "Take a few days or a week to think about all your options. Abortion is legal and that would mean that you could have an abortion and it would be confidential. No one would ever know about it, including your parents and your brother. Just think about your options and you may want to tell your cardiologist as well. He'll advise you on what to do.

"I must tell you that if you do decide to have an abortion, you will need to have an ultrasound because they will want to know how many weeks pregnant you are for the procedure. Other than that, like I said before, just think about your options, you DO have options."

And that was that. I left Dr. Clugston's office, completely different from when I had entered. I was pregnant. I was a statistic: a pregnant teen. I was devastated and ashamed. I got in my car and called my girlfriend.

"Tara… I'm pregnant… It came back positive. I'm pregnant."

I was such a bawling mess. I was sobbing furiously and I couldn't catch my breath. My face was soaked in tears. I had no idea I could cry like that. I was hysterical and freaking out.

"Oh Chicken," Tara sighed. (She had nicknamed me Chicken earlier because she wished she could put me in a cage so no one could hurt me. She always thought people took me for granted because I was too nice and I never stuck up for myself.) "Come over and we will talk about it."

I drove over to her house, sobbing the entire way. Finally, catching a break from the tears, I parked; knocked on her door and she opened it to a fresh batch of my tears.

"I'm freaking pregnant!!!!!!" I wailed. "Now what?"

Like a child, I went into her bedroom and lied down on her bed and covered my head with blankets. I wrapped myself in a cocoon, trying to disappear. Tara was right beside me, holding me. I cried and cried. She cried. We cried some more. Then we laughed and I cried again.

I don't remember how long we stayed in her bed but I know it was a pivotal and emotional time in my life. I felt fortunate to have someone beside me, who had known me since childhood. This was the girl who had lied for me after I peed my pants and was embarrassed about it. All through elementary I peed my pants because at recess we would have so much fun on the tire swing and I would laugh so hard, I'd end up peeing my pants. Tara told the other kids that I had spilled water on myself or that I fell in a mud puddle. In Grade Six, she was helping us move and she made me laugh so hard while carrying a box that I peed my pants right then and there. I couldn't help it! We laughed about those days and we cried about the future. I cried when I thought of who I had become pregnant by: Josh. We hadn't been dating for very long and I wasn't sure if he would be supportive.

This was going to be the hardest journey of my life. Heart transplants… they seemed minor now, now that I was pregnant. Almost 19 years old and pregnant. Tara and I made a pact that morning: no one else would know, other than Josh. She wouldn't tell a soul. I wasn't sure how the heck I was going to go home and eat supper with mom, dad and Billy and pretend nothing was wrong. I told myself I needed some time to figure everything out. Then I would tell them.

I decided to do a timeline and put events in chronological order. I was hoping that I could estimate how many weeks pregnant I was. It was the end of March and I hadn't been with Josh very many times so I estimated I was approximately four weeks pregnant, which gave me a few days to take some time to think things over.

I told Josh that day about the pregnancy and he seemed to be understanding. He said he wanted to keep the baby. This didn't surprise me but I didn't think he was thinking about me. I had a lot of medical stuff to consider. This wasn't going to be a "normal pregnancy" for me. I still took a couple of days to think things over and think about what were the best options for me and what my future would hold if I kept the baby.

I was sitting at Josh's house in Medicine Hat a few days later. He lived with roommates in a trailer park community in the Southridge area. I was in the kitchen, staring at the phone and wondering if I should call home. Once I told mom and dad about the baby, there would be no going back. They would know I had sex. Josh's trailer was not fancy, in fact, it was pretty much a crash pad; everyone who was drunk ended up there. It was a party house, to say the least. Instead of calling my parents, I decided to confide in Tara's mom, Sharon. She would give me some adult advice, which is what I needed.

I talked to Sharon on the phone for a few minutes. She listened to me and told me exactly what Dr. Clugston had said: I had options. Then Josh came inside. The door swung open and he yelled out, "Honey, I'm home!"

Josh was in his typical attire: black cowboy hat, black Wrangler jeans, a white shirt tucked in and… a beer in his hand. That was when the vision came. A nightmare vision of my future life flashed before my eyes.

I have a baby on each hip. I'm living in this trailer and there are three more kids fighting and screaming in the bedroom. I'm living off welfare because I can't work because I've just popped child after child out. Josh is yelling at me, "Honey, I'm home!" and, as always, is half-cut. He has a white t-shirt on and there are mustard and ketchup stains all over it. He isn't working either and he is completely drunk all the time and does whatever he pleases.

I shivered. That vision stuck with me for days and that was when I made my decision. Abortion was the best option if I wanted to do anything with my life.

CHAPTER TWENTY THREE

You make your bed, you lie in it

Before I was pregnant, I had been against abortion. Now being in the situation I was in, I had a totally different perspective on it. I had sinned by having sex out of wedlock and I knew that I had to face the consequences. I prayed God would forgive me for having an abortion but at this point, it seemed like my only option.

I called and booked an abortion appointment for April 14, 2001 in Calgary. There was only one slight problem. I had to have an ultrasound before the abortion but when I called to book the ultrasound, I couldn't get in until May. Another snag: I had to have this abortion before May 15 because that was the date for my annual biopsy. This created panic and I wasn't sure what to do. I left the abortion appointment booked for April and I took a couple more days trying to figure out what to do. That was when I decided to tell my brother.

It was late in the evening and I was lying in my bed with Tinker. (Tinker knew my secret.) Mom and dad were out socializing but Billy was home. I decided that maybe this was the time to tell him.

"Billy?" I called out.

"Ya, Kris, I'm on the phone."

"Oh. Sorry, can you let that person go? I have something really important I need to talk to you about."

"Okay, give me a few minutes."

Those few minutes seemed like an eternity. Every second of every minute I went back and forth, arguing in my mind,

"Tell him."

"Don't tell him."

"Tell him."

"Don't tell him."

Billy walked into my pitch-black room and sat on the edge of my bed.

"What's up?" he asked.

"What I am going to tell you is very important but you can't tell mom and dad. I am so serious, you really can't tell them. I'm in so much trouble. Oh Billy… I am in so much trouble."

I started crying.

"What? What is wrong?"

He probably thought I was losing my mind.

"I'm pregnant."

There was silence. Pitch-black and silence.

"It's Josh's," I said, if my brother was wondering who the father was but didn't know how to ask the question.

"Have you told him?"

"Yes."

"What does he think?"

"He wants me to keep the baby."

"Well, you know that it's your choice. This will affect your life more than it will affect his. You know that, right?"

"Yes, I know that… I don't know what to do."

"Well, I think you should have an abortion. You're so young and this is a lifetime commitment. You need to think about your future and mom and dad are not financially in a position to help you raise a child."

I didn't tell Billy I had an abortion appointment booked. I didn't want him to know that I was considering that option when a part of me was having a hard time accepting that I was going to have an abortion. My head was spinning and I was fighting with myself over the choice to go through with it. I just wanted this to all go away: the pregnancy, the doctors, Josh, everything. I wanted it all gone. I wanted to be 14 again.

"You can't tell mom and dad," I repeated to Billy.

"I won't. I promise."

There, I had told someone other than a friend. I had told a family member I was pregnant. The next few days it got harder and harder to keep my secret from my parents. Everywhere I turned I saw babies. There were babies on T.V., advertisements for birth control and pregnancy tests. I saw staggering statistics about teenage pregnancies and what percentage of students finish school if they become pregnant: not many. After days of tears and heartache and pain, my thought process changed. Seeing all the babies on T.V. I realized that an infant was a life. A life that my parents might actually want. They were my biggest advocates and what if they were more supportive than I thought? I knew that I no longer had three options, only two options: keep the baby or have an abortion. Adoption was not an option. I couldn't go through a high risk pregnancy only to give the baby away. As well, I couldn't live knowing that I had a child out there who was being raised by another family. Adoption is a selfless act and I marvel at those who have the strength to deliver their infants to other people but adoption just wasn't for me.

I made the choice to tell mom and dad about my pregnancy. Two things would happen, either they wouldn't accept it and they would be furious with me, or they would accept it and be completely supportive of me. Deep down inside, I knew they would be disappointed in me either way.

I didn't want to tell my parents my news together. I could handle them better one-on-one and they wouldn't feed off each other then. I thought if I could get them separated, I would tell mom first, dad later. That day finally arrived about a week and a half after seeing Dr. Clugston. It was Thursday, April 5 and mom was going to Great Aunt Lynn's house. I offered to drive her there. This was the perfect opportunity to talk to her. Number one, she was alone. Number two, she couldn't hurt me because I was driving the car.

"Mom, I have something really important to tell you," I said shortly into our 20 minute drive.

"What, Kristy, what? Do you want to move out again?"

"No... I wish it was that simple. I truly do."

"Just tell me."

"Well, you are probably going to be really mad at me."

"Uh... Oh my goodness. You're not pregnant are you?"

The last sentence, "You're not pregnant are you?" felt more like a statement than a question to me. At that moment, we fell silent. I didn't flinch or say one word. Then I turned my head and looked at her, although she couldn't see my eyes through my sunglasses, my eyes were full of tears.

"Yes, mom, I am pregnant."

"Don't tell me! Oh my gosh, Kristy. Who is the father?" Mom was clutching her hands against her chest, as if her heart had broken right then and there.

Could news of this sort make someone have a heart attack? I thought about dad's weak heart and wondered if I would get the same heart clutching reaction from him.

"Mom, Josh is the father."

"Oh my gosh, I need a drink."

"Only a few people know," I said and named the four people in on my secret: Josh, Tara, Tara's mom and Billy.

"You have to tell your dad."

"I know and I have also thought about my options. I have two options…" before I could list them she cut in.

"Options? Well, if you choose adoption there is no way that is going to happen. Your dad and I will adopt that baby before some stranger. That is not an option. I won't have it. I will not allow it."

"Mom, that isn't on my options list. My options are abortion or keeping the baby."

As I pulled up to Aunt Lynn's house, mom looked at me and said, "You need to tell Aunt Lynn. She'll notice that I look stressed."

"Fine," I said.

***

"Come in," greeted Aunt Lynn.

"Oh Lynn," said mom. "I need a drink. We need to have a drink."

"Kristy, would you like some wine?" offered Great Uncle Eddy. He always offered guests his special homemade wine. The wine was good but in the past, one glass was my limit, anything more than that and I would start to feel buzzed. At this particular moment, I kind of wished I could have a drink too. That was definitely not an option.

"Lynn, Kristy has something to tell you."

"Aunty Lynn, I'm pregnant."

No one said a word. Then we all started to laugh and joke about my pregnancy.

"You just wait, you will have twins or something," chuckled Aunt Lynn. She joked some more and then we all joked about the thought of me having twins. We settled into chitchatting but that came to an end when dad arrived about an hour later. He was stopping in on his way from work. I had been relieved for a bit after telling mom, Aunt Lynn and Uncle Eddy my news. Now my heart sank and I was nauseous when dad walked through the door. He came in and sat down at the kitchen table. I knew I wouldn't be able to look him in the face and tell him I was pregnant.

"Blaine," said mom. "Kristy has some news."

"What? Is she moving out?"

They laughed.

"No," I said.

"Well, what is it? I don't care what it is as long as she isn't pregnant."

Silence.

"She better not be pregnant," repeated dad.

More silence.

"WHAT! Are you pregnant?"

"Uh hem, uh yes, dad, I'm pregnant."

"Oh boy, I don't know if my heart can handle this," said dad as he clenched at his chest as if he was massaging his heart.

Both my parents now knew about my pregnancy and to my disbelief, I was still breathing. I was alive and well. Telling my parents was huge but I was numb. I wasn't sure if I was happy or shocked that I had told them. There was relief but I was shaken up and had so much anxiety that it left me exhausted. Plus, I hadn't told them about the abortion appointment yet. I would tell them soon though. Next on the list of people to tell were my doctors and this was almost as daunting as telling my parents. I didn't want to disappoint Dr. Coe. (Dr. Coe, my pediatric cardiologist, knew me better than Dr. Isaac, my adult cardiologist. I had only met Dr. Isaac twice at this point.) I would take my time getting to Dr. Coe although mom wanted me to call the cardiologist immediately.

"Kristy, I think you need to phone Dr. Coe right now."

"What? Mom, are you serious?"

"Yes. I think he needs to know."

"What do I say?"

"You call him up and you tell him... well, you tell him that you are pregnant."

I couldn't believe she was making me tell him. I knew that it was the right thing to do; I just didn't feel ready. I had just told my parents I was pregnant. I needed some time to breathe. Possibly a part of me thought mom would tell Dr. Coe for me. How could I have been so stupid though when I was the one who got pregnant? As the saying goes, "You make your bed, you lie in it."

I left the kitchen with Aunt Lynn's cordless phone. My mind was racing, my hands were shaking and my heart was thumping. I walked slowly down the hall of my aunt's house and turned left into the guest room. I positioned myself comfortably on a chair and I dialed the numbers mom had written down on a piece of scrap paper for me. Then I lifted the receiver to my ear.

RING, RING, CLICK.

"Dr. Coe speaking."

"Hi Dr. Coe, it's Kristy."

"Oh. Hi Kristy, how are you?"

"I'm good, thank you. Um, I have something I need to discuss with you that is urgent."

"Okay, I have time now. Would you like to discuss it now?"

"Sure, well, I don't really know how I should tell you this… Dr. Coe, I'm pregnant."

"Pardon me?"

"I'm pregnant. I have booked an abortion appointment for April 14 but I can't get in to get an ultrasound done until the middle of May."

"Oh. Oh dear, okay. What have…oh. Okay, let me make a few phone calls and we will get you in for an ultrasound right away. Have you taken some time to think about your options?"

"Yes, I have. I have known about this for a couple weeks now. I am leaning towards an abortion."

"Do your parents know? Have you told them?"

"Yes, I just told them right before I called you."

"Okay, call me tomorrow. In the meantime, I will call for an urgent ultrasound. You need to keep taking your medications as usual too and it would be a good idea to go for blood work tonight."

"Thank you, I will do that. I will call you tomorrow."

"Bye."

"Bye."

I hung up the phone. I had to say, the conversation had gone a lot better than I thought it would. I had expected Dr. Coe to be upset and maybe scold me, almost like a father. He sounded shocked indeed but he never read me the riot act on the dangers of pregnancy for transplant patients. Perhaps he was concerned about my health and just didn't have the time to list off all the possible complications.

I sat in the guest room for a few minutes after the call and reminisced about the days before I was pregnant. However, I was no longer only one person. How could I take care of a baby when my life wasn't exactly easy now? I still had good and bad days in regards to my health. As well, I couldn't afford a baby with the work I was doing. I knew I wanted a job in transplants somewhere in the future but how would I get there with a baby in tow? I felt alone. No one could understand what I was going through although I was comforted by the fact that I had the support of my parents. I stood up and left the room. I walked slowly down the hall, regretting every minute of the mess I was in. I went into the kitchen and everyone stared at me.

"So… How did it go?" Mom asked.

"I think he sounded shocked and disappointed but he said he would make some phone calls and put in an urgent request for an ultrasound."

"Okay, good," said mom. She knew an ultrasound would be the first thing ordered to make sure the baby was alive. It would also give us some answers as to how far along I was. "When will we know the appointment date?"

"I am supposed to call Dr. Coe again tomorrow."

"Okay, good."

It was that simple. My big secret was out.

The next day I called Dr. Coe and he came through like always. I was scheduled for my first ultrasound in two days at the Medicine Hat Regional Hospital. Dr. Coe was the only one who knew that I had an abortion appointment booked. I wanted to wait until the ultrasound was done and then tell mom and dad about my plans. Waiting would show them that I had some sense of maturity: the abortion wasn't a last-minute decision; it was something I had contemplated for a while.

Mom accompanied me to the ultrasound. I was extremely nervous and a part of me was in denial that I was pregnant.

"Hi, I'm here for an appointment," I said to the hospital receptionist.

"Yes. Your name please?"

"Kristy Plotsky."

"Hi, Kristy. Please fill out this sheet, front and back, and then return it to me."

I filled out the necessary paperwork and once I was finished, I handed it back to the receptionist. I sat down. Mom and I didn't say much in the waiting room. We were both apprehensive about the ultrasound and really couldn't believe what was happening.

"Kristy Plotsky?"

My name was called and I was guided to an exam room by a nurse. I motioned mom to follow us.

"Kristy, can you please remove all clothing from the waist up. You may leave your bra on," said the nurse.

"Okay, thanks."

"Once you are done, you can cover up with this white sheet."

I did as instructed by the nurse and lay on the bed with the sheet covering my stomach. Mom was beside me when the ultrasound technician walked in and introduced himself. He told me he would be the one taking the pictures today.

Some cold gel was plopped onto my belly, making me flinch. I had decided that I wouldn't look at the ultrasound screen because then the experience wouldn't be real. But I couldn't help it and I looked. I needed to know this was real. I wanted to know if I was pregnant or if this was just a dream.

Then I heard the sounds, the same sounds you hear when you have an echocardiogram: a swishing and swashing noise. I heard fluids moving through my body and my heart beat.

"Okay, so Kristy if you look here, you will see the embryo," said the technician pointing at an area of the screen.

"Oh wow! Yes I see that." Despite the stress of being a pregnant teen, it was captivating to think I had a baby inside me, thanks to my donor family. I couldn't believe that my body, one that once held a diseased heart, could provide life. It was my new heart that was the reason for me being able to have this miracle.

"Okay, so do you see those two lights?" asked the technician.

"Yes. They are kind of flickering a little and it's hard to see them, right?"

"Correct. Those lights are their hearts."

"Hearts? I'm sorry; did you say hearts, as in plural?"

"Yes, Kristy. You are carrying twins."

"I am pregnant with twins?"

I looked at mom, who had turned pale and was in shock.

"Okay, Kristy. We are done here," said the technician while handing me a towel. "Use this to wipe off the excess gel. Then you are able to go. The results will be sent to Dr. Coe."

"Thank you," I said.

He left the room and I wiped my belly and looked at mom.

"Can you believe that?" I said. "Can you believe twins?"

"No. I don't know what to say. You just wait until I tell Aunt Lynn. She was the one joking about it."

We left the hospital and drove home. The discovery of the twins had punted me into outer space. I was beyond shocked. It was too early to tell the sex of the twins but that didn't matter. In the car I told mom about the abortion appointment and my plans for the future, which had changed from only an hour ago.

I was going to go through with the pregnancy and keep the babies. Being pregnant with twins changed everything; the fact that I couldn't get pregnant and I did was a miracle but having twins – that was the grace of God. Two babies were a gift from God telling me that Grandma Crockford was watching over me. She had had twins but, unfortunately, only one survived at birth. I knew twins ran in our family and I was blessed to carry that on. The babies were a gift from Dawn too. God doesn't give us more than we can handle and so I was going to go through with the pregnancy. I didn't know if both twins would survive but I prayed it would all go smoothly.

The first thing I did when I got home was call the abortion clinic in Calgary and cancel my appointment. Mom was relieved and proud of me and a little scared for me and the unborn babies. It wasn't going to be a straightforward pregnancy. Josh thought I was joking when I told him we were having twins. Again, he didn't comprehend the concern for my health. At any rate, it was my decision.

That summer of 2001, I was in and out of doctors' offices just like the "old" days before my heart transplant. Dr. Coe gave me literature to read about the risks of pregnancy and heart transplants. Needless to say, the risks were huge…and scary. Rejection symptoms could be similar to morning sickness. The side effects of transplant medication on babies was concerning, specifically physical birth defects such as head deformities. (I had read about a study that did research on rats and one side effect of the drug was skull abnormalities.) Twins placed the mother at an increased risk in general but add on having a heart transplant and there were a myriad of more problems.

There were articles about transplant recipients who had given birth but no one fit my profile: twins. I was the first known woman in the world to have had a heart transplant and then be pregnant with twins. That was why I had a multidisciplinary panel of doctors caring for me. I had a nephrologist (kidney specialist), an obstetrician (a doctor who specializes in pregnancy), a family physician in Medicine Hat, a cardiologist (heart doctor) and an internal medicine specialist (a doctor who specializes in the treatment of diseases). These doctors were doubled too because I was in two different locations: Medicine Hat and Edmonton. I saw a set of specialized doctors in Edmonton and then a different set in Medicine Hat. Sometimes I would see a few different doctors in Medicine Hat if I was visiting, particularly my family physician. I saw all of my doctors on a regular basis and was scheduled for blood work on a weekly basis as well.

My pregnancy was categorized as high-risk. The doctors didn't know what my heart would do while being pregnant. High-risk also meant that I may have to be admitted to the hospital some time during the pregnancy. I had to quit my job, which at the time was working in a group home. I loved my work because I felt like I was helping people. The children I looked after gave me reasons to smile. They had heart wrenching stories and I felt protective of them, like we were a big family. I looked forward to going to my job every day but the demands of working in this type of setting were too risky for me to continue, especially being a high-risk pregnancy. I had to lift kids and do other chores that might tax my body.

I started maternity leave early and therefore, wasn't able to receive much unemployment. I was only getting roughly about $200 a month to cover things like my cell phone bill and gas. That money didn't do anything to cover what the babies would need. To file for maternity leave, I needed to supply Josh's social insurance number. This is when I realized that having children with this guy was the biggest mistake of my life.

I asked him for his social insurance number but he wouldn't give it to me. (He never gave me a reason. He just said no.) We ended up having a huge fight about it. The next few days I didn't hear from him at all: he was on a drinking binge. I did hear he was telling people how stressed he was and how much pressure he was under and how he was so worried about everything. I don't think he worried about me.

Friends called me and told me that they had seen him at the bar. I should've known he'd end up there. Despite being upset with myself because I knew better, I had it in my head that since we were having kids together, I needed to stay with him. I really wanted Josh to have some drive to get a career. I thought that if we both got help and worked on our relationship, we could be a family. I didn't come from a broken home and I couldn't imagine being a single parent. I had to stay with Josh because that was what people did. They stayed together for the kids.

My parents had been trying to sell their house for about nine months. They wanted to move away from the farm. It was too difficult to look out the window and see grandma's house. On June 1, 2001 the sale went through. I was excited in the beginning. Then I realized that my dreams of raising a family of my own on the acreage would not happen. I realized that my roots were on the farm… but it was no longer my home.

My parents moved to Red Deer where dad got a job as an electrical inspector and mom worked in the home. Billy was living in Calgary with his girlfriend and, well, I had some Grade 12 schooling to finish in the next few weeks. By now, people in my community and students at my school knew what was happening with me. Mom had called Coral and Remi, Dawn's parents, to let them know and they were thrilled. It was actually old news to them because they had already heard I was expecting from people they knew in Medicine Hat. My good friend Cheryl was a big support but I didn't have a close group of friends. Janine actually called me one day to find out if the pregnancy rumour about me was true. Other than that, we rarely spoke.

While my parents lived a few hours away, I stayed in Medicine Hat, living at Josh's mom and stepdad's house. Josh was there too, on and off. I stayed at his parents' place for about three weeks. It wasn't awkward without Josh around as I wasn't there a lot, only to sleep. (I often went to Tara's for the day.) After my exams were finished, I packed my stuff and moved to Red Deer. I never did graduate. I didn't have enough credits. Not only was I was a teen pregnancy statistic but a high school dropout. I regretted being about eight credits short from crossing the stage with my peers.

Going to Red Deer to live with mom and dad was like starting a new life. Janine and I were no longer speaking so moving was the best thing for me. In August, Josh and I decided to try to make our relationship work and he moved to Red Deer and into my parents' home with me. Things seemed okay from the outside. Josh had quit drinking while I was pregnant. (In the past, I had felt that his drinking interrupted everything to do with us.) He reassured me that he hadn't given me his social insurance number because he was scared I would leave him. He finally handed the card over. I had always felt that at the end of the day, everyone should feel sorry for him and things were never his fault. He always had excuses for behaving the way he did. He told me he drank because life was stressful and alcohol was an escape. I think sometimes we do have valid excuses but eventually, you need to take responsibility for yourself. I once heard Dr. Stephen Covey, an American educator and businessman, say responsibility is "the ability to respond." We all have the ability to respond to events in our life. I was doing it and he wasn't. It made me burn knowing the pregnancy had changed my life drastically yet, didn't have a big impact on his.

CHAPTER TWENTY FOUR

Hello

I will never forget September 11, 2001. The entire world changed on that day, that sad and terrible day. It was a chilling and sobering thought to know I was bringing new and innocent life onto this planet when there were despicable people, terrorists, attacking innocent people. My own world changed that day too.

I was approximately 26 weeks pregnant when I went for a check-up with my obstetrician. We found I had high blood pressure and there was some discharge from my vagina. I had a few months to go before my due date of December 6 and the doctor told me that I needed to be admitted to hospital as soon as possible. He said I should be on strict bed rest for the rest of my pregnancy due to preeclampsia (hypertension. It causes high blood pressure, water retention and other complications for expecting moms.) I had known I might have problems with my pregnancy but add in my transplant and then the twins, it was all cause for extra concern.

I was going to deliver my babies in Edmonton by Caesarean section (C-section) so Dr. Coe could be close by. (I had stopped going to Dr. Isaac at this point and was just seeing Dr. Coe.) I was having the C-section because there was a concern that a vaginal birth (all that pushing) would put strain on my heart. We called Edmonton and said we were on our way. I left for the city that same day and made the hour and a half drive to the Lois Hole Hospital for Women (part of the Royal Alexandra Hospital) where I ended up staying. I was not happy being back in the hospital. As you know, I hate them. Plus, I didn't feel like I needed to be there. It put more strain and stress on me and my family by disrupting our lives. My parents were worried about me though, mom worried a lot, so the Royal Alex was the best place for me.

I was able to go home to Red Deer on a pass for the first weekend that I was in the hospital. Josh was working as a welder at a company in Red Deer and it was nice to see him and get out of the hospital. It was tough being there when I felt fine. It was my blood work and other levels telling the doctors that something wasn't right. I felt too good to be constricted to bed. I was tired of course, and feeling down about the acne that had popped out all over my face (pregnancy hadn't given me glowing skin!) but otherwise, I was fine. My belly wasn't gigantic and it was hard to believe there were two babies in there. My stomach looked barely big enough for one baby.

The next weekend mom and I begged for another pass. The doctors seemed hesitant about letting me go but mom insisted. It was easier on our family to have me home in Red Deer. Besides, I was only in the hospital to be watched and my family could do that at home. The doctors were worried about my health and the babies and wanted to try to get me as close to full term as possible. They didn't want me exerting myself in anyway. But bed rest is bed rest no matter where you are. With reservations, the doctors allowed me to go home where I rested in bed.

I had found out my twins were girls during one of our "family" echocardiograms. I would see the transplant team, including Dr. Coe, to have my echo and then after that, they would do an echo on the babies. The doctors were making sure the hearts of the babies were developing and that there was no sign of heart disease. It all looked good. Terri, the technologist, asked me if I wanted to know the sex of the babies. I said yes and she told me it looked like I was having girls. I was excited as were mom and dad. Josh didn't care what we had. We all just wanted the twins to be born healthy.

We started calling the girls A and B. The doctors could actually determine who was who by the way they were sitting. Baby A was always a little smaller than Baby B. I knew from the moment I was keeping A and B that I would name my firstborn after my heart donor. That was a given. I had had Baby A's name picked out since

August. She would be named Shaylynn and her middle name would be Dawn. Mom had called Coral and Remi and asked permission to name one of my daughter's after their daughter. They said I could use Dawn's name and were happy about it. They were thankful that I was recognizing Dawn because this pregnancy was a result of her being an organ donor.

On Saturday, September 29, I decided that the second baby would be named McKayla. Both McKayla and Shaylynn were names I had found in a baby name book. I saw Shaylynn and loved it right away. I knew McKayla would have mom's middle name, Mona, but I wasn't sure if McKayla went with Mona. I kept hemming and hawing about it and I finally made the decision. McKayla Mona it was. I went to bed that night and fell asleep peacefully.

At about 5:00 a.m. I woke abruptly. I was peeing the bed. Not a regular occurrence since I was a little kid. I got up and went to the bathroom, peeing the entire way to the toilet. I couldn't stop peeing. I had heard stories about women having their water break in the middle of the night but I didn't imagine it would be like this. I had no pain and I felt fine. I decided to go back to bed.

About a half an hour later, I started to have some cramping. It was bearable but something wasn't right so I woke up mom and dad and told them that I thought it was possible that my water had broke. This was way too early for the babies. I had two more months to go. My parents rushed around frantically getting dressed and we raced to the Red Deer General Hospital. As soon as we got there we told the nurses that I was a heart transplant patient who was pregnant with twins on a pass home from Edmonton and that my water may have broke. The Red Deer nurses were kind. They had a room in emergency that was open and had me lie down on the bed. The cramping was getting worse, thus my pain was getting worse. Josh was with me but had faded into the background. He was unfamiliar with all the hospital commotion and unsure of what to do.

The nurses hooked me up to a heart monitor and then hooked up a fetal Doppler (a handheld ultrasound device used to detect a baby's heart rate) to my stomach. Things seemed to be going well and I knew that I would be delivering my babies that morning and meeting them for the first time. I was scared and excited and completely overwhelmed. Mom and dad were handling things pretty well although mom looked stressed and worried.

It was about 6:00 a.m. when the nurses checked to see how dilated my cervix was. (As the cervix dilates, it opens wider and thins out; this is what happens before labour begins.) At this time, it was about two centimetres dilated. The attending nurses called the doctor on-call, who happened to be a retired obstetrician. He was a pleasant man who came in and checked my heart rate and the dilation of my cervix. Everything seemed to be going as planned, other than the fact that I was not in Edmonton. Where I was supposed to be for labour.

The obstetrician called an ambulance to transport me to Edmonton. Then I started to have more contractions and more pain. I was experiencing some major discomfort. I had attended labour classes but what I was going through wasn't anything like my lessons. My labour was happening really fast. The doctor checked my cervix again and noticed that I was four centimetres dilated. The obstetrician knew those babies were coming quickly so he cancelled the ambulance and said we would need the STARS (Shock Trauma Air Rescue Service) Air Ambulance instead. STARS would take me by helicopter to Edmonton so I could deliver my babies there.

About 15 minutes had passed and the time was now 7:00 a.m. and I was starting to have extreme pain and discomfort. The doctor checked my cervix once again and this was when the commotion started. I was seven centimetres dilated. Five minutes later, there was no time for the air ambulance. There was no time for anything. Baby A was coming. Baby A was coming feet first. Fast.

"Cancel that ambulance," said the doctor. "We are delivering right NOW!"

I couldn't remember when to push and the nurse was telling me not to push, just breathe. I looked to the left of me and mom was standing there holding my arm. It gave me some comfort, especially when I was in such disbelief. I couldn't believe this was happening and I couldn't wait to meet my little babies. I was still in an emergency room because there wasn't time to move me to an actual delivery room. Dad was in the hallway pacing. Josh was out there too.

"PUSH Kristy...," coached the nurse. "Okay... Breathe... Breathe... One. Two. Three.

"Push... Okay breathe... In... Out... Breathe... In... Out..."

I saw blood, lots of it, coming from my vagina. It was not something I expected to see. I had had this perfect idea of how my labour would go and this was as far away as you could get from it. I cried and said I wanted drugs but mom told me that I didn't need any. I was in a lot of pain and it was a different kind of agony than what I had ever experienced with my transplant and other procedures. Delivering a baby was like taking my vagina and stretching it over my head. I knew the torment would eventually end; at least that was what I was hoping!

Then... there she was, my baby. I didn't hear her cry. I didn't hear any baby noises. Was she okay? I couldn't hear anything.

Then... her first noise... Her first tiny little cry.

"PUSH...," ordered the nurse. "LAST PUSH!

"Okay... Relax... Kristy... Okay, breathe... In... and out... Breathe in... and... out..."

I looked over to where mom was and she was gone. I was scared. Where was she? "MOM....MOM...MOM?"

"Ya. I'm right here."

She had almost fainted. All the blood and the ruckus and stress had nearly knocked her out. (Mom had never fainted before and she had seen a lot before this.) She was now sitting in a chair next to me.

Baby A was whisked away by the nurse to be cleaned up and given oxygen as her little lungs were not yet fully developed. She would need to be put in an incubator.

I caught a glimpse of her as they took her away. I could see she was tiny but she was moving. A complete sense of relief washed over my body. We were all going to be okay. One more thing to do, deliver the other baby.

Baby B was on her way. She was coming out head first but the umbilical cord was tangled around her body. Although not breech like her sister, Baby B's delivery was harder because I knew I was in for some misery.

"Push Kristy...," said the nurse. "Okay breathe... in... out...

"Breathe... in... out...

"Breathe... in... and out...

"Wait... Okay push... One, two, three push... One, two, three...

"Breathe..."

Baby B was out. She cried at first and then nothing. She turned blue and the doctor flung her diminutive body onto mine and made an incision in her umbilical cord. (I don't think the umbilical cords of my girls were cut completely because both of them required an umbilical artery catheter and an umbilical venous catheter. These were to aid in blood transfusions if required and also to give medication.) I half sat up, using my elbows to wrench myself into a sitting position to watch the medical team take care of Baby B.

Baby B was lifeless. No sounds, no cries, no movements... The doctor and nurses were very good at reassuring me that she was fine but I was worried.

Was she alive??

Is she okay?

I was panicking. I couldn't do anything to help her, not even touch her. Oh my God. I didn't hear her cry. Was she okay? Was she okay? Oh my God. She didn't look good. She was all blue. Was she going to live????

If you're a mom and you have been there, you anticipate the cry and you need to hear it.

"Mom, is she okay?" I ask my mom while crying. I didn't understand, I didn't understand what was happening. Was my baby okay?

The nurse whisked Baby B away and cleaned her up and then I heard the most beautiful sound, the sound of an angel. Baby B cried for the first time. Relief. The tears of my baby calmed me in ways I can never explain. There's something about a baby's first cry. I couldn't believe that I had just given birth to two baby girls. I was in a dream.

The girls were born September 30, 2001 at Red Deer Hospital after 30 weeks gestation, two months premature. Shaylynn Dawn Plotsky weighed in at 2 lbs 2 ounces (1145 grams) and McKayla Mona Plotsky weighed in at 3 lbs 2 ounces (1445 grams). McKayla's heart had a small hole but it wasn't a cause for alarm because it can happen with preemies.

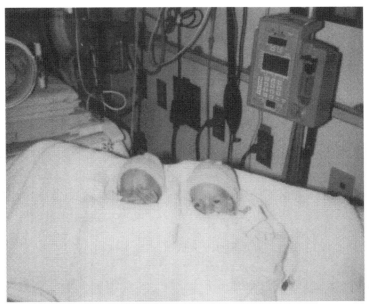

Shaylynn and McKayla October 7, 2001.

The labour and delivery was over, which I had thought was the worst part, but boy was I wrong. I had to now deliver the placenta, the organ that connects the developing fetus to the uterine wall to allow nutrients to pass to the baby. I had to push and breathe just like I was delivering another baby. This part took a long time but in reality, it probably only lasted for 15 minutes until the placenta came out. This was a moment my stomach will never forget.

Imagine a big round mold of Jell-O with nothing but air inside. If you took a pin and pierced one side of the Jell-O, it caves in. It completely falls in on itself and withers once all the air's let out. That was exactly how my stomach felt when the placenta came out. It came out so forcefully that there was blood splattered everywhere. Seriously. It was crazy. There was blood on the ceiling and blood on the walls.

The doctor cleaned me up and stitched my vagina because there had been some tearing during the delivery. I didn't have any meds for pain and while I was in some discomfort, it didn't seem too bad because I was in shock. I had gone from being pregnant to being a mom rather quickly.

My babies were transported to Edmonton via ground ambulance and taken to the Royal Alex neonatal intensive care unit. There was no room for family in the ambulance because of all the babies' equipment so they went up with just the nurses. The Royal Alex neonatal had been newly renovated that year and was a beautiful place where the girls would stay until they were healthier. We didn't know their prognosis at this point but I was hopeful all was well. (I was happy that they looked healthy.) I was transported by ground ambulance to the Lois Hole Hospital for Women, where I had been staying prior to giving birth. Josh went with me, riding in the front of the ambulance, and mom and dad drove behind us. I would have to stay at the Royal Alex for a couple days, enough time for my vagina to start healing and to make sure that my heart was okay. It had done an outstanding job while I was delivering my daughters and I was hoping it would keep on ticking.

The next few weeks were difficult for me. I saw my daughters every day, spending many hours with them. Josh was with me and mom had stayed too. Dad visited as much as he could be. (He had to work.) I was struggling with my raw emotional state. I was out-of-sorts from the pain from the stitches. It was hard to sit and be comfortable. I also couldn't hold my babies because they were in an incubator. All I could do was stare at them through the clear plastic walls protecting them and keeping them warm. It was strange for me, as a new mom, having all the professional health care staff watching me. I felt judged because of my youth and I thought that maybe the nurses and doctors didn't think I could care for my babies properly because I was young. I couldn't wait for the day to come when I could hold my daughters in my arms. That was my focus.

A couple weeks after their birth, they were placed in my arms. I was overcome with joy. I couldn't hold them for too long but even a short time was good enough to cement the mother and daughter bond. With what I had been through, I told mom that I wanted to have my girls blessed. I wanted to have a small prayer ceremony for them with me, Josh, mom and dad around the incubators. My parents had a close friend who knew someone who performed blessings. They asked if he would do us the honour of blessing the babies and he said yes. I was given two beautiful christening gowns for the girls, which I am sure you can imagine, were extremely large on my tiny daughters. Their little bodies were swallowed up in white, lace-trimmed garments.

Given the variety of medications I was on, especially the rejection drugs, and the research I had read about the drugs causing head defects, I had been significantly worried about abnormalities. I had readied myself early on about the huge possibility that my babies may have birth defects. I was ready to take on the responsibility as I am an extremely loving person and these were my babies and they were a miracle. Thank God they were born perfect. The first things I noticed, as I peered down at my beautiful baby girls, were their little tiny hands and beautiful squinty eyes.

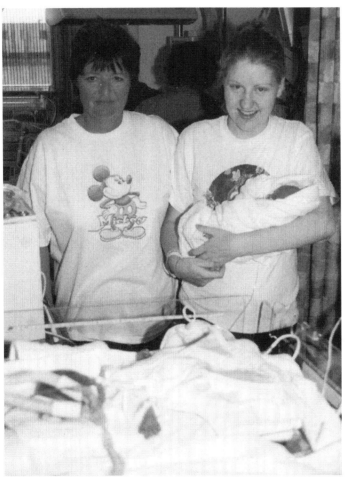

Mom and me just after the Blessing of the girls.

CHAPTER TWENTY FIVE

Delta Dawn

I met Dawn's family in October of 2001 when they came to meet the girls at the hospital. Dawn's mom Coral, her older sister Heather and her Aunt Maureen visited me. I kept staring at Coral. All I could think about was that Coral gave birth to the heart that now beats inside my chest. It was her daughter's heart that kept me alive and allowed me the opportunity to have twins. When I was pregnant I would say that I had three hearts inside me and not one of them was my own.

We wanted a photo as a group and outside the Royal Alex, we asked a stranger if she would mind taking our picture. The lady was more than willing and as she was about to snap the photo, she poked her head from around the camera and asked, "How do you all know each other? Are you related?"

Silence.

I had no idea what to say. Then Coral said, "Why don't you take the picture and then we will tell you."

The lady snapped a couple of pictures and then walked towards us to hand back the camera. That was when Coral pointed to me and blurted, "She has my daughter's heart."

Oh my goodness! If only you could have seen the look on the photographer's face: one of complete surprise. She definitely wasn't prepared for what Cora had said. The woman didn't really know what to say after that. We spoke to her a little about the transplant and then thanked her for her time. I bet the next few hours she was replaying the scene with us over in her mind.

Meeting Dawn's family was amazing and I learned so much about Dawn then. She had wanted to have twins and spoke about it often. I also learned a little about what kind of person Dawn was: kind. She would do anything for anyone. She was much beloved by her family and friends. I was proud I had her heart and I knew deep down my girls were a miracle all because of Dawn. I never met Dawn's dad Remi – that was to come. Remi wasn't ready to meet me yet... the pain of losing his daughter was still difficult.

Coral and Heather holding Shaylynn and McKayla.

Meeting Coral, Heather and Maureen for the first time.

The news about the birth of the twins had spread quickly. The media kept people updated on how I was doing. The girls were a medical miracle and it was important to share my transplant story and give other recipients hope that they could have a family too. We held a press conference on October 5. The media came and took photos of the girls and interviewed me and my family. I can't believe how big a deal it was that I had twins.

The headlines in newspapers this time read:

Heart-warming Twins
Red Deer Advocate

Transplant Mom's Twin Miracles
Transplant Recipient Makes Medical History
Twin Girls: 'A Medical Miracle'
Edmonton Journal

It was an amazing day. One of the best moments was seeing Dr. John Mullen, the man who transplanted my heart. It was incredible that he was here supporting me and he got a chance to meet my girls. The last time I had seen him was five years earlier when he was removing the staples from my chest after my transplant.

Josh saw me and the girls on and off. I was too wrapped up in motherly duties to really notice him. Health-wise I was healed and I didn't mind having visitors but not a lot of people came to see me. Mom was with me and Josh's mother and grandmother met the girls. Having kids when you're a teenager kind of makes some friendships fall apart. Plus, I had moved to Red Deer and was a few hours away from Medicine Hat.

My hospital stay was set apart from all my other times because I wasn't the patient. I got a family room where I could get some rest and be close to my babies. The girls were finally transferred from the neonatal intensive care at the Royal Alex to the Red Deer regional at the end of October. I couldn't go with them in the ambulance because there wasn't enough room for me with all the medical equipment and incubators. They would be in Red Deer for about a month and then be able to come home for good once they passed the car seat test. (That means they sit in a car seat for a length of time and their heart rate, breathing and oxygen levels are monitored. This is also known as a tolerance test typically done for babies who are born premature.) Mom and I picked out the cutest outfits for Shaylynn and McKayla to wear on their car trip home. McKayla was bigger and passed the car seat test so she was discharged from the hospital first, which was extremely heartbreaking and not to mention strenuous. She left her sister behind. I was trying to flex my time between being home and caring for McKayla, and being at the hospital so I could spend time with Shaylynn. Thank goodness for my parents because they supported me and also provided me with a lot of breaks in-between sleepless nights, poopy diapers and doctor appointments.

About three days later, Shaylynn was finally able to come home. That day, mom and I packed up McKayla and took her to the hospital to get her sister. The nurses were absolutely amazing and thought the world of my girls. We got Shaylynn ready and left. I remember walking through the door at home with both girls, I had a car seat in each hand. Life was going to be a tad more difficult than I had imagined. Carrying two car seats and a giant diaper bag was going to take some practice. In hindsight, perhaps it was a good thing that the girls' diapers were extremely tiny and the same could be said for their outfits. At any rate, it was home sweet home for the three of us.

The girls arrived early but we weren't unprepared for them. They didn't need a whole bunch of stuff anyway, mainly diapers and milk. I couldn't breast feed them due to my heart medication. Preemie stuff was expensive though. Luckily, they just wore sleepers.

Billy had bought me a really nice "fold'n go" playpen. I set it up in the middle of the front room in our townhouse. I carefully took off McKayla's winter jacket and then put her in the playpen. (I was afraid I was going to break the babies because they were teeny and seemed fragile.) Next was Shaylynn and I tenderly repeated the entire process. Mom had put a red soft fluffy blanket on the bottom of the playpen to cover up the vinyl fabric and add some warmth. The sisters were both lying together beside each other for the first time since they were in the womb. I left the room for a moment and when I came back, I saw the most amazing and cutest thing I had ever seen in my entire life. The girls were both lying on their backs but McKayla had her face positioned towards Shaylynn and she was sucking Shaylynn's thumb. Tears of joy formed in my eyes and I couldn't help but smile. I was truly blessed.

Shaylynn and McKayla finally home together.

My relationship with Josh was already strained before the birth and things were only going downhill after the babies were born. He started drinking again. Christmas was near and it was going to be my first as a mom. I wanted to have a family holiday with us altogether. I was scared to lose Josh and be a single mom. If he left me, I would never find anyone else to love me because I had kids now.

Dad had been offered a job with an electrical inspection company in Calgary and it only made sense that he accept the position as Billy was in Calgary too. Red Deer was beautiful but we didn't have the supports there that we needed. Josh's grandparents did live in Red Deer and I visited them often but other than them, we had no family in the city. I didn't have any friends there either. My parents decided to look at buying a house in Chestermere, a small town of about 2,500 people located approximately 23 kilometres east of Calgary. Mom and dad purchased a home in the West Creek area of Chestermere with a move-in date of January 5, 2002. My daughters and I would go with them. I had no other options. The move took me closer to Medicine Hat and that made me happy. I wanted to be back in the 'Hat.

My brother's girlfriend had invited my entire family to spend Christmas Eve with them and also to have Christmas dinner with them in Calgary. We stayed at the house Billy was renting in Calgary. By this time, Josh and I were no longer. I had kicked him out. I know, it sounds childish, but things between us were not getting any better and there were a couple of episodes where things had escalated. We argued over his lack of motivation. I wanted him to get his welding ticket and pushed for it. He didn't want anything to do with that and it ended in us breaking up. I was scared and felt sick about being single forever.

I was now a 19 year old single mother of twins. I was heartbroken and ashamed. I had wanted a normal family and – in my head – that consisted of two parents; mom and dad and the children, perhaps even a dog at some point. I had a hard time wrapping my head around the idea of parenting on my own. I was devastated and didn't feel that I could raise two babies as a single mom. Don't forget, that having children before you're married was not typical in my family. Great Grandma Hilda Plotsky was disappointed I wasn't married. She was worried about my health and the babies more than anything. (No one in my family ever said anything bad about me having babies out of wedlock. To my face anyway.) Great grandma loved me and she passed away shortly after my daughters were born. Her death reminded me that our time on earth is finite.

My dark cloud came back with Josh out of my life. (Maybe my depression had never truly gone away.) He went back to Medicine Hat and I spent Christmas with my family in Calgary. I longed for normalcy but there was none. I tended to my babies as best as I could. I didn't do any research or join classes on child rearing. I was too ashamed. Who has twins at 19? I did the best I could. I watched my babies while they slept. I fed them and cleaned up their diaper messes. I played with them and cuddled them. We did a lot of cuddling. Mom and dad were always a great help and I'm not proud to say it, but I don't think I treated them all that well. I was rude to mom and we argued a lot. I wanted to move back to Medicine Hat and give Josh another chance. Mom didn't think that was wise. We also argued about what I should be doing with my life. I needed some time to think. I was grieving the loss of family, my own family, and with Josh gone, I felt like no one would ever love me again.

Tara had invited me to Medicine Hat for a New Year's Eve bash at a bar. Mom and dad said they would look after the girls. I promised my parents that I was not going to the party with the hope of running into Josh. But that was a lie and, of course, I ran into him. Medicine Hat isn't that big.

The next day I woke up feeling sick to my stomach and I was determined to make our relationship work because that is what you do. Josh had told me he thought it was best if I moved back to Medicine Hat with the girls. I think I wanted to hear that more than anything. We'd be a family again. The next sequences of events were not shining moments for me, beginning with my decision to move me and my daughters in with Josh. (Into a new place, not the trailer.) I didn't have a job and without a high school diploma, employment pickings were slim. Mom and dad were furious with my decision.

To save you some time, living in Medicine Hat didn't end well. To make a long story short, my relationship with Josh deteriorated and while he never hit me, it did become violent in other ways. I'm not going to pretend that I was innocent and did nothing wrong because sure, I was verbally abusive. However, that being said, Josh did things that weren't suited to a family man. He was lazy and only around us when it was convenient for him. He put a lot of stress on me physically and mentally and it jeopardized my health, certainly my heart. One particular evening in February of 2002, we got into a massive fight at a local laundry mat over something trivial. Josh stranded me and the babies there. He just up and left us.

I believe there are things that happen in our lives that change our course. These pivotal moments are perhaps God's way of intervening and redirecting us. I believe he spoke to me through the laundry mat attendant who had witnessed everything. The attendant knelt down beside me, and said, "Honey, you deserve better. Where is your mom?"

I told her that my parents lived in Chestermere. She put one hand on my knee and lifted her other hand to my head and swept my hair out of my eyes. She looked straight at me and said, "You need to go home and be with your mom to raise these beautiful babies. You need to pack your stuff and go be with your family where you are loved."

Then she stood up and helped me to my feet. She wrapped her arms around me and I let it all out. All the tears I had been holding back came pouring down my face. Despite her advice, I didn't listen. I believed in the white picket fence and the dad being in the picture. I also didn't have any confidence that I could do things by myself.

A month later in March, there was another incident. I had moved out of Josh's and was renting a one bedroom apartment for my girls and I. (My bedroom was large enough to have a crib set up in it. The girls were tiny and slept in the same crib.) When Josh left us this time, my cell phone was gone and my patio door broken. I called 911 after he left. He was picked up later that night and charged with assault.

There was a restraining order put in place for a specified amount of days. Eventually, we both broke it and started talking. I partly blamed myself for his actions so when he said he was sorry, I accepted it. I wanted to make everything all right. I wanted to prove we could do this, be a family. I sure wasn't thinking of my girls. I was being selfish and I see that now. I knew I needed help but I didn't know where to turn.

Josh and I tried to make things work again and moved back in together. He did put some effort into being a father and I was hoping our family wouldn't unravel once more. I could hope and wish all I wanted because the inevitable happened. I'm not sure what the tipping point was for leaving Josh. I think one night I must have had an epiphany or maybe we had another big fight and I decided I needed to leave.

I'm not ashamed to tell you that this was a time in my life when I had to access social assistance. Under Alberta's Income Support program (welfare), I was encouraged to register with the Maintenance Enforcement Program (MEP), a process to make biological parents pay child support. (The province could cut you off of welfare if you didn't register for MEP.) The child support amount goes against what you receive from social assistance. For example, if a biological parent is paying $200 per month, that payment amount is calculated towards your social assistance, therefore providing you with less money. I went through MEP and did get some payments from Josh. While I was nowhere near rich, I could cover essential bills like food and rent for me and my daughters.

***

Late that spring I had to go to Edmonton for my regular biopsy. Mom was gracious enough to come with me and help out with the girls. When we returned to Chestermere the next day, I remember thinking, "Hmm, gee. My right leg sure hurts." Perhaps it was just sore from the biopsy but usually it was my groin area that was sore after a check-up, not my leg. I brushed the pain off. I was overreacting.

Mom talked to me about moving back to Chestermere because she knew things weren't going well in Medicine Hat. She offered to take the girls. It was a relief knowing I had support. I wanted a better life for the girls and myself. Over the phone, Josh told me that I'd be sorry if I didn't bring the babies back to Medicine Hat with me. Well, I didn't give into his threat. I left the girls with my parents for the weekend and headed to the 'Hat to pick up our things.

When I got to Medicine Hat, I knew I had to get my leg checked out. It was tingling and numb and I could barely walk. It had been about six years since my transplant and I didn't think the problem with my leg had anything to do with rejection: this was probably about circulation. I went to emergency and the doctor told me I might have a blood clot. If I felt any chest pain, I had to return to emergency immediately. That would mean the blood clot moved or I was having a heart attack. The doctor said I needed an ultrasound for my leg the next day. I had so much on my mind with Josh that I just said, "Fine."

Josh wasn't at the home I shared with him. He was in jail for the previous assault charge. (He had to spend 90 days in jail and served the time on weekends.) That night there was a big thunder and lightning storm and I was scared to stay in the place so I stayed with Janine. By this time, Janine and I had patched things up and we were becoming close again. The next day, she drove me to my ultrasound and the doctor identified a major blood clot in my leg. I had to be taken to emergency right away and be admitted to hospital. Great. Another hospital stay.

It turned out that I had a deep vein thrombosis (medical jargon for blood clot). If a blood clot breaks free, it can cause significant complications, even death. My whole right leg was clotted and tingling and numb. Plus, it was swelling. My one leg was the size of my two legs put together. Janine and I joked about how big my leg was. I couldn't walk and as soon as I tried, it became very painful.

My parents were supposed to be coming down that weekend to help me pack up my belongings and move (yup, again) but instead, they visited me at the hospital. I was there all weekend and given heparin (a blood thinner) intravenously. Once the weekend was over, I was given Coumadin (a brand name for warfarin, an anticoagulant) by my family physician, Dr. Jeraj, and told the blood clot would subside and therefore, the swelling would as well. Meanwhile, my parents, along with Aunt Lynn, Uncle Eddy, Brenda (their daughter) and Rob (their son-in-law), had done a marvelous job of packing my stuff. Janine was a big help too and watched my girls throughout the day while my family got my things.

That was the last time I ever lived in Medicine Hat although it would be a lie if I said I hadn't thought about going back. I missed some of my friends, specifically Janine. That June of 2002, I was living in Chestermere with mom and dad and my daughters. This is where I should have been all along.

CHAPTER TWENTY SIX

Nothing to worry about

As the weeks passed, my leg wasn't getting better. It was still significantly swollen and I couldn't put pants on. We didn't know why my leg was continuing to swell so mom contacted my family physician again in Medicine Hat. We arranged to have an ultrasound at Mayfair Diagnostics, a clinic in Calgary. The blood clot had not resolved and when the technicians scanned higher up my leg, they realized that my entire leg was one huge blood clot. They also found that I had a blood clot in my abdomen and in my lungs.

I had felt tired but I was the mother of baby twins so that wasn't unusual. In any event, I was a health mess and there was no way they were letting me walk out that door. The ambulance came and took me to the Peter Lougheed Centre, a large hospital in Calgary. I was flabbergasted that I had blood clots that terrible. Josh never reached out to me during this time and it made me angry.

I was at the Lougheed for at least a couple of days and then discharged with a strict medication regime. I was told to take Innohep (a brand name for tinzaparin. An injection given daily for deep vein thrombosis and pulmonary embolism.) Mom injected the medication into the area surrounding my stomach once a day.

We later learned that the blood clot was a result of the Depo-Provera injection (a contraceptive injection) I had recently received prior to my biopsy. I took the Depo-Provera shot because I wanted to gain weight and I didn't have regular periods. There was speculation that the Depo-Provera would add some pounds onto my frame and provide some relief (more of a break) from my menstrual cycle. I stopped the shot right away and have never taken it again. In fact, I have never taken any oral contraceptives again for that matter because they increase my chances of developing blood clots.

The blood clot eventually dilated but not without leaving a trace. My upper right leg has a tremendous amount of varicose veins protruding through the skin. When I wear a bathing suit I have been asked on several occasions, usually by strangers, where I got the "horrendous bruise." I tell them it was the result of a blood clot.

***

Living with my parents, I spent my days caring for the girls and helping clean the house. I couldn't expect mom to tidy up after us, after all, we were living there basically for free. I helped pitch in for groceries but I wasn't making much money. Josh wasn't contributing financially and I had a hard time finding work in Calgary. (I was looking in the city because Chestermere was a small community at the time and didn't have much to offer in terms of jobs.) I took on a series of meaningless jobs like working the graveyard shift at A&W, experience I already had from my younger years. My work there wasn't too bad. I was scheduled for the nightshift from 11 p.m. to 7 a.m. When I came home, mom let me sleep until about noon. The hours weren't great but they allowed me to be home during the better part of the day when the girls were up and playing.

The summer of 2002 I decided it was probably best to pursue giving mom private guardianship. It would give her the ability to make decisions without me. It was more of a "just-in-case-anything-happened-to-me" thing. Josh didn't have an option when it came to the private guardianship plans. I wanted mom to have the rights to care for the girls, not him. With my roller coaster health and the recent blood clot scare, I was worried about what would happen to my girls if something happened to me. My parents and I got a lawyer and pursued private guardianship.

Josh came to Calgary to attend court for the private guardianship proceedings. Private guardianship was granted to mom and provided me with peace of mind. I also did up a will. I wanted to make sure that I had everything in order: just in case.

When I saw Josh at court that was the first time I had seen him in months. You know what happened; we gave our relationship one more go. He moved in with a friend in Calgary and we were seeing each other. You might be asking, why did I do it? As you well know by now, I couldn't shake the "perfect family" picture: a dad, a mom, two kids, the dog and the white picket fence. The thing was, Josh wasn't really interested in being in that picture with us.

That summer flew by and on September 30, 2002, the girls celebrated their first birthday. My family rented a room at the Chestermere Regional Recreation Centre and we held a party. Josh was there and lots of family came to mark the day. It was fun.

In October I headed to college. I enrolled at the Business Career College in Calgary to study for my diploma in medical business applications. I didn't need a high school diploma or an Alberta Education High School Equivalency Diploma (GED) to attend. I was moving forward with life.

Things with Josh were going backwards. Our reunion wasn't going well and there were lots of fights and he turned to drinking again. I was determined my girls would have a father in the same home as them and you cannot fault me for trying. In the end, Josh and I weren't meant for each other. I knew it from the start and I had to accept it in the end. There were other circumstances that pushed me away from making our relationship work.

Just before I had the girls, I noticed some bumps surrounding my vagina. I spoke to a nurse about them and was told that they were simply odd changes due to pregnancy hormones. I never thought much about the bumps again until after the girls were born. Several months after I delivered the twins, I noticed the bumps getting larger and there were more of them. Perhaps they got worse the more stress I had? I only knew they were growing in size and number around my vaginal area. I was concerned and sought out other medical opinions.

I was told by three different doctors in Medicine Hat that the bumps were skin tags. My family doctor at the time told me that skin tags were hereditary and nothing to worry about. I was even given the option to have them cut out but I would have to pay for the surgery since it wasn't covered because it was deemed cosmetic. I opted for no surgery, mostly because I knew I couldn't afford it and I thought the bumps were nothing serious anyway. However, after my blood clot fiasco I noticed the bumps were spreading and getting bigger. I was persuaded again by previous professional medical opinions that they were only skin tags. No need to worry.

In the early winter of 2002, I was in Edmonton at the U of A for a check-up for myself and the girls. Restrictive cardiomyopathy was not thought to be genetic but doctors routinely monitored the hearts of the girls given my diseased organ. (It was convenient to check the girls too when I was at the clinic anyways.) During this routine visit, I decided to tell Dr. Coe about the festering bump situation down below. He looked at them and began grilling me with questions like how long had it been going on and when did I first notice the bumps and had I seen anyone for them? I answered his questions one by one and then he told me something I didn't want to hear.

"Kristy, um... You have a virus," he said. "These are not skin tags. This is a virus and you need to see a dermatologist right away. Kristy, you have venereal warts."

"Excuse me?" I cleared my throat. My blood started rushing and my heart was thumping. "Pardon me? What did you say?"

"These are not skin tags, these are genital warts," he repeated. "This is a sexually transmitted disease."

I was diagnosed with HPV (human papillomavirus), a sexually transmitted disease that can cause health problems like cancer. I had never heard of HPV before and didn't know anything about it. I did know Josh must have had something to do with it. The news that I had an STI was another shot to my already low self-esteem. Now who was ever going to love me? Here I was, a single mother and a high school dropout with warts on her vagina.

I was booked to see a dermatologist in Strathmore, a town near Chestermere, where I could see a specialist without a significant wait time. At the appointment, I found out that the warts had moved right in and had taken up residence in my vagina, vulva and labia as well as surrounding areas. The dermatologist gave me some topical ointment called Condylox (used to treat genital warts on the outside of the body). Oh my goodness, this stuff was horrible and caused a lot of pain. I was attending college and sitting through class was uncomfortable from the constant itching and stinging from the mixture of medication and warts. It was like the Condylox was antagonizing the warts and they were becoming inflamed – it was just horrible. To my dismay, those darn stubborn genital warts were not getting any better... they seemed to be getting worse. More and more and more grew and none went away.

On my next visit to Edmonton, Dr. Coe arranged for me to see Dr. Romanowski, a gynecologist there. Due to the distance and expense of travelling from Chestermere to Edmonton, they realized I should be seen by a doctor in Calgary. Dr. Romanowski referred me to Dr. Read at the STD clinic in Calgary. There is nothing like opening a door that has the giant letters "STD" stenciled on the front. There was definitely no room to be inconspicuous here. I had to deal with it.

Every two weeks, the STD clinic put liquid nitrogen directly on the warts. The first spray of liquid nitrogen was usually cold but then the second or third spray stung. (I think that was because it was getting to the root of the warts.) We were hoping the treatment would kill the warts and I could take back my vagina. There was no way that was going to happen with the small liquid nitrogen bottle. It was like we were using a little pistol in a battle that called for a bazooka.

Dr. Read was concerned about the cell changes from the warts. They were changing shape and some were changing colour: from pink to white. I didn't have a lot of time to think about having cancer. I was only just getting over the fact that I had a sexually transmitted disease. Mom was worried about cancer but dad didn't say anything.

My regular gynecologist, Dr. Brain, referred me to the Tom Baker Cancer Centre at the Foothills hospital in Calgary. (I don't know why I didn't see Dr. Brain to begin with. I think the referral time was fairly lengthy for her because she was also an obstetrician.) After my transplant, the possibility of being diagnosed with cancer was a horrible nightmare. At the Tom Baker, I met Dr. Ghatage and the amazing team of oncology gynecologists.

On February 26, 2003, I had a laser vulvectomy for HPV with dysplasia at the Tom Baker.

Dysplasia, a medical term, is abnormal cell changes in tissue. Dysplasia is the early stage of developing cancer and my cervix, vagina and labia showed dysplasia. There was a significant area of the vulva that was lasered due to the amount of dysplasia that was now beginning to appear. The surgery was agonizing. I cannot begin to express how torturous it was. The doctors went deep into the tissue in some areas because the wart virus lives beneath the skin. I was discharged the same day with morphine to treat my pain. Dr. Ghatage knew that I was on top of my current medication for my heart transplant and knew I wouldn't abuse the morphine and take too much. (I was used to following doctor's orders.) I wanted to be home because I had my twin girls to look after. It would have also proved extremely difficult for mom to visit me at the cancer centre and also look after the girls.

A couple days later at home, my vaginal pain became so unbearable that mom rushed me to the Foothills emergency. After that, Dr. Ghatage always made sure I had a supply of morphine.

After surgery I took a look down below and, gee, I sure wished I hadn't. It was awful. It looked like my vagina and the surrounding area was a charcoal grill. To make it worse, I had something that looked like grill lines burned into my skin. It was sore to touch. I was in a lot of pain and exhausted too. I couldn't pee either, it stung my skin.

When I did urinate, I had to use a peri bottle at the same time. (A peri bottle, or perineal irrigation bottle, is a bottle with a spout at the end that you can regulate water flow through.) I filled the bottle with lukewarm water and squished out the water at the exact same time as I peed. This helped dilute the urine and made it less irritating to my skin. I had to thoroughly wash the area afterwards because as I was immune suppressed, I was already at a heightened risk for infection. I had to make sure I cleaned my groin well so I didn't increase my already high chances of being susceptible to infection. I couldn't use toilet paper to wipe everything dry – nope... I had to pat myself and then use the blow dryer to take care of any excess water.

Going pee was usually a two minute activity. Not for me. It took at least 45 minutes to an hour to complete. Some days this task made me nauseous because I got dizzy (a side effect of the morphine). I definitely couldn't wear any underwear as anything near my vagina made me scream.

Mom made me a makeshift bed on the couch downstairs for the day and by night, she would transfer all my pillows upstairs to my bedroom. At least during the day I could lie on the sofa and watch T.V. or recline in a chair. I was also able to be part of what was going on with my daughters. I could hold them on my tummy, watch them play or watch shows with them. Mom waited on me hand and foot and even got the bathtub ready so I could bathe. Bathing was my escape and it eased my pain. There was something about the warm water that helped with my discomfort: physical and mental. Over the years, the bathtub has turned into my sanctuary. Back then, it was the place where I cried and, I hate to say it, but it was the place where I felt sorry for myself. I would self-loathe in the bathroom about my body and life. This wasn't how my life was supposed to go. I was upset with God because lots of people make the same choices I did, like have unprotected sex before marriage, and yet I had to endure both consequences: pregnancy and an STD. I wouldn't change having my daughters for the world but the STD... I would change that. I sometimes swore at God and sometimes I prayed to him and asked him to make the warts disappear. Most often, I soaked in the tub, sprawled out with the water up to my neck, and cried. No one was ever going to love me, especially with a warty vagina.

It was two months before I could wear clothes again like jeans and underwear. The first time I got fully dressed, I put on make-up to run a couple of errands for mom. I wanted to feel like I was a human being again. Wearing pants for an extended amount of time was painful but I fought through it. Beauty hurts, right ladies! I soon regretted being beautiful and had to take it easy on how many hours I wore pants. Finding the right fitting underwear was difficult, I am definitely a "no thong" kind of girl. My warts didn't appreciate the thong and neither did my vagina.

After my first vaginal surgery, I had this preconceived idea that the warts would all go away by the magic of laser. I was wrong. Prior to my first laser, I never had any warts in the anal area. However, after, the warts spread to my anus. They were fighting back. They had spread like wild fire and had invaded my entire behind. After that laser appointment, it was like I was doused in gasoline and a match was set in my butt. This was fantastic, not. All my private parts were diseased. I was beginning to understand that the STD wasn't going to go away.

As the days passed and turned into months, I started going crazy. The warts were becoming worse and I never got a break from the itching. The treatments that were currently on the market, Aldara and Podophyllin, were doing me more harm than good. The itching and prickling was driving me insane and making me aware that I had a dirty little secret below the belt. I don't know why I was ashamed of having an STD. Right around this time is when HPV was starting to be discussed in the news. I read many books to educate myself on the disease and what it was doing to my body. Nothing could take away the itching and it became so severe that it drove me out of my mind. I expressed my concerns to Dr. Ghatage about it. It was becoming so bad that wearing any clothing of any kind was proving to be extremely uncomfortable. However, I couldn't just walk around naked. I thought to myself that there would be no way that I would ever be able to wear jeans or dress pants on a daily basis again. I wanted to enjoy being with my girls but it was difficult when the HPV itching consumed my life. I wasn't even sure how I was going to keep going to class. Sigh. I couldn't and had to take a few months off. I'd finish my program later but not on schedule. I never did get rid of the warts and am still being followed by the cancer clinic at the Holy Cross Centre in Calgary.

CHAPTER TWENTY SEVEN

Gasping for air

Tinker used to be the centre of my life. Now that I had two daughters, my dog had some major adjustments to make. One summer night in 2003, we let him out in our Chestermere yard to go to the bathroom. He was good on his own and would let out a little bark and paw at the door when he wanted back in the house. Tonight he seemed to be taking a little longer to finish his business. A good 15 minutes had passed and we figured he was surely done by now. We opened the front door and called him. He was an obedient dog and always came when he heard his name. We called him again… and called him again. He never came.

I went out to look for him but there was no trace of my dog. I was upset and crying. I regretted not checking up on Tinker sooner. He was 10 and getting older and I thought maybe he got lost and didn't know how to find his way back home. I also thought maybe he left us so he could go somewhere and pass away by himself. Animals do that. Tinker had had a stroke a few months earlier. In the middle of the night he made a terrible noise and lost control of his bowel and bladder. The vet had actually given him only a week to live... several months ago. That night I went to bed without my dog sleeping by my side.

The days passed and there was no sign of Tinker. I drove around the neighbourhood praying I would find him but I thought I would probably never see him again. Mom decided to call all the pounds in

Calgary. She also called the SPCA (Society for the Prevention of Cruelty to Animals) and someone there told her a lady from Chestermere had called to say they found a dog – with Tinker's description. Mom called the lady right away and told her that we had lost our dog and described all of Tinker's behaviours. Mom said that if you hold a treat out, he would stand on his hind legs and beg by rotating his front paws.

"Oh my goodness!" said the lady. "He does that."

Mom went to look at the dog and miraculously it was Tinker! Mom was hysterical with happiness when she called me at school to tell me the amazing news.

"We found Tinker."

I couldn't wait to get home and see him and give him the biggest hug ever. Mom also had more exciting news for me. Somebody from *Glamour* magazine had contacted her and wanted me and the girls to be part of an article about "real life heroes." Apparently, they found my name in some archives and wanted to interview me and bring me to New York City to be part of the story about amazing real life heroes. They were making arrangements to fly me and the girls to the Big Apple for a glamour photo-shoot in July. My parents were invited as well because it was too much for me to travel all by myself with both of the girls. We agreed to share my story with others. I was excited to go to New York City. It was one place I had always wanted to visit and now I was given the chance.

Mom and dad had never been to New York either and we took advantage of the opportunity. We paid our driver to take us to some of the "hot spots" in the city. We visited Ground Zero and took pictures of us at the site where the Twin Towers once stood. There were steel beams standing there as a symbol of what happened on Sept. 11, 2001. Some of the people who visited Ground Zero signed their name on the steel fence that barricaded the area. There were thousands of names on the fence. It was a sobering moment to think about the people who lost their lives in the tragedy.

Our cab driver took us to an area where we could see the Statue of Liberty. We didn't go to the statue because tours were closed due to the terrorist attacks and the high alert of another one. The driver also showed us the Empire State Building and we drove across the Brooklyn Bridge. We toured Wall Street and then the driver dropped us off at our hotel.

Mom, dad and I took turns going down to Times Square. Mom and dad went first while I stayed in the room with the girls. When mom and dad were finished walking around and checking out the lights of New York City, mom and I visited the square while dad watched the girls. The girls were toddlers and don't remember the trip. I enjoyed playing tourist immensely.

I was interviewed by *Glamour* about my transplant and life. I didn't share anything about the HPV because I wasn't at the point where I could accept that it was something I was going to have to deal with forever. Psychologically, I was not there yet. I couldn't admit I had an STD to the world, especially when I had a hard enough time admitting it to myself.

Glamour Magazine 2003   *Photo credit: Jayne Wexler*

Glamour hit shelves in late September 2003. When it came out, mom picked up several copies for her scrapbook. It was weird seeing the magazine on the racks in the grocery store and knowing my story was inside. (I liked the piece but it was very short.) It was truly an amazing experience and one I will never forget. I even learned some great make-up tips from when the make-up artist did my face. My friends were excited to see the photos and read the article too.

Around this same time, we received a call from The Sharon Osbourne Show, a talk show hosted by singer Ozzy Osbourne's wife Sharon. The show wanted to have me on as a guest and were trying to make arrangements to fly me and the girls and another adult down to California. They didn't have a show date scheduled but were thinking about having me on in the next few months. I said yes because I thought it was a good chance for me to advocate for organ and tissue donation. Meanwhile, that September the girls and I went to Edmonton for our annual checkups. Dr. Coe was still monitoring their hearts and everything seemed to be going well. The girls were gaining weight and the echocardiogram of their hearts looked unremarkable: nothing indicated restrictive cardiomyopathy.

What we knew of the disease was that it was not genetic. McKayla's heart was looking healthy and the hole she had at birth had closed up all on its own. Other than my chronic HPV, things were going well for me. I was attending the career college and moving along with my courses. It was taking me longer to finish my seven month program because I had to take two months off due to the laser surgery. I completed the rest of my program in the summer and obtained my certificate.

I felt sorry for myself occasionally but every time I experienced self-pity, deep down I knew I was really lucky because I received a heart and was able to have twins. I always tried to change my focus from the negativity of the HPV, to the amazing miracle of my daughters. That pessimistic inside voice was hard to tame though. Sometimes it would latch onto a bad thought and not let go. My inner voice was telling me nobody would ever love me because I was damaged goods.

Josh was way out of the picture and I did go on dates with other men. Nothing ever lasted. I always told any potential partners about my HPV diagnosis, usually on the second date. I didn't want to mislead anybody and I would have wanted the same respect done for me.

In the fall of 2003, mom got me a job at the place where she worked. United Prescription Service was a company that shipped medication to the U.S. My job was mostly packing and placing shipping labels on packages. I did some data entry too. The job worked out well because mom and I could car pool. The girls were two years old and attended a day home in Erin Woods, a residential neighbourhood in Calgary's south-east. The home was regulated through the government, which allowed me to receive a subsidy. These were tough financial times. I was receiving hardly any money from Josh and I was a single mom without a high school diploma. I only had a certificate in Medical Office Administration through a private college.

November 10, 2003 was another typical day. I never ever dreamed in my wildest fantasies that my life would change drastically in the next 72 hours. I was at work when I received a call from my day home lady around 10:00 a.m. Lynn told me over the phone that Shaylynn was throwing up and not keeping anything down. I thought she probably contracted some kind of stomach bug: it was that time of year. I picked Shaylynn up and by that time, she seemed fine. To be sure, mom and I decided to take her to the Strathmore General Hospital, a local rural Alberta hospital. We'd leave after my liquid nitrogen appointment at the Calgary STD clinic. (Yep, I was still trying to go that route to get those pesky warts under control.) In the Strathmore emergency department waiting room, Shaylynn was running around and playing with McKayla. It really seemed like nothing was wrong with her and we were overreacting. (Honestly though, I think from what we had been through so far with me, there was no such thing as overreacting.) The doctor at the hospital told me that kids throw up one minute and then the next, they are fine.

"Kids are very resilient," he said. "Typically, if kids are smiling and running around we tend not to worry too much about them because it was probably just something they ate."

I was relieved and annoyed by this doctor all at the same time. I realized kids were resilient but I really wished the doctor would have done an ECG on Shaylynn, especially with my family's heart disease history. We left the hospital and went home.

On November 11, Shaylynn was back to her normal self. Perhaps the doctor was right. Kids are pretty resilient. I had that day off and I spent it with my daughters hanging out at home. The next day, I was rushing to get the girls to daycare so I wouldn't be late for work. Shaylynn and McKayla were their typical selves, fooling around and getting into things and making me run behind. When I stepped outside, I heard the crunch of crisp, new snow cracking beneath my feet. The footsteps of my little girls were imprinted on the porch steps as I quickly helped each innocent small girl to the vehicle. We left mom and dad's that morning not knowing that our entire world was going to change by that afternoon.

I dropped the girls at the day home and headed to work. I peered down at my clock in my 2002 Chrysler Neon; it was 7:35 a.m. The major highway going into Calgary, Deerfoot Trail, was going to be backed up but I was going to enjoy the drive anyway. (I like being behind the wheel.) I made it to work around 8:00 a.m. and began my usual duties of packing boxes with medication and printing labels. Mom was already at work by the time I arrived. A couple of hours in, Lynn called.

"Kristy, Shaylynn is throwing up again," she said. "I have tried giving her crackers but she won't keep anything down."

"Okay," I replied. "I will be right there. Does she have a fever?"

"She feels a little warm but I took her temperature and it read 38.9 Celsius so she might be starting to get a fever now."

I hung up the phone and quickly went and told mom what was happening. I was worried but I blocked the loud voices of negativity telling me something was wrong. I had to keep myself together.

"Mom, Shaylynn is throwing up at the day home again. I am going to go get her but I am going to take her to Children's."

The Alberta Children's Hospital has way more experience with kids: it's who they specialize in. I thought they'd have a better understanding of what was going on with my daughter.

Mom said she would meet us there. By the time I arrived at Lynn's house, Shaylynn seemed fine. I was going to take her to Children's anyway. I left McKayla with Lynn, who was a great help and more than understanding. (In fact, she pleaded to have McKayla stay at the day home as we didn't know how long I would be at the hospital with Shaylynn.) I got Shaylynn settled in the vehicle. She wasn't throwing up anymore and said she was hungry. I decided to stop at Denny's for a quick bite to eat. It was lunch time by now and I was starving. Mom met us at the restaurant. If Shaylynn was still feeling under the weather, we would take her to Children's.

We ate quickly and Shaylynn ate mostly crackers and drank ginger ale. She complained on and off about her tummy being sore and not feeling great. We asked for the bill and made our way to Children's.

Shaylynn was vomiting frequently on the way to the hospital. My poor baby. She hadn't eaten a lot and didn't really have anything to throw up. When we arrived at Children's, we were triaged and then called into emergency. We didn't have a long wait and were in front of a physician in no time. I provided the emergency doctor with my heart history and the miracle births of Shaylynn and McKayla. I shared that an echocardiogram had just been performed at the U of A for their yearly checkups. I added that my dad had told me a couple weeks ago that he thought Shaylynn's heart was racing. I told the doctor that I had turned down any cause for concern because young kids typically do have a higher rate of heart beat than adults. Perhaps I had become desensitized to anything that would be concerning, especially regarding what I had been through myself. I had seen so much that I didn't worry about things like other people did. My experiences lowered the bar for worry. The doctor decided it would be a good idea, given my medical history, to have Shaylynn visit cardiology and get an echo and ECG done.

I wheeled my daughter over to cardiology while mom went outside to have a smoke and call dad on her cell phone to update him on what was happening. He'd have to pick up McKayla and take her home. I was anxious to find out what was happening with Shaylynn but didn't want McKayla to be forgotten. In emergency, doctors gave Shaylynn some medication to help calm her vomiting. Not many minutes later, mom joined us back in the waiting room and we were called in for the ECG.

It was surreal to see Shaylynn get hooked up to all the machines I was hooked up to as a young child. She also had the very same technologist perform her test. It provided me with some memories of good times and some sad times. I told my daughter about having the test done to me and I think it reassured her. (I had told my girls my heart transplant story but they didn't understand as they were too young.) We finished the ECG and moved straight to the echo room. By this time, it was getting late, around 7:30 p.m., just passed my med time. (I took rejection medication twice a day: 7:00 in the morning and 7:00 at night.) Mom brought me some water to take my pills and then she went to call dad.

Shaylynn was a trooper. She was perfectly still while the echo technologist stuck the electrodes onto her chest. The technologist then put some gel on the sonographer wand (a diagnostic tool) and gently pressed it on the left side of Shaylynn's chest, by where her heart was. As the technologist pushed down on Shaylynn's chest, I pushed my daughter's hair back from her forehead and gave her a kiss, reassuring her I was there. I remembered mom doing this for me most times and how it calmed me.

The technologist performed the echocardiogram and then once she was all finished, she took out a white towel and gently wiped the gel off Shaylynn's chest. We headed back towards the emergency department. At this point, we didn't have any news about anything. We had to wait. It was an all too familiar feeling.

When the doctor finally came in, he said that they were going to admit Shaylynn for the night. She was significantly dehydrated and needed fluids intravenously. Once the IV fluid was complete, they would do another echo in the morning. Shaylynn didn't react to spending the night away from home. She was too sick to care.

I stayed with Shaylynn in her room. I went over the day in my head. I didn't know what to expect but a diagnosis of restrictive cardiomyopathy was the furthest thing from my mind. I thought that she probably had a bad flu or stomach bug. I needed a friend to talk to and called Janine, who was in Calgary visiting her grandparents. Janine said she would visit us in the morning.

Morning arrived after a not-so-great night. Shaylynn hadn't got much sleep because she had vomited a few times. I hadn't slept at all. When I wasn't busy taking care of Shaylynn, I drifted off to sleep, only to be woken by her whimpering. My wonderful mother arrived around 9:00 a.m. with my toothbrush, hairbrush and a change of clothes. I quickly freshened up because I didn't want to miss the call for Shaylynn's echo. (It was nice taking away the feeling that hair was growing on my teeth.) There wasn't a scheduled time for Shaylynn's test but it would be sometime in the morning. Janine arrived shortly after 10:00 a.m., about the same time they called Shaylynn. I carried my daughter in my arms down the hospital hall while mom and Janine shared the duty of pushing the IV machine on the IV pole. We sat in the cardiology clinic waiting room for about five minutes and then Shaylynn's name was called again. I carried her into the room, not realizing it would be the last time I carried my little girl with a healthy heart. I was not prepared for what was about to happen next.

Mom accompanied us into the echo room while Janine waited in the waiting room. I carefully put Shaylynn on the stretcher while the echo technologist wasted no time prepping her. First the electrode stickers: six went on her chest by the breast toward the armpit, and then there was a sticker on each leg just above the ankle. Next came the gel for the sonographer wand and then it was placed towards the chest and finally, the technologist pressed down. The interesting thing was that the technologist performing the echo wasn't the same technologist as last night. Nope, it was Dr. Patton. I knew him from when I was first diagnosed. I don't know if you recall, but you met Dr. David Patton in the beginning pages of my book. He was the resident doctor when I was diagnosed in 1996 and advocated having the extremely expensive medication flown in from Edmonton to dissolve the blood clot in my heart. Here it was 2003 and Dr. Patton was performing an echo on my daughter. He remembered me from the years before.

I sat beside Shaylynn with my hands gripped and tangled around her tiny and delicate hands. At the beginning of the test, everything appeared good. Her heart was fine and there had been no changes since September. I then realized that the echo was taking a lot longer than expected. (I knew this from my own echoes.) My thoughts raced and the little voice inside my head kept saying, "This is taking way too long. Something isn't right."

Dr. Patton had a serious look on his face and was concentrating hard. I sat directly across from him and the only thing separating us was the stretcher that my two year old little girl was lying on. I gently stroked Shaylynn's hands, like my mom used to do to me when I was having a medical test done. I never knew that I was about to experience the same scenario mom and dad faced seven years ago. The only difference here was, I had been the patient too.

No one was talking in the room until Dr. Patton broke the silence. He slowly turned his head my way and gently nodded up and down as if to say, "Kristy, she has it."

It was if we could communicate without speaking. Everything went into slow motion. The room felt like it was closing in on me. I tried hard to choke back the lump in my throat and stop the rush of tears. I couldn't let Shaylynn see me cry. I didn't want to scare her. I couldn't breathe. It was like I was drowning and I couldn't get my head above the water.

CHAPTER TWENTY EIGHT

The Heart of Michigan

Dr. Patton gently hung up the sonographer wand. He was finished Shaylynn's echo. He grabbed a towel and slowly swiveled his chair towards me. He lifted his head and looked me straight in the eyes.

"Kristy," he whispered, "she has restrictive cardiomyopathy."

I couldn't move. The whole world stopped for a moment. I only wished it had stopped before this moment. Before the moment of the terrible and tragic announcement. Tears tried to push their way out of my eyes and I struggled to hold back the deluge. To find out my daughter had the same heart disease as me was all too much. I felt lightheaded but I had to get out of this place. I rose to my feet. The walls were closing in and I could barely breathe.

Mom and I knew what restrictive cardiomyopathy meant. Shaylynn didn't. She was scared of the hospital and machines and IVs but not of the diagnosis. That is why I didn't want her to see me cry. I didn't want to frighten her. Mom was devastated. I could see it in her eyes. She was silent, probably trying to be strong for Shaylynn too.

"I need a moment," I said softly and got up.

There was nothing but silence in the dark echo room. I walked unsteadily to the heavy sliding door and somehow managed to open it. I exited slowly but then picked up my pace as though I was about to be trapped in that place forever. I closed the door behind me and made my way down the hall to the waiting room. I could barely see as my eyes were clouding over from the threatening tears. Janine got up and walked towards me. Once we met, I stood in front of her and the tears rolled down my face. I barely got the words out, "She has it," between my heavy sobbing. We walked over to a more private area of the waiting room, leaned against the wall and slid down it until we were sitting on the floor together. Crying.

Over the next few hours, the cardiology team in Calgary collaborated with the paediatric transplant team in Edmonton to make arrangements for Shaylynn to be seen there for transplant assessment. Shaylynn was scared. At two years old, she didn't understand what was happening. I told McKayla that her sister was sick but she didn't understand either. The plan was to have Shaylynn flown by medevac to Edmonton the next day, November 13, 2003. Unfortunately, there wouldn't be any room for me to go along because of all the medical equipment and the medical staff accompanying her. (I found out later that my daughter wasn't too stressed about being without me on the flight. We had started a book for her like my family had done for me when I had my transplant. An ICU nurse from Alberta Children's Hospital wrote in Shaylynn's journal that Shaylynn entertained everybody with her contagious laugh on the flight from Calgary to Edmonton.)

We were fortunate that Billy was working in Edmonton at the time. He met Shaylynn at the U of A's Stollery Children's Hospital (it opened in October 2001) and waited with her until mom and I arrived. We drove to Edmonton together while dad stayed home with McKayla.

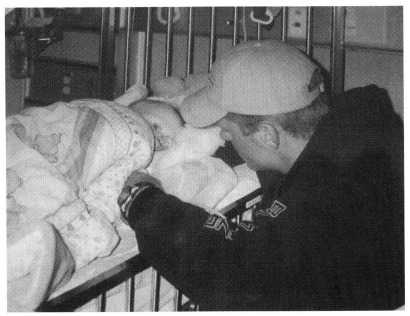

Uncle Billy with Shaylynn at the Stollery hospital October 2003.

Shaylynn had to complete several different tests, the same tests I had went through for my assessment including x-rays, holter, ECGs, blood work and echoes. It was definitely a totally different feeling watching your daughter have an echo, knowing that she has your same heart disease. Restrictive cardiomyopathy was not supposed to be genetic but I blamed myself for Shaylynn's diseased heart.

At the assessment, we found out that doctors don't like to do transplants on kids who haven't been vaccinated. With the girls being premature and then me moving back and forth, I never got around to making sure the twins were vaccinated. That was terrible of me. However, there wasn't enough time to get Shaylynn vaccinated before transplant but it would go ahead anyway.

Receiving Shaylynn's diagnosis was as if I had travelled back in time. It was like I was walking through a living nightmare – one that I had already been through myself. After we came back to Shaylynn's room there were so many emotions coursing through my body. The sharpness of the pain and sadness was dulled by shock. I never ever thought about the possibility the girls might need a heart transplant. If the thought had ever entered my mind, I brushed it away as quickly as it had arrived.

That evening, I stayed with Shaylynn at the hospital. The doctors weren't letting us go anywhere other than Edmonton. Mom and dad were still with me and while Shaylynn was getting some much needed rest, my parents and I strolled down to a familiar area of the Alberta Children's Hospital where I could use the pay phone to call family. Yes, this was the exact payphone that I had used to contact my family years earlier with the news that I needed a heart transplant to live. Now, only eight years later, I was using the same phone, sitting in the same chair and telling my family the same news. There were a lot of similarities then and today. The only difference now was it wasn't me who needed the heart transplant: it was my daughter.

As I called family and friends back in Medicine Hat, I stared blankly at the ground. I held the phone tightly against my ear while the present and past swirled around me. I squeezed my eyes shut and the voice on the other end of the phone faded away. I wasn't in 2003 anymore.

It was all so familiar, too familiar, like it was yesterday. I could see my parents standing not too far away from me. I could hear the same busy sounds and the hustle and bustle of the children's hospital: doctors and families of patients being paged, medical staff walking by, perhaps on their break or just finishing their breaks and going back to work. I couldn't believe I was in this space again, in the fight for life – but this time it was my daughter's life. Her life meant way more to me than my own. How was I going to get through this, especially knowing what I knew as someone who had already received a gift? What if a heart wasn't found in time? We knew we didn't have much time. We knew what this disease did. I opened my eyes, hoping I would wake up and find it had all been a horrific nightmare.

It wasn't. It was real and this was my reality. I looked straight ahead of me, thinking this was exactly where I was in 1996. But it was 2003. I re-focused on the present and the voice on the other end of the payphone. I quietly say goodbye to the person and hung up. My parents had left to take a smoke break (yes, they still have that bad habit) so I sat quietly by myself and watched people walk by me. I took a deep breath and stood up, about to make my way back to Shaylynn's room. I had been gone for several minutes and she probably had woken up from her nap. My baby needed me and I needed to be strong. I looked up at the ceiling and then stretched my back and shoulders. I took another deep breath. As I let it out, I asked God to give me and my family courage.

***

The assessment tests were all completed within about a week and Shaylynn was now on the Edmonton transplant waiting list. Her tests had revealed the restrictive cardiomyopathy was progressing rapidly. We weren't given a pager. Doctors had my cell number and mom and dad's cell and home phone numbers and would go down the list until they got a hold of us one way or another. My family had fought to have me double listed but that wouldn't be the case with Shaylynn. Changes had been made to the system and organs could be procured from other centres. If nobody was a match for an organ on a local list, then a search was done to find a suitable recipient further afield.

I stayed with Shaylynn while my parents stayed at the Travelodge. (The hotel company offered discounts for people visiting the hospital.) We were sent home with Shaylynn after assessment and I was told to keep a close eye on her. I definitely would as I was worried about her heart. She was a lot like me when I was sick. We both didn't look ill on the outside but inside, our hearts were rotten.

It was nice to be home in Chestermere. I was especially excited to see McKayla. However, everything felt different. The first thing I did when I got home was pack two bags of clothes – one for McKayla and one for me. I stored the bags in the front closet. This way when we got the call, I was all set and didn't have to waste any time packing.

Shortly after Shaylynn's diagnosis, I went to a doctor at the U of A and was prescribed antidepressants. I was upset about Shaylynn and the emotional turmoil piled onto the depression I was already struggling with. I often cried myself to sleep. Nothing was making me feel better. Being home did lift my spirits somewhat.

In Chestermere, we settled back into our old routines. We had to be vigilant about taking the cell phone with us in case we got the call that a donor heart was ready for Shaylynn. I was always on alert waiting for the phone to ring. It was incomprehensible that Shaylynn needed a new heart. I prayed she would get one in time.

Despite it being several years since my diagnosis of restrictive cardiomyopathy, there hadn't been much research done on the disease. We did find out it was genetic. Other than that, there was nothing. Doctors didn't know what gene caused it and this was concerning since Shaylynn's restrictive cardiomyopathy came on so quickly. McKayla would need to be checked often.

I couldn't believe I was going down this road again. This time, it was much worse. This time, the disease was affecting my daughter. I would give anything to be able to change places with her. I talked to my parents about what they went through with me. They gave me advice but the major difference now was: I had also been the patient. I had an overwhelming feeling of helplessness not being able to protect my own child. I didn't know if it made it worse or better that I had gone through the same experiences that Shaylynn was going to go through. I was sick thinking of the hardships she'd endure. All the times I had wished I was healthy so that I didn't have to go through certain things or miss out on certain activities, I was now wishing for Shaylynn. Having a heart transplant was a lifelong journey – it never ended.

I guess you're wondering how Josh reacted to the news of Shaylynn. He was concerned as a father and did see her but we needed more than that. When I tried talking to him about child support (as this was going to be difficult financially), he said that I should sell my car. That wasn't the kind of support his daughter needed.

While I wanted a heart for my daughter, another family's child would have to die in order for that to happen. I was overcome with unfathomable grief thinking about a mother and father losing their loved one. I thought about Coral and Remi and what they went through losing Dawn. I cried at night to Tinker, just like I used to when I was a young child.

***

I've said many times that Christmas is my favourite holiday because you get to spend it with family and eat delicious home baked goods. That Christmas, I went to Costco with mom and bought my daughters beautiful Christmas dresses. (It's a tradition now.) I had so many things to be thankful for and celebrate.

We spent Christmas with Billy's girlfriend's family in Calgary. Christmas Eve we did a fun gift exchange. Everybody brought an inexpensive wrapped present. Then you would draw a name and whoever's name was picked, could open a gift. But if someone wanted your gift, they could take it. It sounds like the opposite of the "season of giving" but it created a lot of laughs and we needed them.

During the holiday we talked a lot about Shaylynn needing a heart transplant. I didn't want to think about the possibility of not finding a suitable donor for Shaylynn in time but my thoughts wandered there from time-to-time. Someone predicted Shaylynn would get her heart in January. I prayed her prophecy was correct.

Shaylynn rang in the new year, 2004, with her old heart. January was dragging on and on and the waiting was pushing me to the edge of reason. I had anxiety every time my cell or house phone rang. Our packed bags remained in the front closet, ready. We needed that call.

Mom and dad's house phone rang early on the morning of January 23. It was 3:40 a.m. and I must not have been in a deep sleep because the ring woke me. I heard mom talking but her voice was muffled and I couldn't make out what she was saying. I repositioned my head hoping to catch a word or two. It was no use. I told myself it was probably my brother needing a ride or something. I put my head back down on my pillow.

There was some commotion coming from my parent's room and I heard them whispering. I couldn't decipher what they were saying. Then mom poked her head into my room, "Kristy, that was the U of A hospital. They may have a donor heart for Shaylynn."

I sprung to my knees on the bed.

"What? Oh my gosh! We have to get ready. Mom, what do we need to do now? Do we need to drive to Edmonton?"

By this time, I was standing up on my bed. Mom told me that Edmonton would call us in a couple of hours to give us instructions. She added the nurse had said the donor was still on the breathing machine and they were waiting for the family.

The thought of a little boy or girl lying on a stretcher and attached to a breathing machine about to die broke my heart. I started bawling and drilled mom for information about the donor and family.

"Mom, did they say if it's a boy or girl? How old are they? Mom, where are they right now? Where are they from? What happened? Was it a car accident?"

I had all these question that mom couldn't answer. She turned and started to head downstairs. I was about to follow when she stopped me.

"Kristy, you should really try and sleep because it may be a really long day."

There was no way I was going to be able to sleep under these circumstances. I went to get out of bed but with the excitement tangled with the overwhelming grief I was feeling, I miscalculated how far the floor was from my bed. I was wearing OR scrubs (given to me by a doctor several years earlier) and I hooked my left foot in the bottom of the right pant leg, ripping the pant leg and sending myself tumbling to the floor. It hurt but I didn't have time to deal with the pain. Mom helped me up after having a chuckle about my fall and lack of grace. All I could think about was what the donor family was going through and how badly I wanted to hug them and cry with them.

Edmonton called around 5:00 a.m. with good news. The heart was definitely a match for Shaylynn, however, it wouldn't be in Edmonton for several hours. I told Shaylynn what was going on but she didn't understand. McKayla was confused about the whole ordeal and wondered why I paid so much attention to her sister. I wasn't working then and when I was given the go ahead to travel to Edmonton that morning, we got our things together and left right away.

The hospital made arrangements to have Shaylynn, me and mom fly out of Calgary on a medevac flight with a medical professional onboard. Shaylynn's new heart wouldn't be arriving in Edmonton until after 4 in the afternoon so we had some time. We could drop McKayla off at the day home but couldn't pick her up. Billy was a great help here because he lived near the day home and could take care of his niece. Billy and dad would come to Edmonton as soon as they were done work and bring McKayla with them.

We got to the airport and boarded the medevac plane a little after 9:30 a.m. Shaylynn had been on a plane before so it wasn't scary for her. She was hungry but eating was out of the question before surgery. I prayed to God for two things while I was on that plane: for the family who had lost their little one… and that this wouldn't be a dry run for us.

We arrived at the airport and then took an ambulance to the Stollery shortly before lunch. Operating room preparations got underway for Shaylynn and she was connected to an IV and had blood taken. The media had learned about Shaylynn and at the hospital we met with a reporter from the Edmonton Journal. The headlines from various news agencies' shouted:

Mother Relieves Transplant Drama

Mother, Baby Share *Transplant Miracle*

She's a Fighter Just Like Mom

The donor heart was not due to be at the Stollery until about 5:00 p.m. I learned then that it was from an older child and coming from Michigan.

"Wow!" I thought. "That's a long ways away."

The distress of the donor family filled my mind. I wondered what they were going through. I wondered what happened to their loved one. I wondered if their heart would help my loved one.

Shaylynn would be going into the operating room at 4:00 p.m. even though the heart hadn't arrived yet. She would be prepped for surgery but nothing would be done that couldn't be undone in case something happened to the heart. There was a possibility that it wouldn't work or it could fail testing once it arrived at the Stollery.

Mom and I took Shaylynn into the operating room and we both cried while giving her hugs and kisses. Dad and Billy hadn't arrived in Edmonton. They were on their way with McKayla but wouldn't see Shaylynn until she came out of surgery. The heart arrived at the Stollery at 6:00 p.m. I wasn't stressed out that it was late. What was bothering me was the surgery more than anything. It was a big and risky surgery and brought a flood of emotions back for me.

Shaylynn was readied for surgery. The doctors told me they had already opened her chest and were finalizing the tests on her new heart prior to transplant. The hardest part for me was keeping positive during the surgery. I was helpless as I sat and waited for my daughter's heart transplant. I drank litres of coffee and this is probably what started my addiction to caramel macchiato drinks (steamed milk with vanilla-flavoured syrup, espresso and caramel drizzle). There was a coffee place on the main floor that brewed the specialty coffee and I frequently visited the café. I also whiled away time talking to my family about my surgery way back when and we started a book for Shaylynn, like we had done for me. My stomach was growling and I realized I was starving: I hadn't eaten all day because Shaylynn wasn't allowed to eat. Mom and I went to the hospital cafeteria to get some food. I found it difficult to eat because my anxiety level was sky-high and it was tough to sit and focus on food. The events of Shaylynn being sick, her diagnosis of restrictive cardiomyopathy and the waiting for a new heart had taken a toll on me. I was drained.

Shaylynn's surgery took about five hours to complete, a little quicker than mine, and she was transferred to ICU after 12:00 a.m. once she was stabilized. Dad, Billy and McKayla arrived just as Shaylynn was moved. She had to have an external pacemaker because her Michigan heart wouldn't pump on its own. To help it, doctors had Shaylynn use an exterior pacemaker to aid the heart's rhythm. After a week, her new heart started beating on its own.

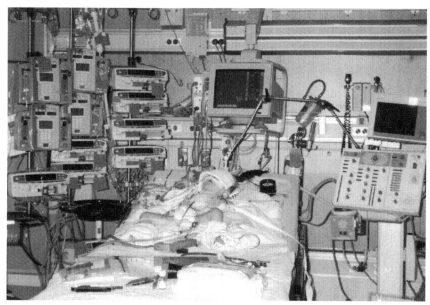

Shaylynn hours after her heart transplant.

The doctors told me that Shaylynn might require an internal pacemaker. They gave me all the information about the internal pacemaker because this was something I had never dealt with before. I never had a pacemaker. In the end, the decision to insert the internal pacemaker was left up to me.

The really big pro in terms of a permanent pacemaker for Shaylynn was that she'd have a backup, just in case. The cons to a permanent pacemaker were that it would add to the already lengthy list of doctor appointments. Shaylynn would have to be followed up by another doctor in another clinic. As well, the pacemaker battery may need to be replaced at some point, which would mean more surgeries. Another con was that we had to make sure she didn't go near anything magnetic. For instance, at airport security she would have to get a pat down instead of going through the scanners. The one pro outweighed the cons and my decision was a no-brainer. I agreed with the doctors to have the pacemaker permanent by putting in an internal pacemaker.

The permanent pacemaker was a good idea and provided my family with peace of mind. If the new heart didn't beat properly, then the pacemaker was there to send signals to the heart to help get it into the correct rhythm and rate. The downside of Shaylynn having the pacemaker permanently meant she would have to have another surgery. Her transplant incision was reopened and the permanent pacemaker inserted.

Once Shaylynn was moved out of ICU and into the main hospital ward, I was able to stay in her room. (Our family had been sleeping in a downtown Edmonton hotel.) The risk of infection after transplant was significantly high, which meant Shaylynn was given a private room. This helped our situation a lot, especially having McKayla with me. No roommate provided us with more space and room to move when anyone came to visit. My parents saw us regularly and some of my friends visited too.

It was surprising to me that Shaylynn never pulled out her IV or any of the other tubes. It was hard for her to suck her thumb with the IV in her tiny hand. The film, *Finding Nemo*, kept her distracted. I'm not exaggerating when I say we watched that movie every day, twice a day. It became her favourite movie. McKayla was a big help around the hospital. It was cute how she always wanted to wear the nurse's hospital badge or give Shaylynn her meds. On days when McKayla was fussy and needed a break from the hospital room, I borrowed a pull-wagon and pulled her up and down the U of A hospital halls until she fell asleep. I also took Shaylynn for strolls to give her a break from her room. One day Shaylynn was in the wagon when she saw a Nemo balloon. She started yelling, "Nemo! Nemo!" and pointing to the balloon.

Past the patient rooms there was a play area called The Beach. Kids could go here during specific hours and play with dolls or colour. I took Shaylynn and McKayla to The Beach often. If I needed a break, mom or my old friend Judy (the same University of Alberta Hospital child life specialist Judy Dahl) would take the girls for a while.

Two weeks after Shaylynn's heart transplant, we received requests from journalists across the country for interviews and updates regarding Shaylynn's health. We even received a phone call from Canada AM (a CTV national morning show) asking for an interview with me and the girls. (After the girls were born in 2001, the television program had asked for an interview but there were scheduling issues and we were unable to do the interview.) I was more than happy to talk to Canada AM because I was thinking about how many individuals I could reach about organ donation. I wanted to provide help and hope for other families waiting for transplants too.

It was really cool being interviewed by host Seamus O'Regan. I remember we were interviewed at 6:00 p.m. on February 3, 2004: the day before the segment aired. We had to pretend that it was actually 6:00 in the morning instead of the evening.

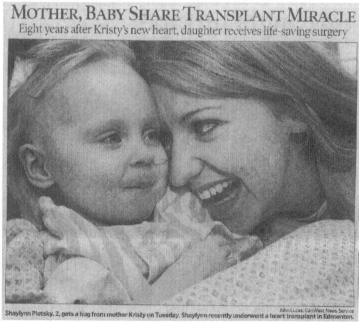

MOTHER, BABY SHARE TRANSPLANT MIRACLE
Eight years after Kristy's new heart, daughter receives life-saving surgery

John Lucas, CanWest News Service
Shaylynn Plotsky, 2, gets a hug from mother Kristy on Tuesday. Shaylynn recently underwent a heart transplant in Edmonton.

Reprinted permission of the Calgary Herald, a division of Postmedia Network Inc.

The same day as the Canada AM interview, I was sitting with Shaylynn in the hospital waiting room when a nurse came in with a gentleman. He was holding a trophy… the Grey Cup! (The Grey Cup is the trophy won by the top CFL team.) I don't recall the name of the man who brought the trophy into the hospital but I do remember he played for the Edmonton Eskimos and had also just finished his medical degree. Edmonton had won the 2003 Grey Cup over the Montreal Alouettes and the cup was on tour. The nurse asked me if I would like to hold it and of course I wasn't going to pass that opportunity up. Shaylynn was feeling under-the-weather and couldn't sit up so I leaned over and showed her the shiny trophy.

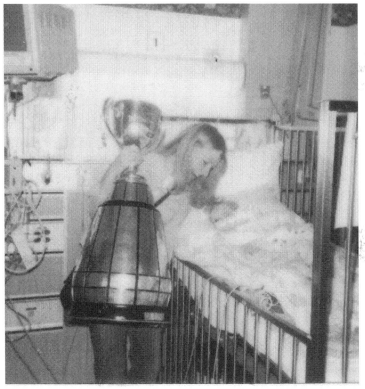

Holding the grey cup beside Shaylynn's bed at the Stollery.

Shaylynn was in the hospital after her heart transplant for approximately four weeks. She was discharged on February 10 but because of the risk of rejection and the multitude of tests she needed routinely, from blood tests to echoes, we had to stay close to the

Stollery. (Shaylynn did have physio but because of her young age, we went to the playroom instead of physio.) We ended up staying in an apartment near downtown Edmonton. The apartment was specifically for patients and families and was subsidized by Family Supports for Children with Disabilities (FSCD is a provincial service.) My apartment wasn't as close to the hospital as the Campus Tower Suite Hotel (where my parents stayed during my heart transplant) but it still worked out great. There was plenty of space for when mom and dad came up.

At the beginning of March, we were cleared to go home to Calgary. We still had to trek to Edmonton for check-ups every month because there was no pediatric transplant clinic in Calgary. Really, it couldn't have worked out better because I was still being followed by Dr. Coe and was supposed to see him every six months. Whenever Shaylynn had to go to Edmonton, we made sure to book some appointments for me on the same day and the doctor would squeeze me in for an echo at the last minute. Shaylynn was the priority though and we were travelling to Edmonton for her most of the time.

Shaylynn was on an awful lot of medication and because she was a toddler, all her medication was in liquid form and had to be given by syringe. She didn't like taking the meds and made faces when I gave them to her. Right from the beginning though, while I was stern, I was empathetic. Some of the medication Shaylynn took tasted terrible. I knew from experience that tacrolimus (an immunosuppressive drug) was far from yummy. I gave her chocolate milk right after her dosage to rinse the bad taste away. We didn't think there was a need to colour code anything this time around. I had become somewhat of an expert administering medication. However, there were so many that mom and I decided to go back to colour coding until we got the hang of it.

Shaylynn was a trooper. I made a pact with myself to always teach her how important her medication was and to not feel ashamed about taking it. From the beginning, I told her why she was taking the drugs and what they did for her body. I didn't focus on what would happen if she didn't take her meds until she was older. She still takes medication to this day and will for the rest of her life.

McKayla liked to help administer Shaylynn's medication. The younger twin would take the syringe and stick it in her sister's mouth. I have to say, it was the cutest thing. Sometimes I would let McKayla be the doctor and sometimes I wouldn't. I had to watch when McKayla gave Shaylynn her medicine to make sure it made it into Shaylynn's mouth.

McKayla helping Shaylynn at the Stollery.

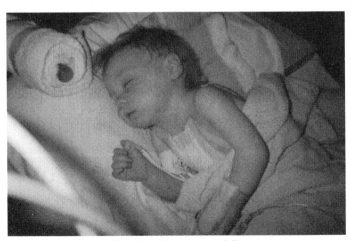

Shaylynn sleeping peacefully.

McKayla making sure Shaylynn takes her medication at home.

CHAPTER TWENTY NINE

Kick in the pants

At home, between Shaylynn's doctor and hospital appointments, I tried to keep a regular routine. I also booked things for myself that coincided with what my daughter needed such as blood work. The timing of blood work was crucial because blood had to be drawn prior to taking our medication. We had to get up early to make sure we were at the lab right as it opened. Otherwise, we'd be stuck waiting in a long line.

To make it to all of Shaylynn's appointments and mine, I took a leave from my job. United Prescription was incredibly understanding. Josh never offered to take Shaylynn to the doctor nor did he visit his daughter. It was me who had to call him and update him on Shaylynn's recovery and health.

I attended Tara's wedding in Medicine Hat in April 2004 and brought a Bartholin cyst along with me. The Bartholin glands, or greater vestibular glands, are found on each side of the vaginal opening. The glands secrete mucus that moistens the outer genital area. When a gland becomes blocked, it's called a cyst. I had one of these cysts and it was painful but I was determined to attend my friend's wedding.

It was at the wedding that my cyst ruptured. I was sitting and noticed a wet feeling in my groin. Right away I thought, "Oh no!"

Intuition and my background kicked in and I knew what had just happened wasn't good. I wasn't sick or anything but I was humiliated: the back of my dress had a huge wet spot on it. I went to the bathroom immediately and noticed the gland area wasn't as swollen as it was earlier. I also saw pus coming out so I grabbed some toilet paper and drained the spot.

The next day I went to the Medicine Hat hospital. Being back in that emergency room was odd. I had spent so much time there as a teenager. I was waiting for the doctor to see me when a nurse came in, a woman I knew. We had gone to school together but weren't good friends. I didn't feel comfortable having her look at my *nanner* (that's what Janine and I called our vaginas). I told the doctor I wanted a different nurse. My former classmate was as relieved as me because she also didn't feel comfortable treating me. I wasn't ready for the world to know about my hidden HPV secret. Only people extremely close to me and medical professionals knew what I was dealing with.

The doctors operated on me. They gave me a general anesthetic and then cut an opening to drain the cyst. I wished mom had been there but Janine visited me and that was comforting. Nothing against Tara but I have always regretted going to her wedding. I went by myself when Shaylynn was in the hospital. She was having uncontrollable diarrhea and I should have been in Calgary with her.

Three days after being admitted to the Medicine Hat hospital, I was discharged. I went home and wouldn't you know it, the cyst came back. I was seen by a doctor at the Foothills who operated on the cyst and drained it once more. More medical procedures were in my future. At the end of April, Dr. Ghatage, my gynecologist oncologist, discussed the possibility of admitting me to the hospital for intravenous 5-FU (Fluorouracil - a type of chemotherapy drug frequently used to treat many types of cancer.) I was concerned about the possibility of having vaginal, cervical and anal cancer and there had been reports that intravenous 5-FU worked well fighting cells turned pre-cancerous by HPV. The intravenous 5-FU required hospitalization for four days and then the chemotherapy would be repeated one month later.

The intravenous 5-FU was started in June 2004 and repeated again in July 2004. Being away for four days at a time was crummy, especially because I wasn't sick, I was just sitting in a hospital room getting chemotherapy treatment all day. (The free time did give me some hours to work on my book.) My parents took care of my girls but I couldn't see them. There were many immune suppressed people also getting chemo and the medical staff didn't want young kids visiting and spreading germs.

I was discouraged that the chemotherapy wasn't helping the HPV (although I have yet to develop vaginal cancer.) In August, I received another laser as the warts refused to budge from my butt. Mom and I spoke to the Dr. Ghatage about letting me recover at home. It had become fairly difficult for both my parents and me to attend appointments and surgeries. Shaylynn was struggling with health problems too. She was spending a significant amount of time in and out of the Alberta Children's Hospital due to constant diarrhea. We were also having difficulty getting her medication levels just right. Other than these setbacks, the girls were thriving. Their growth was behind but they were getting taller and gaining weight.

I wasn't working and if I had been, I would have had to quit: I didn't have child care.

Shaylynn wasn't allowed to go to the day home because of the threat of contracting chicken pox, mumps, measles or rubella (any viruses fought off with a live vaccine). Shaylynn can never be vaccinated as most are live vaccines. When you're given a vaccination, you're given a tiny piece of the live virus or bacteria and your body fights it and becomes, hopefully, immune. Being immune suppressed, Shaylynn couldn't fight the virus/bacteria and so the twins were never given their vaccinations. We also knew the girls had my medication in their systems, which was another reason they weren't vaccinated. They had been medicated in utero. However, since Shaylynn was immune suppressed and not vaccinated, we needed to be extra-careful and kept her home. (McKayla was eventually vaccinated.)

It was good I was home too because the warts were getting worse and worse and worse. The constant itching and discomfort they were causing made me want to cut off the lower half of my body. I was going crazy. CRAZY. I scratched at them with toilet paper when I was in the bathroom but there was never any relief.

In October, Dr. Ghatage performed an alcohol injection to try to provide some numbing to the vaginal area, hoping it would lessen my discomfort. It was a painful process that did not work. I had confronted Josh about giving me HPV. I never had any symptoms until him and because I'm immunosuppressed, my body shows symptoms right away. Josh admitted that I more than likely got the warts from him. In his defence, he probably didn't know he had HPV: guys typically don't show symptoms, especially if their immune systems are healthy. The same goes for some women.

That December, Dr. Ghatage discussed the possibility of having a denervation of the vulva. The denervation would cut the nerve supply to the vulva and hopefully provide relief from the itching.

"Hallelujah!" I said, "a way to get rid of the torment."

On April 28, 2005, I went into the Foothills and had a laser of the vulva and merring (surgical term for cutting vaginal tissue), a procedure for surgical denervation of the vulva. This was probably one of my most memorable surgeries because it was incredibly invasive and the scar was huge. The incision extended from the mons pubis and ended at a level that was lateral to the anus. The exact same incision was made on the opposite side. The line of incision was required to completely transect each nerve branch, which resulted in a denervated vulva. Suction drains were then placed in the wound and held in place with sutures. Those suction drains were extremely uncomfortable and the positioning made it very difficult for me to lie on my back. The nurse would come in and drain the suctions every four hours or as needed. Basically, it was like a cipher hose suctioning out blood. The suction drains were removed after about seven days. I also had a catheter for urinating as the vuvla area was significantly swollen due to the denervation and laser. I felt like a big mess although my vagina was numb and I didn't feel any itching.

The denervation was supposed to give me much needed relief from the itching. I think it was the constant itching that caused the HPV to become worse. If the itching subsided, I thought maybe there would be less irritation to the area, which would help clear up the HPV. I was out of the hospital in just over a week.

On May 26, I went to Dr. Ghatage to have my sutures removed. I told him that the denervation had helped the itching by 95 per cent. My vulva was numb and swollen but at least I wasn't being driven mad by constant irritation. The bad news was the denervation didn't stop the HPV from spreading. Warts were growing on warts and there were a lot of them.

I had multiple lasers that year as I had developed severe dysplasia (a pre-cancerous condition). I had yet another laser in December. Mom and I had become pros at managing my postoperative care so there was never any reason for me to be admitted to hospital. It was much better to recuperate at home, especially because my girls were there. A couple days after my laser in December 2005, I had got up to go to the bathroom mid-morning and then carefully waddled my way back to the couch where mom had set up my makeshift bed complete with soaker pads (absorbent pads) and blankets. Mom brought me a popsicle and as soon I as finished it, a terrible pain started pulsating through my abdomen. My initial thought was that it was cramping as it was that time of month. (Lucky me to have this all at once – a laser and my period. I couldn't use a pad because the laser left me really sore and uncomfortable. The only pad I could wear was one that was kept in the freezer, which I used as an ice pack down below.) The pulsating pain was steady and didn't stop. I called for mom and dad.

"The pain is bad. I can barely breathe."

I heard dad yell for mom to call the ambulance. By this time, my hands were tingling and cramping. My vision was going blurry and a big bright light started to shine. The pain continued to get worse and the worse the pain got, the more my hands and feet tingled. My hands were cramping intensely and my fingers curled into claws.

"Oh no!" I thought. "Does this have anything to do with my heart?"

The ambulance arrived several minutes later. The paramedics were able to give me some pain medication through intravenous but because we didn't know exactly what was wrong and given my complex history, they didn't want to give me too much of anything. They took me to the Peter Lougheed in Calgary, as that was the nearest hospital. It was here I had the worst experience ever in a hospital.

I waited in the emergency department all night: at least eight hours without pain meds because the medical staff didn't want to give me something in the event I needed surgery. They originally thought my pain was caused by passing kidney stones. Finally, after hours of waiting, I was given a room. I was taken there on a stretcher and had to be transferred to the hospital bed. I told mom that if I stood up blood would flood out because I was on my period and wasn't wearing a pad or tampon. We tried to tell the nurse but she wasn't listening and insisted I get up and move to the bed. As soon as I stood up, blood dripped out, like I had told her it would. Instead of being concerned, the nurse was furious and demanded I wear a pad. I tried to explain the situation to her; that I had just had a laser of the vulva for severe dysplasia caused by HPV. The nurse didn't care and was so rude to me and mom that I started crying. Thankfully, that nurse was off her shift shortly. I prayed I wouldn't have to deal with her again.

But life isn't fair and the mean nurse was back a couple days later. One particular morning I was feeling very unwell but I had to take my medication (no matter what, rejection medication is important and must be taken). Because I had a catheter in, I couldn't get up to get water or juice to take my meds. I reluctantly rang my call bell for help. The mean nurse walked into my room and said, "What do you want?"

I told her my predicament, thinking she might show some kind of compassion. Nope. She handed me some water like I had asked for the moon and walked out. I took my meds and tried my best to keep those meds down. I was nauseous already and it was a fight to keep the pills in my stomach. I didn't want to have to deal with this mean nurse again.

The meds stayed down for about 15 minutes and then… I threw up all over myself. I didn't want to ring the call bell but I had no choice. The mean nurse came back, looking as annoyed as ever, like I disrupted her day and I was nothing but a burden. I told her that I had thrown up on myself and she replied, "What do you want me to do about it?"

I was dumbfounded and didn't know how to respond to that. I was 23, not a child, and should have been treated accordingly. I wished nothing more than for mom to be there and tell this lady where to go. (Mom would have whipped that woman into shape. She didn't have a problem telling nurses or doctors what she thought of them.) I looked up at the mean nurse and calmly said, "I need to take my medication again. Those are rejection drugs and I need to keep them down for an hour and if I don't, then I will have to retake them. Because I have a catheter in and I am hooked up to several machines, it is hard for me to get my medication so can you please bring it to me?"

I would be lying if I said I didn't say any of that with any kind of patronizing tone. After that, the nurse treated me a little better but not much better.

It took at least two days for doctors to learn that I wasn't passing kidney stones. Instead, I had an E. coli (bacteria) urinary tract infection (UTI). I was given intravenous antibiotics to fight the infection and hospitalized for 10 days. The crummy part was that the infection had damaged my only good kidney. My left kidney already had scarring and didn't work one hundred per cent. During my transplant, I needed dialysis (dialysis removes waste and excess water from the blood.) The right kidney was the only kidney I had that worked to its full potential. Rejection drugs, specifically tacrolimus (an immunosuppressant), are also extremely hard on kidneys. Long-term use of rejection drugs is not good for kidneys. Down the road, I might need a kidney transplant. For now, I was referred to a nephrologist (kidney specialist), who would follow-up with me after the course of oral antibiotics.

Those few years it was like if it wasn't Shaylynn who was sick, it was me. If it wasn't me who was sick, it was Shaylynn. McKayla was still being monitored frequently as we didn't know if the restrictive cardiomyopathy gene had been passed to her: early detection was crucial.

I had been battling and battling the warts and they were winning. As you know, the HPV had developed into severe dysplasia around my left and right labia. The warts in my anus bled frequently, especially after a bowel movement. I stayed up to-date on all the latest research about HPV and one of the books I read was *What Your Doctor May Not Tell You About HPV and Abnormal Pap Smears* by Dr. Joel Palefsky. After reading his book, I was convinced that I had anal cancer. Many of the things I had read regarding HPV talked about how anal cancer can go undetected but I had all the symptoms like blood in my stool, anal itching, anal warts and dysplasia. Given my health history I thought, "Why wouldn't I have anal cancer?"

Due to the constant blood in my bowel movements, I advocated to see a gastrointestinal physician to make sure that my colon was normal and to complete an anal pap smear. The results? I didn't have anal cancer. One less thing to worry about.

CHAPTER THIRTY

Warts and all

McKayla and Shaylynn were both four years old and Shaylynn was almost two years post-transplant. Because Shaylynn was older, we didn't have to be constantly concerned about her catching something. We still had to watch her but she could watch out for herself too. I put the girls in a day home in Chestermere, not too far from mom and dad's house.

Since the girls were getting older, I started asking myself what I wanted to do with the rest of my life. It was November 2005 when I decided I needed to put some serious thought into the future. I thought about all the obstacles that I had been through. I had had many hardships and yet I persevered. I think things happen to us for a reason and there was a reason for every single thing I had gone through. If I could help someone else with their troubles and pain, that would be good enough for me.

I contemplated options like teaching. Teaching hours work for moms. I could have the same schedule as my girls. However, I knew I wanted to do something within healthcare. With my background, I could help patients journey through the healthcare system. I also wanted to do something with organ donation and maybe start a foundation. I took some time to seriously think about who I was and what I wanted for my girls.

I was a woman who had seen a lot in terms of the healthcare

system. I had tons of knowledge about the system that I could use for good. I knew what it was like to be a patient and I know what it was like to be a parent of a patient.

I wanted to make a difference in the world. I wanted to provide for my girls and not rely on a man, especially in our patriarchal society. I wanted to provide opportunities for my girls and I knew I wouldn't be able to do that without an education. I regretted not graduating from high school though I was never fond of going to class. Not having a diploma was something that I wasn't proud of and it was always a huge regret for me. Then I found out about Athabasca University, a school in Athabasca, Alberta, that specializes in online distance education.

I had failed some of my Grade 12 final exams and I didn't finish high school because I was pregnant. I decided to apply to Athabasca anyway as a mature student and see what happened. I was shocked and extremely happy to learn that I didn't need a high school diploma to apply to the university. I was accepted. To pay for classes, I applied for a student loan and got one.

Hmmm, what did I want to study? I wanted to help people and with the experiences I had I thought maybe I could be a counsellor. I registered at Athabasca University for a four year Bachelor of Arts degree with a major in psychology. I was going to be a psychologist.

The New Year was ushered in with big and bright plans. As of January 2006, I was a student and registered in three university courses. I took an introductory psychology course, a criminal psychology course and an English course. I was excited about my foray into learning, however... I didn't realized how much work it was going to be. I was studying by long distance and completely self-directed. Another factor was that because I had received a loan from the government, I only had three months to complete my courses. That put some pressure on me but since the girls went to bed early, I got time to do my reading and course work.

I wrote a lot of papers at night while the girls were sleeping or on my days off when they were napping. I had a part-time job too on top of it all. I was applying to jobs when I found one that looked interesting: administrative assistant for Healthy Minds/Healthy Children program with the Calgary Health Region. The interview for the position was at the children's hospital where I had spent countless hours. It was fate. I got the job!

The Healthy Minds/Healthy Children program was a continuing professional development program for children's mental health. (In the early days, we were mandated to reach family physicians. Eventually, our mandate changed when we saw the overwhelming need to also support practitioners working within the field of children's mental health.) My job included registering people in courses, providing support to staff and updating the program's website. I also attended meetings and took minutes. (The job was part-time: two days one week and then three days the next. That schedule lasted for at least six months and then I was offered a fulltime position. I couldn't pass up the paycheque even though I was extremely busy already.) I was 24 years old and at last, getting somewhere in life.

Shaylynn had a health blip just after the new year. Her pacemaker wasn't working and doctors weren't sure if there was something wrong with the leads (wires) or if the battery was dead. In the end, they replaced the battery as if it was dead. The surgery was fairly minor and they re-opened a small portion of her previous scar. We were discharged from the U of A hospital after a couple of days.

Besides work and family, I had found love. This is the first time you're reading about him and that's because he's not that important to my story but he's worth a footnote. I met him through a friend at the career college and he made me feel like I wasn't completely damaged goods.

That winter, I spent the days with my girls and then in the evening I had my head in my books. I wanted my degree terribly and it motivated me to work hard. I felt like once I had my degree then people would listen to me. I was still dating my boyfriend at the time and he was with me when I celebrated a significant milestone: my 10 year heart anniversary.

Just over half of organ recipients make it to their 10 year transplant anniversary. According to the Heart and Stroke Foundation of Canada (2011): 86 per cent celebrate one year, 75 per cent make it to five years, 62 per cent to 10 years, 47 per cent to 15 years and 36 per cent to 20 years. I had lived for 10 more years because Dawn had given me her heart. Amazing and terrifying things had happened in those 10 years. I had so much to be thankful for.

My parents planned a party for me. We rented a room at the Chestermere Regional Recreation Centre for May 27 (the day after my transplant date) and my family was there along with cousins and friends. Annalies and her mom came and my friend and I took pictures of our signature gesture: our hands clasped together like a heart. Mom secretly invited Dawn's mom Coral, Dawn's sister Heather, her husband Paul and their kids to attend the event. Remi came too and I got to meet Dawn's dad for the first time.

I was in awe of Remi. He is a genuinely nice man, a caring man. I didn't want to stare at him but I couldn't believe I was meeting Dawn's father at last. I couldn't believe it had been 10 years since my transplant and 10 years since Dawn had died. It was touching to have both Remi and Coral at my anniversary with my family when they could have been remembering Dawn at home with their own family.

My donor family and I at my 10 year heart transplant anniversary.

Annalies and I at my 10 year heart anniversary

I continued working on school but I realized that taking three courses was a lot for me. I was too busy. I didn't pass my classes with flying colours, I struggled. I got a B in English, a B- in criminal psychology and a C- in psychology. University wasn't easy.

In September of 2006, Shaylynn and McKayla started down their own road to education. My babies were old enough to go to school. I had to be extra careful with Shaylynn's health as she wasn't vaccinated but I told her teachers about her medical history and made sure they understood her situation. The girls and I have developed a ritual for first days of school. They both get a "first day of school outfit" and then I take a lot of pictures before we leave the house. I get them to pose with their arms around each other and I always say, "That one is going in my scrap book." The photos haven't made it in yet... maybe after this book. I'm probably more excited than my daughters are on the first day of school.

***

Tinker's health had started deteriorating early 2006. We thought we might have to make a tough decision soon. My dog could no longer do certain things on his own like climb stairs and go to the bathroom. At Christmas time, he pretty much required help with everything. He was also getting sores on his body. My parents knew it was time to have the talk about saying goodbye to him. I pleaded with them to wait until after the holidays. Mom and dad agreed. I got to spend one last Christmas with Tinker. I cherished the time that I had left with him.

Mom and I took him to the Chestermere veterinary office on January 12, 2007. The drive to the vetrinary seemed like the longest drive of my life. I held Tinker firmly in my arms as I knew this was the last time I would hold him and feel his fur against my skin. It would be the last time I peered into his eyes. I wished he could tell me what to do. Were we making the right decision?

Part of me wanted to yell, "STOP! I can't do this." Part of me knew that was selfish because I knew my dog was in pain.

Tinker was my best friend. I would never forget the day I got him when I was around eight or nine years old. Tinker made a big impact on my life. He was always there for me, especially when I was sick and fighting for my life. Now, I needed to be there for him.

When we arrived at the vetrinarian's office, a staff member led us into a room with a metal table. I carefully positioned my friend on it. My face was burning and my eyes were clouding. I looked up at the lady helping us and asked if we could have a few minutes alone with him.

She smiled and said, "Take as long as you need."

The lady quietly closed the door. It was just mom, Tinker and I. Mom said her goodbyes by giving him a hug and telling him how much she loved him. He was a big part of our family. He had been through so much with us.

I said Tinker's name and slowly caressed my fingers through the curly black and white hair on his head. I lowered my head so I was close to him and looked him straight in the eyes. I told him how much I loved him and that he was such a good boy. I thanked him for always being there for me and my family. By now, tears were trickling down my face. Mom left to let the lady know we were ready. I held Tinker as snug as I could until mom returned with the veterinary assistant.

My dog was taken to a back room and given an IV. We could hear him yelp from the needle poke to start the IV. It was sad. He was brought back to us. We carefully laid our boy on his side on a towel we draped for him over the metal table. While the assistant and the vet prepared the syringe, I cupped his little head in one of my hands and stroked him with the other. I didn't want him to be scared.

Mom placed her hand by his tail and softly massaged his back. It was time. The vetrinarian explained that once the medication was injected, Tinker would close his eyes, go to sleep, and then stop breathing. The vetrinarian explained that Tinker would feel no pain once the medication was injected. I nodded my head and indicated I was ready. The vet smiled and nodded back.

As the medication was slowly being injected into my dog, I stared down at him, reassuring him that it was going to be okay. I felt his head become heavier in my hand. His eyes started to slowly close and open, like he was drifting off to sleep. The syringe was emptied and the tubing from the IV dangled over his lifeless body.

Tinker was gone.

Tears poured down my face. I gave him one last kiss and whispered, "I love you," as I slowly lifted his head off my hand. I turned and looked at mom. We gave each other a hug and then walked away. We got in the vehicle and drove home.

On the way home, we reminisced about Tinker, all while tears poured down both of our faces. We talked about the time we snuck Tinker into the Alberta Children's Hospital. How dad had put him in a duffle bag to get him past security. Poor Tinker. He didn't know he was supposed to stay still. He walked to the left of the duffle bag and it tilted sideways to the left. Then Tinker walked to the right and the duffle bag tilted sideways to the right. It was definitely a funny sight to see. We cried and laughed the entire 10 minute drive home.

Walking into our house was a very somber moment. We tried our best to explain to the girls, who were five at the time, where Tinker was. We told them Tinker had been sick and we had to make a tough decision to ask the vetrinarian to give him medication to take away all his pain. I don't know if the girls understood. They asked about Tinker for several days and weeks afterwards.

Our home was pretty lonely without a dog. I've always had an animal around. I grew up with them my whole life. When I was little, I had lots of cats and then dogs. Now Tinker and Chuck were both gone. It was a major transition.

Mom felt we were all sad and moping around. (Not to mention I had another laser booked a couple weeks after we put Tinker down.) We definitely weren't over Tinker but mom thought we needed something positive in our lives. That was when she found some people in Chestermere selling shih-tzu bichon frise puppies. Well, wouldn't you know it – the one we picked (actually mom picked) looked just like Tinker, black and white and cute. The only difference was this puppy was a female. Maggie became part of our family on January 22, 2007.

I was going to become part of another family after my boyfriend proposed and I said yes. We went through the motions of an engaged couple but by 2007, our engagement ended. We weren't right for each other and we parted with no hard feelings. Looking back, if our break-up hadn't happened, I wouldn't have found "The One" and the girls would have never found a great father. The end of my relationship gave me more drive to work harder and finish my schooling. I never wanted to rely on a man again. School was my ticket out of living with my parents and providing for my own family.

I was a single mom with twins, working and going to school. I pushed myself because I wanted to prove to people (and myself) that I wasn't a screw up. I was going to break down the stigma of being a teen mom statistic and get a university degree. I was motivated to add more chapters to my memoir. (I thought people would be more apt to buy my book if I had credentials after my name.) However, school and the girls took up the majority of my time and I decided to put my story on hold until I had my degree. Never in my wildest dreams did I think it would take me 10 years to publish my book.

In the spring of 2007, just when I was hitting my stride, something happened to Shaylynn. She was five years old when HPV signs started to show. One morning she was getting ready to have a bath when she came to me and said, "Mommy, my bum hurts."

I asked if it would be okay to have a look and she agreed. (We had already had the speech about when it was okay for people to look at your private parts.) I was horrified at what I saw: my daughter had warts in her anal area. How could this have happened? I was devastated. I didn't need a doctor to diagnose the bumps because those annoying things were all too familiar to me. However, I knew this was something that needed to be looked at and I contacted Dr. Ghatage. He arranged for Shaylynn to be seen by one of his pediatric colleagues, Dr. Mannsfeld.

Dr. Mannsfeld was able to get Shaylynn an appointment fairly quickly. During our first visit, the doctor said Shaylynn definitely had warts and they were definitely caused by HPV. The news was the worst thing I could have heard. Of course, I was basing the diagnosis on my personal horrible experiences dealing with HPV and all the pain and sadness the virus caused me.

I didn't know how I was going to explain HPV to my daughter. How do I tell Shaylynn that her mother gave her a sexually transmitted disease? (HPV can be passed from parent to child during birth.) Shaylynn was immune suppressed and I knew that was partly why she was showing symptoms. Dr. Mannsfeld suggested a "watch and wait" approach. (Like mother, like daughter.) After several months of waiting, we noticed the warts were spreading in the anal area. After much discussion with Shaylynn's cardiologist, we decided to take her off one of her two rejection medications: CellCept (mycophenolate mofetil). It was the least important. About a month after being off the medication, Shaylynn's warts miraculously disappeared.

You know that saying "it could always be worse?" Well, before Shaylynn's diagnosis, I didn't think that was possible. But after learning about Shaylynn having HPV, I realized that that was the worst. I cried many times when I was by myself.

Shaylynn's plight did have a silver lining. I was on CellCept too and after seeing how Shaylynn reacted to being off the drug, I asked my cardiologist if I could stop taking it as well. (I didn't see Dr. Coe though, I saw Dr. Isaac at the heart transplant program in Calgary. I still talked to Dr. Coe on and off in regards to Shaylynn. It was bittersweet saying goodbye to him in 2007. It was the end of an era and I realized I was getting older .) Dr. Isaac said I could go off the drug since I was on a low dosage. Unfortunately, it didn't turn out to be the answer for me. Stopping the drug did nothing except give me one less pill to swallow.

I still had frequent lasers and kept a watchful eye on my HPV. I continued to be screened by my nephrologist, cardiologist, dermatologist and gastrointestinal physicians. I continued to be a single mom with a job and working towards my psychology degree.

***

We got a royal surprise in March. Judy Dahl had put Shaylynn's name forward to the Children's Wish Foundation and we found out she was going to be granted a wish. When I asked Shaylynn what she wanted, she said she wanted to "meet a real princess at Disneyland." So, that was it.

The wish foundation was the same one that sent me to meet Reba. For Shaylynn, we were going to Disneyland Park in California. Of course, mom and dad were coming with us because there was no way I could fly to the Golden State with six year old twins by myself. With the recent death of my beloved dog and the break-up of my relationship, the trip couldn't have come at a better time. The Haskayne School of Business, at the University of Calgary, raised money for the Children's Wish Foundation of Canada by selling high-end cutlery from Cutco Corporation. All the money the business students raised went to fund Shaylynn's wish trip. On April 9, 2007, the school presented me with an oversized cheque for $22,000. Jason Evanson, Children's Wish Chapter Director, Alberta and NWT, was there as well to accept the cheque. I attended the media event that was held at the University of Calgary and thanked the students personally. I was excited and grateful that they were giving my daughter the opportunity to go to Disneyland. Shaylynn's news hit the newspapers on Wednesday, April 11, 2007:

Students Make Girl's Dream their Biz

Calgary Sun

Heart-felt Drive Nets $22,000

The Metro

We left for Shaylynn's wish trip on Friday, April 22. We stayed at the Residence Inn Marriott Hotel in Anaheim. We had a large place that was able to sleep mom, dad, me and the girls. Billy flew down too for a couple of nights to take in Disneyland Park with his nieces.

The hotel was near my favourite coffee place. Yep, you've probably guessed it by now – Starbucks! Every morning after we got up, mom and I walked to the Starbucks and grabbed a coffee to go. We "needed" the caffeine because we had a pretty hectic schedule throughout the week. We had tickets for SeaWorld, LEGOLAND, Disneyland, Disney California Adventure and Universal Studios. Exhausting but fun.

Our trip to LEGOLAND was a scene right out of the movie

National Lampoon's Vacation (1983). We drove 70 miles (112 kms) to the theme park only to arrive and find it was closed. We even had tickets for that specific date! Well, we didn't want to waste the day so I suggested we drive to Los Angeles and check out Hollywood and the Walk of Fame. We ventured into the celebrity city and took a tour to see where the stars lived. I was kind of hoping we would see someone famous but alas, we didn't.

The highlight of the California trip was seeing the girls meet the Disney princesses at the Royal Hall in Disneyland Park. My little girls' faces beamed with joy. Of course, you can't visit Disneyland without taking a boat through the water-based ride *It's A Small World*. Oh my gosh, it hadn't changed a bit. It was the same as when I had been on it as kid when I visited Disneyland with Aunt Terry, Uncle Steve, Jen and Billy in 1991.

The trip was incredible. Shaylynn did get sick at the end of the week but it didn't spoil her whole adventure and I know she had a fantastic time.

Shaylynn and McKayla with Cinderella.

With the diagnosis of Shaylynn's HPV, coupled with our ongoing medical tests for our heart transplants, my 25 year old brain was on overload. It made me work harder on school though and I learned about how physical health impacts emotional and mental health and vice versa. I took many courses based on human behaviour and adolescent development. I really wanted to focus on the family and I'm sure it also helped with my own countless health experiences and other emotional times such as saying goodbye to a friend when Billy and his fiancée broke-up that summer. It was difficult as she had been close to us.

In November, I had another laser surgery. I was having them pretty regularly by now. Christmas came and went. It was low key: just mom, dad, Billy, me and the girls. That was okay with me though. I liked being at home and being with family.

In February of 2008, my brother casually re-introduced me to a friend of his, Wade Thackeray. Billy was having a small get-together at his house to watch a Pay Per View boxing match.

It's kind of funny how life works out sometimes. I had met Wade in 2006 at my brother's engagement party but I was seeing someone then. Wade had a girlfriend too. After my relationship ended, my brother's fiancée always said I should date Wade. She thought he was a nice guy and I deserved a nice guy. I had met some real winners (sarcasm here) and with everything I had been through, she wanted me to have someone who would treat me well. I wanted nothing more in the world to settle down but I was hard on myself for having kids before I was married. I felt like I had let many people down and I wasn't worth the trouble.

Wade was five years older than me and already knew half of my family. An electrician by trade, he had met dad, an electrical inspector, on jobsites. By April, Wade and I were hanging out and talking about the future a lot. He wanted kids but was completely okay with me already having children. (He said if he could have more children, great. If not, that was fine too.) He officially met my daughters when we went to Tim Horton's in Strathmore. The girls and I were on our way to Medicine Hat to visit Janine. Tim's was a pre-planned meeting and I introduced him to the girls as "mommy's friend."

The meeting went well: the girls liked him and he was good with them. Wade and I spent more time getting to know each other and seeing how our complicated dynamics would work. As I got to know him, I fell for him. We had many things in common and we fit. I didn't know what his reaction would be to me having HPV though. Sooner or later, I would have to tell him.

I never ever dated a guy without telling him that I had HPV. Having HPV meant that I had a responsibility. It was never a question of IF I would tell someone but rather WHEN. My secret was a potential deal breaker with Wade. I thought no one would want to be with someone who could give them an STD. He might say to me, "No way. You have way too much baggage – kids, medical stuff, HPV – too much. See yah."

There's never a right time to tell someone you have warts but at the beginning of May at Wade's house, I spilled the beans. We had gone for supper and when we pulled into his driveway, I told him. We sat in his truck for about an hour while I explained what I was dealing with. He had no reaction at first because until then, he had never heard of HPV. I gave him all the information about what it was and why my body had a hard time fighting it. By now, I was an HPV expert. (I took HPV quizzes online that determined what you knew and I would get all the questions right every time.) This was probably information overload for Wade but he seemed to take it all in. I left that night thinking that that was the end of our relationship.

I was upset but it was here I discovered my self-esteem. I realized that I was not my HPV. HPV didn't make me a bad person. Many people have sex before they're married (without protection) and keep doing it and never have anything bad happen to them. Me, well I got pregnant and got an STD. I couldn't change that. What I needed to change was my attitude. I was who I was. I am who I am.

I talked to Wade the next day. He didn't bring up our previous conversation and it was like I hadn't even said anything about HPV to him. Later in the week, he called me to see if I wanted to meet him for a drink at a local Chestermere pub. I had already made plans with a friend to see a movie but after the film she was more than happy to stop for a drink. We met Wade and when my friend left to go to the bathroom, he leaned over and told me that he accepted everything: warts and all. I'm pretty sure my heart skipped a couple beats. It was a romantic gesture and I was shocked that he was okay with everything.

Wade accepted the whole package: me, my kids, our various medical issues, and the fact that if we had sex he may contract HPV... but then he may not. Here he was, sitting in front of me, accepting me for who I was and what I had. This was as romantic as romantic gets.

CHAPTER THIRTY ONE

All in the family

Wade and I spent the summer of 2008 dating and hanging out with the girls. We took them to the Calgary Stampede and that was a blast. My parents liked Wade and thought he treated me and the girls well. The first time I met his mom, Audrey, was in Calgary on a summer evening. Wade and I, along with Audrey and Wade's youngest sister Terisha, went to see the horror film *The Strangers* and then we went out for supper at Chili's. Audrey asked me many questions about Shaylynn and McKayla, who were six at the time. She told me she couldn't wait to meet my kids and this made me happy. The girls and I were invited to the family cabin in Fernie and that was where we met the rest of Wade's family.

I met the entire family in July at their Fernie cabin. I already knew Audrey and Terisha and was introduced to a few more people: his dad Barry, his sister Shannon, Adam, his brother-in-law, a niece and nephew and his paternal grandma. I called her Grandma immediately. They met my two girls and they fit in right away. I've always wondered what his family thought about him dating a girl who already had kids. Having children before you're married is like telling the world that you've had sex before vows. This definitely wasn't something I was proud of but I would never change being a mom for anything in the world.

One day, the guys left to go quading and I was sitting on the back deck with Audrey, Shannon and Terisha. They were talking about marriage and somehow got on the topic of HPV. It was a topic that was uncomfortable for me. I just sat there with my secret and hoped no one would ask my opinion on the subject.

At another point in the visit, we were all sitting in the living room and I was talking to Audrey when a commercial for Proactiv Plus Acne Treatment came on TV. I had had bad acne from time-to-time and my kids knew zits caused problems for me. Shaylynn turned her head and said to me as she frantically pointed to the screen, "Mom, mom, mom! You need this stuff. Mom, this is what you need for your face."

It was so funny and I couldn't help but laugh. I was embarrassed but what can you do when kids say the funniest things.

Things were going well between Wade and I. He had a house in Langdon, a hamlet just east of Calgary. He had recently purchased the home and when we didn't have things going on, I visited him and picked weeds in his backyard so he could get ready to build a deck. I didn't know I was helping to improve the house that would be mine in two months.

I had another laser surgery at the end of August. This time I couldn't recuperate at home. I had to stay in the hospital. Dr. Ghatage lasered a fairly significant amount of my vulva to try and keep the pre-cancerous cells under control. We had talked about how it would be best for me to stay in the hospital as we could manage my pain better. Wade came to see me later that day after my surgery and it was the first time he saw how the HPV affected my life. It didn't deter him from loving me and my girls. In fact, he was so worried about me that it showed how much he cared.

I knew Wade was "The One" when he asked if he could take the girls to Chuck E Cheese (a restaurant chain geared towards kids) when his sister Shannon and her family were up from Pincher Creek, Alberta. It was one of the nicest things anyone has ever done for me. It was a relief to have someone helping mom and dad with the girls while I was in the hospital. This was something I wasn't used to and neither were my parents. The girls had a blast at the restaurant and Wade got to bond with Shaylynn and McKayla on his own.

If you're wondering how Josh felt about having another man parent his children, he seemed to be fine with it and even liked Wade. Josh saw his daughters when it was convenient for him and he never called them except on their birthday and at Christmas. He was giving me some money towards the girls that I used to pay for their day home and that was nice.

The girls started Grade Two in September 2008, just before their seventh birthday. They turned seven at the end of that month and I couldn't believe how big they were getting. They were growing so strong. It seemed weird to think about how small they were when they were born. That year, we had their birthday party at Wade's house in Langdon. Wade and I went together and bought the girls a trampoline for their birthday. They absolutely loved it!

Wade visited me at mom and dad's house that fall and asked if we could talk. He said that he wanted me and the girls to move in with him. He said he knew that we loved each other and wanted our relationship to continue. I had been living with my parents for a long time but I would be lying if I said I wasn't sad about living with Wade before we were married. I also knew that if we were going to try to be a family, we needed to see if living together was going to work. In our eyes, living together was a commitment and one that we weren't taking lightly.

We moved in with Wade in October. Langdon was home now. Shaylynn and McKayla liked their new place although they did miss their grandparents. I was happy about the change but it was all so new. Part of me worried that Wade's family thought I only wanted to move in with their son so I didn't have to live with my parents. I wanted people to know I was paying my way. Wade and I split our bills and since he made a lot more money than I did, he covered the mortgage while I paid for things like the phone, cable and internet.

The first few weeks of living together were stressful as we tried to get everything organized. It was also overwhelming figuring out how the four of us fit together as a family. Wade was used to peace and quiet (something I craved a little of too) however, with three extra people in the house, silence was not easy to find. Wade was allowed to parent and I told him it was okay to say no if the girls were doing something he didn't like or agree with. Blending a family takes time and we joked that his kids really grew up before his eyes.

Our first Christmas was spent together at our house in Langdon along with my mom, dad and Billy. Wade's parents, Audrey and Barry, his sister Terisha and Grandmother Caroline were with us too. I really wanted both families to get to know each other and get along.

Spending the holiday together was heartwarming for me as we all came together.

Wade and I combined our first Valentine's Day with our first trip in February 2009. We travelled to New York City. Wade had never been to the Big Apple and while I had visited the city, it was only for a few days during the *Glamour* shoot. We both thought New York would be a fun place to go together.

While in New York, we toured the hotspots and got along well while navigating the busy NYC streets. We even had the opportunity to see the *Late Show With David Letterman* (a comedic late night talk show). I had entered a contest to win tickets for *Letterman* and won when I answered a trivia question correctly. (Over the phone I was asked, "What deli does Dave eat at frequently?" Thank goodness I was at a computer because I had to google the answer: Hello Deli.)

My HPV plague continued to get worse. (Actually, it was already terrible and I don't know what is worse than terrible. Somehow, the HPV got worse.) I made the terrifying decision to have another denervation as the last one had provided temporary relief from the itching. The itching had returned with a vengeance. I knew I would be off work for a couple of months but as I had been employed with Healthy Minds/Healthy Children for over three years, I was able to access short-term disability benefits.

The surgery was successful and I had been out of the hospital for a couple weeks. I exercised that morning to start building up my strength again. I had the day all to myself as the girls were at school and Wade was working. I was excited about using my free time to do my school work. I had completed eight courses to date with Athabasca but had switched from wanting to be a psychologist, to being a social worker.

I had researched career options and realized that if I wanted to be a psychologist, I'd have to continue on to a Master's degree. I wanted something that would provide the opportunity to work in the helping profession and also be part of a registered professional body. I had made an amazing connection with one of my colleagues at Healthy Minds/Healthy Children and she opened my eyes to social work. Jessica had her Bachelor of Social Work (BSW) and her Master of Social Work (MSW). When I met her, she was finishing her PhD in social work. She was able to provide me with a lot of information on the pre-requisites of that field. Not to mention, my Healthy

Minds/Healthy Children office was at the University of Calgary (U of C), in the Faculty of Social Work. Here, I established great connections and got to really understand what the profession was all about.

Social work is about looking at the whole person, not just one part of the person. Some aspects of life, like dealing with poverty and being sick, make it harder for people to accomplish certain things such as finishing school or getting a job. Saying this, I understand how marginalization affects people BUT you look at the whole person. I don't judge anyone because I come from a place of compassion and empathy regardless of race, sex, gender and socioeconomic status.

My calling was social work and I changed my whole course of schooling and started taking courses that I could transfer to the U of C or another institution that offered an online Bachelor of Social Work such as the University of Victoria (UVic) in British Columbia. I needed to have 20 courses under my belt to apply to the programs and I had eight. I would buckle down today and finish my homework.

My plans of doing school work were interrupted by Wade when he came home from work early that morning. The economy was going through a downturn and Wade was let go from his position with the electrical company he was working for at the time. He had been with the company for seven years and I felt bad for him. I was a little bit worried too about our financial future.

It was interesting with us both not working and we got to spend a lot of time together. Honestly, the timing couldn't have worked out better because I needed extra help with the kids, making supper and house stuff like cleaning because I was sore from the denervation. I ended up having complications with the incision and had to have homecare come in and clean the area as it was infected. The homecare nurse showed Wade what to do for me and that was great having him help me. I started feeling better and when the incision completely healed, I helped Wade finish our backyard and build a fence. This fence was better than the white picket fence I used to dream about. This fence was sturdy and strong: built from treated wood and six feet tall.

For some time, we had talked about getting a dog to complete our family. We thought there was no better time than the present. Wade would be home all day and could potty-train the puppy. Wade didn't want a small dog though. He said they were yappy. (Secretly, I think he loves mom and dad's dog Maggie. She's a shih-tzu bichon frise.) Wade wanted a dog we could take camping. We both agreed that we would pick a dog that was great with kids and something a little different than what mainstream society owns. (Note: no labs.) While we were in Edmonton for one of Shaylynn's appointments, we went to a shelter to see what dogs were available for adoption. They were all cute but not for us. While browsing for a dog online, I came across some adorable Alaskan malamute puppies in Fort Macleod, near Lethbridge, Alberta. We went to meet them on the way to Pincher Creek to visit Wade's older sister. The four of us fell in love and couldn't resist the fuzzy cuties. Originally, we picked a girl but then decided to go with the boy with the green collar – green was McKayla's favourite colour. We made arrangements to pick him up on our way home from Pincher Creek.

We ended up leaving Pincher Creek early as Shaylynn had started throwing up. We stopped in Fort Macleod on our way back to Calgary and picked up our malamute. We named him Breaker. (The name came out of the blue. It works though because Wade is an electrician.) Breaker was part of our family now.

When we got home, I got Shaylynn settled and then had a big mess to clean up from Breaker. The poor little guy had pooped all over the crate he had been travelling in. He remains with us today and let me tell you, he's no longer little.

In December 2009, Wade was talking to a couple of former co-workers and was offered a job with Entegra, an automation, electrical and instrumentation company. It was welcomed news as Wade had been out of work for about 10 months but there was a catch: the job was in Grande Prairie, a city in northwestern Alberta about a seven hour drive from Langdon. The company was willing to fly Wade to Grand Prairie on Monday morning and fly him home Friday evening. While it sucked he would be away from us during the week, we needed his income and he wanted to get back to work.

He began work on January 4, 2010 as a shop manager. I was a solo parent again and it was crappy but I wanted to be supportive of my boyfriend. My parents were always there to lend a hand and the girls and I ate a meal at their house once a week.

At the end of that March, I decided to fly out to see Wade instead of having him come home. I wanted to see where he was living. I was waiting to board my flight at the Calgary Airport on Friday evening, March 26, when the gate agent called my name. Apparently, the plane was overweight and I was weight listed, which meant that I could no longer fly on that plane. After a few minutes of worry, I was put on a flight to Edmonton that left in an hour. I crossed my fingers and hoped I would make my connection to Grande Prairie.

When I told Wade what was happening, we were both sad. We were looking forward to our weekend and wanted to have the maximum time possible to be together. Wade seemed much sadder than me but I didn't think anything of it.

I did make it to Grande Prairie and Wade greeted me at the airport. We went for supper at The Keg and instead of heading to his bachelor suite; he took me to a hotel room that he had rented for the night. I thought that was sweet of him but I had really wanted to see where he was staying while he was living in the city.

Wade pushed open our hotel room door and told me to go in. I noticed champagne and chocolates on the bed but I thought that was just a nice gesture for our weekend. Wade then shut the door and I turned toward him. He grabbed me and put one of his hands on my left arm and his other hand on my right arm. He held me close yet with some space in-between us so we could gaze into each other's eyes. He looked at me and then shared how much he loved me and the girls. I didn't know why he was saying all this wonderful stuff to me.

As he professed his love, he slowly took his hands off me and reached into his pocket to fish something out. I still had no clue what was going on. Wade retrieved the item he was looking for and then knelt down and asked me if I would marry him.

I was speechless, in a good way. I had no idea he was planning on proposing… in all places – Grande Prairie. Tears, happy tears, ran down my face. I found my voice and said, "YES! Yes, of course I'll marry you and spend the rest of my life with you."

The ring was absolutely beautiful: gold with diamonds. (When I first started wearing it, it got snagged on everything. Sometimes I would even scratch Wade and the girls with it. I wasn't used to wearing something so shiny and big.) I was usually not one for expensive jewelry or large sparkling diamonds but the ring Wade picked out himself was gorgeous. It was and is the most beautiful ring I have ever seen in my life. I phoned the girls right away to tell them about the proposal. They were excited about the engagement. Mom and dad were in on the surprise because Wade knew I was traditional and that I would want him to ask my parent's permission to marry me. The other thing I did right away was contact Coral and Remi to let them know I was engaged. They were glad to hear the happy announcement.

In April, Wade returned home for good. His Grand Prairie stint was over. He still had to go out of town but not for any huge length of time. Over the next few months, we spent some time figuring out when we wanted to get married and where. I didn't want the whole wedding planning thing to drag on and we also knew that we didn't want to go away to get married. There were a lot of people in my life who I wanted at my wedding and I knew if we decided on a destination wedding, these people wouldn't be able to attend.

I hoped Coral and Remi would come to my wedding but I also knew that it would be hard for them. Dawn never had the opportunity to get married and a wedding was one of many things Coral and Remi missed out on with their daughter. Wade and I sent invitations to Dawn's parents when we picked October 2, 2010 to get married. I had thought of asking Remi to walk me down the aisle with dad as well as having Heather as a bridesmaid. I never asked them for the favours because they declined to come. I understood why. It was too hard for them and I also think they didn't want to take away any attention from me. It would be difficult to celebrate my wedding and be happy when they had a lot of grief over what could have been with Dawn. I had other ways to include her in my big day. When Wade and I planned our ceremony, we wanted to symbolize how important Dawn was in our lives. Daisies were her favourite flower, particularly the ones with yellow centres, and all the flowers in the arrangements, bouquets and boutonnieres were daisies.

Our special day was held on October 2 in Langdon at the Langdon Baptist Church. Pastor Paul Jensen officiated our special day. Paul was someone I had known for a few years from a previous church I attended. Wade looked handsome at the front of the church and I walked towards him bursting with love. My dress was from Bellezza Bridal in Calgary and was a white form-fitting gown with sequins and ruffles. I felt beautiful.

Shaylynn and McKayla were ring bearers and I had three

bridesmaids: my cousin Jen and Wade's sisters Shannon and Terisha. My maid of honour was Janine. The day couldn't have been better and I thanked God for everything. God was part of the reason why I wanted to be married in a church: I wanted to be married in front of him. He would be my witness to my marriage. I was not allowed to let him down again.

Getting married to Wade was definitely one of the most amazing days of my life. The weather also cooperated although it was warm for fall and made the record books as the hottest day in 2010: 30 degrees Celsius. We departed the church as a family with the song *Don't Stop Believing* by Journey. We love the song and the lyrics fit: I was a small town girl and Wade was a city boy. Also, we believed in us as a family.

Our reception was at the Travelodge in Strathmore and we walked into the room to the song *Eye of the Tiger* by Survivor. For our honeymoon, Wade and I went to Mazatlán, Mexico for a week. It was a kid-free trip. I was ecstatic to call Wade my husband though the term took a bit to get used too. It made me feel kind of old.

Wade and I on our Wedding day with Shaylynn and McKayla.

CHAPTER THIRTY TWO

Nobody knows it but me (Kevin Sharp song)

I have to say, it was pretty amazing being a wife and also knowing that I was in this relationship for good. Being part of a couple takes work, lots of work. Communication is key and we're constantly growing: as spouses and as people. The girls started calling Wade "dad" just after we got married. They were nine and old enough to choose what they called him. Dad it was. Josh signed over his parental rights and Wade started the process of adopting Shaylynn and McKayla. On December 9, 2010 he legally became their father (it says it on their birth certificates). The girls and I changed our names from Plotsky to Thackeray. (The girls used to think Wade's last name was "factory.") The adoption was a celebration and we went out for supper with my parents to Boston Pizza in Chestermere.

Wade and I talked about having kids together. We tried for about a year after we were married. It wasn't something we stressed over: if it was going to happen it would happen. I told my doctors what I was planning and Wade and I also went to a geneticist who talked about possibly taking my eggs and seeing if they could find any abnormalities and perhaps find the gene that caused restrictive cardiomyopathy. The downside was it would cost about $10,000. We decided against that and to try for kids anyway. What was going to happen, would happen.

When 2011 arrived, it marked 15 years since I had had my heart transplant. For me, 15 years seemed like a pretty big feat and I wanted to do something extra-special with Wade and the girls. I contacted Coral and Remi to see if we could visit them in Elk Point, a town about a four hour's drive northeast of Calgary, and visit Dawn's gravesite. They graciously said yes and we went on my transplant date and Dawn's birthday, May 26.

Coral and Remi were welcoming and even offered their fifth-wheel to us for accommodation but we stayed in Edmonton. When we arrived at Elk Point, we met up with Coral and Heather and went to see where Dawn was buried. This was the first time I had been to the gravesite. Since the beginning of starting to write this book, I've always wanted to see where she was buried and I cannot begin to tell you the flood of emotions I had the moment I saw her headstone. It was surreal to know that I had her heart beating in my chest, keeping me alive. There are no words to portray the amount of gratitude and love that I feel for her and everyone who knew her. Here I was, with my twin girls and husband, standing next to her mom and sister. Dawn was responsible for giving me the chance to have kids and live a (somewhat) normal life. Truly a miracle.

After we stood at her graveside, we went to Coral and Remi's house. I was lucky to be able to meet Brenda Poitras, one of Dawn's best friends. Heather shared some stories of Dawn from when they were younger. We also talked about how kind Dawn was. Heather brought her three kids (Aron, Sasha and Delaney) with her and they played with Shaylynn and McKayla. We all went to a nearby lake and had a little picnic. It was the perfect anniversary and I felt so much love. This was also the first time Dawn's family had met Wade and it all fit so perfectly.

Aron, Shaylynn, Sasha and McKayla having fun at our picnic 2011.

Spending time together at Stoney Lake .

What wasn't so perfect was my HPV. It was the bane of my life and never ceased to cause me a lot of grief. I had plenty of lasers but they didn't work. I was being consumed by the suffering HPV was causing me. I did more and more research on the STD. I wrote letters upon letters to doctors everywhere asking them for information to solve my health problem. I thought maybe there was an off-chance that another doctor had experience treating HPV in immune suppressed patients. As well, I was talking with Dr. Ghatage about doing a vulvectomy: basically removing my entire vulva and labia.

A vulvectomy was a drastic measure. (We had talked about it in my early 20's. He wouldn't do it then. He was worried about me being so young and not married.) Well, I was married now and we needed to have the vulvectomy chat again. By this point, I realized that having kids with Wade was not in the cards. We had the girls and we were both okay with that. Before I went ahead with the procedure, I tried another tactic in my wart war.

HPV had become popular in the news, especially with a brand name vaccination that had come out on the market. I tried the vaccine but it didn't clear up the warts. I was beginning to lose hope the HPV would ever resolve. Wade was a good support but the itching was an uncomfortable reminder that I had pesky warts and they were a problem.

Another option was Botox (Botulinum toxin. Used in some medical treatments.) and I had it injected in my vulva area, hoping to alleviate the itching and discomfort. It relieved the itching for a couple of days but that was it. I prayed God would soon heal me.

I then heard from Dr. Atul Humar, an infectious disease doctor in Edmonton, who had some positive results with a rejection drug called sirolimus. It seemed that sirolimus had carcinogenic agents that actually fought certain cancers. (The warts were pre-cancerous.) This rejection drug also had a different release (over 24 hours) and instead of taking it twice a day, patients only needed to take it once a day.

I corresponded with Dr. Humar via e-mail and was able to make an appointment with him through his administrative assistant. I went to see him in late fall of 2011 and we discussed the possibility of taking me off tacrolimus and putting me on sirolimus and its side effects. One side effect was it prevented wound healing. If I was going to have another laser, I'd have to go back on tacrolimus.

Another side effect of sirolimus was that it can cause severe stomach upset. I hoped I would tolerate the new drug but I was nervous because I had been on tacrolimus for a long time. I didn't want to rock the boat but I needed help with this HPV. Getting rid of the warts outweighed a sore belly.

I saw Dr. Ghatage and he told me sirolimus might take away the itching. I was excited to hear that. After much discussion with Dr. Isaac and my cardiology team, we decided that it was worth switching rejection medications. On an evening in February 2012, I took my last dose of tacrolimus, the rejection drug I had been on for 13 years. The next morning, I started 3mg of sirolimus. I would be lying if I said I wasn't nervous. I had been taking tacrolimus for a long time and I knew the side effects and I also knew what antibiotics I couldn't take because it would contraindicate my tacrolimus level. I was scared and excited about the possibilities of the new medication and the possibility that the sirolimus could end my fight with HPV. The warts were intolerable and something had to give.

CHAPTER THIRTY THREE

Piece of the heart

After a few weeks of taking sirolimus, there seemed to be no change with the HPV as well as no major side effects. (I did get diarrhea.) The month after I switched meds, I had to have a biopsy: the first one in a few years.

When I started going to the adult cardiology clinic at the Foothills around 2007, there was never any reason for a biopsy. The clinic's procedure was that doctors only did a biopsy if there was a reason such as possible rejection or a medication change. The change in my drugs warranted a biopsy. The biopsy would be another first because it would be an adult biopsy: something I had never had before even though I was 29.

I had the adult biopsy about a month after the medication shift to make sure my heart was in good working order. As an adult, the biopsy was done through an artery in my neck and I was awake for the entire procedure. It was weird to be aware of what was happening while doctors inserted a tube into my neck. (My neck was frozen.) The tube with clippers (to take biopsy tissue from the heart) was guided with the echo machine. I had medical drapes over my face and neck and I had to hold very, very still. The crummy part was that I felt the instrument taking pieces of my heart. There was a tugging sensation and then the heart fluttered. It hurt too and I was sore afterwards. When the biopsy was finished, I got up and went home with Wade. A couple days later, cardiology called and told me that the biopsy had come back with rejection. The rejection was measured at a *1R, which meant that the results could have been a lab error or that the piece of tissue they biopsied wasn't a good piece of tissue. The doctors said they wanted to repeat the biopsy in about a month. Hearing the "R" word gave me major anxiety. Wade was worried too but hoped it was the lab's error. My parents were on vacation and I called them right away to fill them in.

Mom and dad were in Scottsdale, Arizona. A couple of years prior, they purchased a condo stateside with Billy. My parents went down to Scottsdale twice a year, once in the spring and once in the fall. I gave mom the news and, of course, she was upset, especially because she was far away. She knew what rejection could possibly mean – that my heart was being attacked by my body. I said not to come home as this was another "wait and see" case.

Shaylynn and I talked about rejection a lot during this time. She was scared it would happen to her. I took it as an opportunity to remind her about the importance of taking her anti-rejection medication.

Living with the possibility of rejection was stressful. It was always in the back of my mind and I definitely thought about it at least once a day. My heart was more than an organ to me, it was special. It had helped me live and become a mother and a wife. I tried to listen to my body to see if there was any change in how I felt – anything different that might assist doctors. There was something different.

By the end of March, I was beginning to have these weird spells at least once a week when I was driving. I got dizzy and the closest thing I can compare it to is feeling like being on a roller coaster: you're at the peak of a climb about to drop down into a deep valley. The next thing you know: you're falling. You have major butterflies in your stomach and your head tingles. Well, that was how I would feel for seconds at a time. It was bizarre.

I thought about possible causes and, given my history, it wouldn't have surprised me if I had a blood clot in my brain. The vertigo soon became more frequent, coming at least once a day, but I brushed it off as nothing to worry about. I still drove and I wasn't nervous to have the kids in the vehicle while I was at the wheel. It was strange that the dizzy spells correlated to only when I was driving. I thought maybe I was having panic attacks due to driving.

I had the second biopsy and it showed the same results as the first one. Receiving the same news about rejection meant it was real. The rejection was really happening. A transplant recipient's worst fear is to hear the word rejection from a medical health professional, especially your transplant cardiologist. It meant being sick again, hospitals, surgeries and waiting for a new heart. It could mean death and I had so much to live for.

I had only heard the word rejection a handful of times since my transplant – the first few weeks after transplant when I was sick and they thought it may have been rejection (although that remains unconfirmed). The second time was after a biopsy about a year after the girls were born. That last time I had rejection it was due to stress and we never treated it because it was a low grade rejection.

Hearing the news again about rejection, I told the cardiologist at the time, Dr. McMeekin, of my vertigo and how it felt like I was falling. Given the fact that I was a heart transplant patient, he ordered me a 24 hour holter monitor. This specific holter monitor recorded the exact moments I had dizzy spells. When I had an episode, I'd push a button and the holter recorded it. I also completed a diary describing what I was doing at the time the spinning feeling came on.

A couple days after I completed the holter monitor test, cardiology called to tell me that it seemed like I was having sinus pause. Sinus pause happens when the heart's sinoatrial node (the heart's natural pacemaker) stops stimulating the myocardial tissue to contract – making the heart pause. Basically, the first few beats of my heart were normal and then there may be a 1.6 second pause before the heart resumed beating again. The sinus pause could be the explanation to why I was dizzy or faintish at times. It was sort of good news but as always; there were more questions than answers. (My life's theme, eh?) Why all of sudden would my heart experience this? What could be done about it? I was regretting my decision to change meds to get a reprieve from the HPV itching (which I had definitely received while on the sirolimus).

During the seconds where my heart paused, I felt the symptoms and because I was symptomatic, it was important to have it looked into further. More tests were ahead and if my heart couldn't beat regularly on its own, a pacemaker would be implanted into my chest.

The only experience I had with pacemakers was with Shaylynn, who still had hers. I felt sad that after almost 17 years, I would need a pacemaker. I was upset that Dawn's heart was failing. I suggested to the doctors that the drug change might be the cause of the problem and perhaps I should go back on tacrolimus. They didn't heed my comments and I understand why now. It's not uncommon for someone who is many years post-transplant to need a pacemaker. However, before I got one, a firm diagnosis had to be made. Cardiology wanted me to complete a stress test to see how my rhythm was doing.

For the stress test, doctors made me walk fast on a treadmill to get my heart rate up. Of course, while I was on the treadmill I didn't have one episode of dizziness. Nothing. Nada. I told Dr. McMeekin that the vertigo and fainting feelings never happened while I was exerting myself. A few weeks before the test, my family and I had gone roller blading and biking and not once did I feel any dizziness. The doctor suggested I should keep running, especially if it helped ward off symptoms. Wouldn't you know it, as soon as I climbed into the passenger seat beside Wade and he drove away, I started having episodes of vertigo.

I had a repeat biopsy in April and this time it was clear of rejection. To be safe, the doctors wanted to make sure that in a month's time, there was absolutely no sign of rejection. Another follow-up biopsy was scheduled.

It was at end of the month when I noticed I was winning the battle against the warts. My HPV was clearing up. In fact, a lot of the warts had subsided and it was as though the sirolimus was curing me. I felt incredible. I no longer associated my vagina as something separate from my body and it also didn't make me feel dirty. I loved my vagina again!

Wade and I were staying at his parents' house in Brooks, a city about a two hour drive southeast of Calgary, and I had a shower and checked down below. When I moved my hand to feel my labia, I was surprised to feel the skin was as smooth as silk and as soft as a baby's bottom. My entire labia had once been overrun with clusters of warts and was bumpy and rough. Now it was as though I was in a dream where my HPV had completely disappeared. I had often prayed to God to heal me and it was through his work that I was treated. Was this the miracle I had been praying for? I shared my discovery with Wade and doing so, I brought up the one question that had been lingering in the back of my mind: was this a sign my immune system was working and therefore I was still in rejection? (Remember, rejection drugs lower immunity to keep the body from rejecting the heart.) I didn't want to think about that possibility. I wanted to think about how this was a miracle.

That week, I called cardiology and told them about the HPV. They thought it was amazing news. (I don't think they ever knew how bad it was.) HPV was not their area of expertise but it was thought that the sirolimus had a different compound or toxicity that warded off the warts. Another bonus was that the sirolimus helped control my sweat. Sweating caused more itching and with less sweat, there was less itching. With less itching, I wasn't aggravating the warts and they started to go away. I can't deny that deep down inside I was a little bit angry that I hadn't heard about this rejection drug before. I may have been able to save myself from a lot of unnecessary laser surgeries. I don't know why I wasn't introduced to sirolimus earlier. It could be that sirolimus is typically used in kidney transplants, not hearts. (It has something to do with the toxicity of the drug and it's easier on the kidneys.) I would have made the switch years ago.

My dizzy spells increased by the beginning of May. I had them more than once a day as well as when I wasn't driving. I also noticed I felt out of breath and crappy overall. A few months earlier, I was fine (except for the HPV). I surmised maybe the switch in drugs was responsible for the sinus pause. I was on very little medication (tacrolimus, aspirin and a multivitamin) prior to the change to sirolimus. But no, the results of my tests said I would more than likely need a pacemaker.

Sinus pause is actually not that unusual and there are a lot of people who have it but because they don't have any symptoms, they don't know they have it. Me, I was symptomatic. If I wanted the vertigo to go away, the pacemaker was my answer. It felt like I was backtracking with my health. Why, after so many years of doing well from the heart perspective, did I need a pacemaker all of a sudden? Was this the beginning of something bad?

I relied on Shaylynn and her experiences to gain some insight into living with a pacemaker. I guess Shaylynn and I could always be patted down together at airport security. (Haha.) There were a few things that I still wondered about like if the pacemaker would bother me, physically and mentally. It would certainly add to my list of physicians and appointments although I could go to the pacemaker clinic at the Foothills. I knew I would have to be admitted to the hospital to have the pacemaker inserted and I hated hospitals. (As a patient. I would be a visitor any day.)

I was on my way home after a nice visit with mom when I turned onto the off-ramp towards Langdon. A spell of vertigo came over me. It wasn't the only one. That drive I fought off the dizzy and fainting episodes over a dozen times until one came on and knocked the breath out of me. I didn't have anywhere to stop and pull over and there was a vehicle behind me. I grabbed my steering wheel, praying I could make it to the next intersection or find somewhere to pull off the road.

Not only could I not breath, I couldn't see. My eyes were blurry. I scrunched them up and barely made out a place to get off the main road. I turned into someone's driveway and came to a screeching halt. I was panting like I had just finished a marathon. I wasn't sure if my heart was racing or barely beating. My hands were shaking and tears ran down my face as I picked up my cell phone to call Wade at work and let him know what had happened.

Wade offered to get me but I declined. It would be silly for him to miss work and come all the way from Calgary to Langdon to get me. I was only about 10 minutes from our house anyway and didn't have much further to go. The vertigo subsided and once I got my bearings, I told him I loved him and that I would talk to him later. I hung up the phone and slowly backed out of the drive way and started for home.

That spell was weird. It was like dizziness and a panic attack all at the same time. I didn't call cardiology about it right away. Sometimes I thought I might be overreacting and didn't want to bother the doctors when they were busy with other patients. Instead, I called mom and she picked me up and took me to emergency in Strathmore. The emergency doctor there spoke with my cardiology team at the Foothills and it was decided that I would be admitted to the Foothills. Ah, Murphy's Law, if anything can go wrong, it will go wrong. I wanted to stay far away from hospitals but that wasn't going to happen. Good fortune smiled upon me though because the Foothills didn't have a bed available for me at the time. I was allowed to go home.

While I had been in emergency, my heart didn't show any signs of sinus pause. By the time I left, the sinus pauses started up again. I went home feeling very uneasy, like something definitely was going on. A part of me hurt because I had had Dawn's heart for so long and all of a sudden, things were happening to it. Another part of me was at peace knowing I was able to have 17 more years than I would have had, had I not received Dawn's gift. Mom dropped me off at home and I took a bath and let my tears splash into the water.

The next day, I called cardiology because I was feeling the sinus pauses strongly. During one episode I was able to take my blood pressure, which was significantly low. I reported it to cardiology and they told me that the only thing they could do was give me a pacemaker. I said, "Okay," right away. I knew it was time.

Wade took me to the Foothills the evening of May 8, 2012 after he got off work. I was admitted because I would get a device faster that way than as an outpatient. I was put into the telemetry room where they hooked me up to monitors so they could collect my heart rate and rhythm data. If I left my room, I had to wear a telemetry pack, a small device that would remotely transfer the data to the computers at the nursing station. This way, they could track all my heart rhythms and any sinus pause.

The room I was in was big and had four beds. Three senior men were my roommates. It was not an ideal situation but it was the room the doctors wanted me in to be able to track my heart. I was in the hospital for a few nights and one evening the fellow to my right had to go to the bathroom. Yep, he had to use the bed pan. Of course, he had to poop and was on the bed pan for some time. The nurse finally came in and asked why he hadn't used his call bell to ring for assistance.

"I couldn't reach it," he said.

I felt so sorry for him. The other fellow across the room was shrieking most of the night. It turned out his pacemaker was defibrillating him. That meant when his heart beat went irregular; his pacemaker sent an electrical current through his heart. Though I've never felt it, I bet it hurt – a lot. (I googled it and apparently it feels like a kick to the chest. Ouch.) Here I was, 29 years old and listening to this all night. I didn't get much sleep there to say the least.

On Friday, May 11, I received a pacemaker, three days after I was admitted. The surgery was done under general anesthetic (I was out) but woke up as they were sewing my incision together. While it wasn't painful, I felt pressure and pulling and tugging on the left side of my chest, below my collarbone. I had to stay in the hospital for a day after the procedure to make sure that everything was working well and that the pacemaker was pacing (pulsing) properly. Basically, the pacemaker would pace if my heart went below a certain number of beats per minute. The doctors had it set so that my pacemaker would pace if my heart went below 60 beats per minute (bpm). After I received my pacemaker, I never had another feeling of dizziness or fainting. Shaylynn was happy to have a pacemaker buddy too. (Just to update you on McKayla's health, her heart was still being monitored every year at cardiology in Calgary. Otherwise, her health was rosy.)

Mom and dad took care of the girls while I was recovering at Foothills. Mom brought them to see me. My manager at Healthy Minds Healthy Children, Harold Lipton, was understanding about me taking time off. Wade's work (now called GlobalFlow) sent me flowers at the hospital.

I was released from the Foothills on Saturday, May 12, the day before Mother's Day. We had made plans that year to participate in a Mother's Day walk the next morning but provided I had just had a pacemaker put in, I wasn't feeling up to it. Wade's family and my parents were going to participate too and instead we decided to have a nice brunch out. We made reservations at the Strathmore Station Restaurant but I had to cancel that as well. I had no energy and my neck was sore from the recent incision. (In keeping with my ritual of looking at my scars, I did check out the pacemaker scar as soon as I was able.) It was hard to do certain things like put my shirt on and I wanted to stay home and marvel at my wonderful family. In the end, we invited everyone to our house.

My chest area was sore for a while: the pacemaker was inserted just beneath the skin on the left side below the collarbone. For six weeks, I wasn't able to raise my left arm above my shoulder because it might rip the leads (wires that attached the device to the heart) out of the heart. I needed to wait until it healed and then I could resume my regular activities. This also meant I couldn't wash my hair for six weeks so Wade washed it for me. The girls helped me too. I cried a lot then and they comforted me. Despite the situation, I loved being home and watching movies with my daughters. That was the best.

It was going to be my birthday soon. I was turning 30 in two days and had been looking forward to it. Most people don't want to leave their twenties but for me, I thought being 30 would bring about great changes. I had the notion that people would listen to me and look at me like I had something important to say. At 30, I would fully be an adult. The other thing that was exciting about my birthday was that I never thought I would ever live to see 30. It was really something to celebrate. I was looking forward to a big bash. That was before I got the pacemaker as an early gift.

Instead of a party, we drove to Wade's mom and dad's place in Fernie the next weekend. The cabin is a beautiful place out in the mountains. There are also several lakes nearby where we waterski. This visit was to celebrate my thirtieth and while I would have loved to get outside and go hiking or quading, I was pretty much laid up. I did sit outside and enjoy the sun. I also brought my school books along and did some much needed reading. I had finished 16 courses and working away at getting the other courses I needed to apply for the social work programs at U of C or UVic. I took most of my courses through Athabasca and a couple through Thompson Rivers University (a university in Kamloops, British Columbia that also offers online programs). My grades were rising and I was obtaining B+'s and A-'s. I needed high scores so my GPA (Grade Point Average) would get me into school. Many people wanted to be in the social work program and it was competitive.

In June, my pacemaker incision had healed. (I was a bit sore and couldn't sleep on my tummy like I used to.) Wade went on his annual fishing trip with the Thackeray men. (Women aren't allowed but I would go if they ever invited me. Apparently, the scenery is beautiful.) Wade, his dad, uncles and cousins drive to somewhere in northern Manitoba and fish for three days. He loves it and gets to spend quality time with his dad and uncles, which is really cool.

The girls and I lounged around the house while Wade was away. I felt crappy most of the time but chalked it up to having been through a lot with the pacemaker. I continued to focus on my schooling, however, it was overwhelming a lot of the time. As a self-directed learner, I had to be dedicated to my coursework. I couldn't slack off and skip a class and get notes from someone else. It was all down to me and I wasn't even halfway through my education plans. Once I was done the 20 courses and if I was accepted into university, I had another two years to go. That meant more papers and studying, etc.

Besides school, I was gearing up for the 2012 Canadian Transplant

Games that were going to be held in Calgary. The Transplant Games are competitive events and activities for people who have had transplants. The Games are put on by the Canadian Transplant Association to raise awareness of organ and tissue donation as well as show that people who have undergone organ transplants, can have healthy lives. I was planning on participating in the Games in golf, badminton and compete in the 100 metre run. I got a chance to take part in the Games in another way as well – as part of the Calgary Stampede Parade.

I had been talking with my former U of A physiotherapist Jennifer Holman and catching up. She was also the vice president (West) of the Canadian Transplant Association. The Canadian Transplant Association was accepted to participate in the prestigious annual Calgary Stampede Parade. Jennifer put me in touch with Patty Hunt, the chair for media and publicity for the Sixth Canadian Transplant Games. I volunteered my time in whatever way possible with the parade and got to help build the float.

When Wade got back from fishing, we worked on the float together. We spent a lot of weeknights meeting with Patti. (Patti's husband Fred had had a double lung transplant.) The slogan for that year's Stampede was, *We're better together.*

We made plans of what kind of float we wanted in the parade and came up with a running shoe, symbolizing the 2012 Canadian Transplant Games. On the front of the runner, it said, *We're better together.* Then we put pictures of donors all around the bottom sides of the shoe. The shoe was going to pull a flat deck trailer where some organ and tissue recipients would sit. I had an idea about an addition I could make to the float.

When I got home, I contacted Coral and Remi and asked if they would be agreeable to putting Dawn's picture on the float. They were definitely okay with it. Coral told me that one of Dawn's friends, Arla Pirtle, would be coming to the Transplant Games because her dad had undergone a double lung transplant. Coral said Arla was going to look for me because they would love to meet me and my family. That was fantastic. I was getting the opportunity to meet another of Dawn's friends.

Wade's company kindly agreed to let us use its bay to decorate and store the float. Building it was the hardest part: trying to attach wire mesh in the shape of a runner to an old station wagon (it belonged to

Patty and Fred Hunt). Once the shoe was formed, there were many small touches that had to be added. It all took a lot of work. Wade was awesome and helped so much in the building of the float. The finished project looked awesome.

On Friday, July 6, Shaylynn and I rode on the float in the parade. McKayla was okay with that and she sat with Wade, mom, Audrey and cousins and waved at us as we went by. So many volunteers made the float a big success!

Shaylynn and I beside the picture of Dawn on the 2012 Calgary Stampede float.

Transplant Corner

This Stampede Parade float promoted organ donation

T his summer proved to be very exciting for many of our heart transplant patients and their families. Three of our heart transplant children were selected to ride in the Calgary Stampede Parade on the Canadian Transplant float promoting organ donation and transplantation.

Enjoying the 2012 Calgary Stampede Parade.

Calgary, Alberta celebrated its Centennial Stampede this year and the Canadian Transplant Association was thrilled to be a part of that celebration.

Thanks to the unstoppable energy and enthusiasm of Patti Hunt, Media and Publicity Chair for the 6th Canadian Transplant Games, we hosted a float in the Calgary Stampede's opening parade July 6, 2012. An estimated 400,000 visitors from around the world lined the streets to witness one of Canada's largest parades as it wound its way through the city center. Prime Minister Stephen Harper, Alberta Premier Alison Redford and Calgary Mayor Naheed Nenshi were among the celebrity guests who donned their cowboy hats to watch or participate in the parade marshalled by country music legend Ian Tyson.

The CTA float, including transplant recipients, transplant program staff and donor families, embodied the Stampede theme that "We're Greatest Together". Participants, riding or walking alongside the float, engaged the crowd as they waved and called out messages of organ donation awareness. The float was pulled by Patti's "brainchild" – a running shoe festooned with photos of our heroes; our organ donors. Congratulations to Patti and her hard-working crew for securing a spot for us in this historic, milestone parade and for bringing Patti's vision to life.

Calgary boasted daily record attendances during the 10 days of its 100th Stampede and our Games Organizing Committee ensured that promotions for our Games, our 25th anniversary and our message of organ and tissue donation were visible throughout the city. CTA Alberta is proud to have been a part of this very special event and would like to acknowledge the hard work and dedication of the entire Committee. Well Done!!

2012 Calgary Stampede Parade.

D uring the same week as the Canadian Transplant Games, the Cardiology Clinic held its 1st Annual Family Transplant picnic. The picnic was held at Sandy Beach with beautiful weather, an abundance of food, but most importantly, fun, fun, fun! It was a great opportunity for the children to see old friends, make new friends and for parents to have a chance to connect with other transplant parents and share stories. As a staff member, I can say it was truly wonderful to see all of the children having fun, running and playing and to have a chance to visit with the parents in a fun, relaxing environment.

Celebratory Cake at the 1st Annual Family Transplant Picnic

Heart recipients Taylor, Sarah and Shaylynn with McKayla at the picnic.

CHAPTER THIRTY FOUR

Poker face

I went for another scheduled biopsy on July 11 to make sure I was still "clear of rejection." Before that appointment, a little feeling poked me in the side and bugged me about my heart. I wondered if the sirolimus might be messing with things. It was the only thing that had changed when all of a sudden – I had issues with my heart. I also wondered if the pacemaker was like putting a Band-Aid on something that was actually much, much bigger than we imagined. I hoped this appointment would put the foreboding to rest.

After the biopsy, the cardiologist at the time, Dr. Warnicka, looked at me and said, "Kristy, I am very sorry to tell you this but you have a blood clot in your left ventricle of your heart. Unfortunately, we are going to have to start you on blood thinners."

What? I had entered the room thinking I was free of rejection and now I have a blood clot? A blood clot in the heart is serious and meant my heart wasn't working properly. Blood clumps when it's stagnant and I wondered what was happening in my body. In 1996 when I had the blood clot in my old heart (when they had to fly in the expensive medication from Edmonton), I understood why: that heart was diseased. Having a blood clot in my transplanted heart (Dawn's heart) was scary. There were so many unknowns. My once-healthy heart wasn't so healthy anymore.

"Can I still participate in the Transplant Games?" I asked with my fingers crossed.

"It's not a good idea," said Dr. Warnicka.

The reason was there was some concern about the blood clot breaking off and moving, potentially causing an aneurysm or major heart attack. Until we had more answers, he didn't want me to do anything to get my heart rate up and put myself at risk. I wasn't allowed to do any physical activity until further notice and that included water-skiing and anything that would cause my body to bounce around. Dr. Warnicka did say that the blood clot looked well-organized, which meant that it didn't look like any pieces were loose and that lessened the chances of bits breaking off. Then he stunned me with the news that the blood clot was caused by a myocardial infarction – in other words I had had a minor heart attack.

People die from heart attacks all the time. I was lucky I didn't die but I was scared and wanted to know why I had just had a heart attack. I was in heart failure and it made me feel bad about Dawn's heart. I didn't want anything to happen to it. I was attached to this heart in a lot of ways and there were so many similarities between Dawn and me. I was going to do whatever I could to save her heart.

I was put on Innohep injections (tinzaparin) until the blood clot dissolved. The last time I was on Innohep was when I had the blood clot in my leg. Mom had given me the shots then. I would have to give myself the needles now and I was determined to do it without too much squeamishness.

Besides the Innohep, Dr. Warnicka prescribed Coumadin (warfarin). I had to wait to start the Coumadin in case I was scheduled to have another biopsy as blood thinners increased the risk of bleeding. You can stop tinzaparin close to the date of the expected surgery, whereas Coumadin you had to stop five days prior.

The cardiologist said the tissue of my heart would be sent to be tested for rejection. Meanwhile, my pacemaker was working fine.

I was bummed about sitting out the Games. (Not about missing golfing. I'm not a great golfer.) I wanted to be a part of this amazing way to advocate for organ and tissue donation. Since I couldn't participate physically, I would have to find another way to be a part of the amazing cause. I decided to put my name and my voice to work whenever and wherever I could.

I attended media events and gave interviews to reporters. I left the part out about having a blood clot. You know me; I didn't want to burden people and tell them I wasn't feeling well. (Except for my family.) Doctors didn't expect to see any changes with the blood clot for months anyway so why bring it up. To showcase organ and tissue donation and to advertise for the Canadian Transplant Games, Shaylynn and I had our photos put on giant posters hung around Calgary. At the top of the poser it read, "Organ Donation Saves Lives." Then by the picture of me and Shaylynn, it read, "Just ask Kristy and her daughter Shaylynn. Heart Transplants saved them both." What better way to showcase how organ donation works than by having a mother and daughter, who were saved by organ donation, on the poster for the Transplant Games.

Organ Donation poster for the Canadian Transplant Games in Calgary, Alberta.

People from all over Canada, representing their provinces and territories and showcasing how organ and tissue donation works, came to the Games. During the event, I met Arla and her family. I was introduced to her dad, Morris Irvine (he received a double lung transplant March 2011), Fae (Arla's mom), Cooper (Arla's son) and Cadence (Arla's daughter). We sat with Arla and her family at Flames Central, a sports bar, where the opening ceremonies for the Transplant Games was held. It was like Arla and I had known each other forever: like we were old friends separated by distance and time commitments. Our relationship came naturally. I guess a part of me has always known her.

Arla and I at the Canadian Transplant Games 2012.

Throughout the weeks of July 16 to 22, I met amazing people with amazing stories. All their stories are absolutely beautiful and if they don't make you consider organ donation… I don't know what will. Taylor Stang was competing in the Games. She had restrictive cardiomyopathy like my family. The Stang family waited seven months for a new heart for their daughter and she received one on June 4, 2006.

Just like my family, Taylor's sister receives testing on her heart because we now know restrictive cardiomyopathy is genetic. We were so fortunate to meet Taylor, her sister Brooke, their mom, Cathy and dad Trent. Cathy shared with me that I had given her hope that her daughter would be able to have children of her own someday.

I met Ryley Mitchell at the Games too. Ryley was born in June 2005 and diagnosed with dilated cardiomyopathy (DMC – enlarged heart). She received a life-saving heart transplant when she was only seven months old. I was fortunate to meet Ryley, her brother Landon, their mom Joanna and dad Jeff.

Heart transplant recipients Shaylynn and Ryley particpate in the Canadian Transplant Games 2012.

Shaylynn was able to take part in the Games. She completed in Track and Field events: long jump, ball throw and the 50 metre dash. She won Bronze in ball throw and had so much fun. She met other kids who had had heart transplants and some of them even had restrictive cardiomyopathy like Taylor.

About halfway through the Games on July 19, I received a call from cardiology – the news wasn't good. The biopsy showed Antibody Mediated Rejection (AMR). What that meant was that the heart's antibodies and my antibodies were attacking each other. Basically, it was rejection and most doctors in Canada remain unfamiliar with AMR. The next step was to put me on prednisone, a steroid often used in transplant patients. I started on 50mg – a pretty hefty dose. I hadn't taken prednisone since I first had my transplant. I continued taking the sirolimus and the Innohep and also started on medication for my blood pressure, which was high. I went from taking rejection pills once a day, to taking multiple medications multiple times a day. In addition to the drugs, doctors wanted me to have Intravenous Immunoglobulin (IVIG) starting on July 26. IVIG is a blood product that contains antibodies and in my situation, it was used to fight my body's antibodies because they weren't working as they should and in full attack against my donated heart. The IVIG would be administered at the Foothills hospital in the day treatment area. I would have to go for IVIG a couple times a week and be treated as an outpatient. The procedure usually took about four hours in total to complete.

The Canadian Transplant Games came to a close with a gala. I attended the event at the Deerfoot Inn and Casino on Saturday, July 21, hoping it would take my mind off the news I had received. I was forcing myself to have a positive attitude and be thankful for my family. Believing in God and having faith helped in that regard. I also focused on how I had cheated death so many times before. Maybe my time was up. Maybe this was going to be it.

I prayed a lot and surrendered to God's plan. There was an incredible peace that came with not wishing anything differently and accepting what it was. Honestly, when you do that, you see all the things you would have missed out on if things had gone in another direction.

We arrived a bit late to the gala but luckily we had assigned seating. We sat with Vickie Chase from CTV Calgary. It was a fantastic evening with fantastic people. I met so many interesting folks. I even met parents of transplant recipients who were excited to meet me and told me how I gave them hope for their own daughters to have kids. It was a touching night. Tears of joy and sadness were evident on a lot of faces. There were many inspirational stories of how organ and tissue donation had touched all the lives there. Donor families and recipients came together and shared their mutual respect, joy and sadness too.

After everything settled down after the week of events with the Canadian Transplant Games, other things came up, especially with my current situation. The clot and AMR were right there with me, reminding me I might have limited time on earth. I had an angiogram (an x-ray image of the heart using dye) on Wednesday, July 25. That next day, Thursday, July 26, I started the IVIG. Minutes after leaving the hospital, cardiology called me and told me to come to the clinic on Friday after my IVIG. Oh, and bring Wade or mom. I knew that meant I wasn't getting good news.

Cardiology had never ever told me to bring someone to an appointment with me. After my IVIG on Friday, mom and I walked over to the Foothills North Tower to see the cardiology staff. This is when they confirmed that I had a minor myocardial infarction and that they wanted me to start plasmapheresis (process of separating blood) on Monday, July 30 at 9:00 a.m.

In some people who are ill, their plasma contains antibodies that attack the immune system. Plasmapheresis is a procedure where the blood is taken out and the plasma cells are separated and then the blood is put back into the body. I would be hooked up to a machine that was connected to a central line that removed my affected plasma and then replaced my blood with good plasma (good antibodies).

That Friday afternoon, Wade and I decided that with the way things were going, it would be a good time to take the weekend and relax. We packed up our camper and headed to Lake Newal for the weekend. Newel is close to Brooks and Wade's mom and dad came by and had supper with us at the camp site. I tried hard to be present and appreciate the moments I had with my family while in the back of my mind I was thinking, "This is it." It didn't stop me from doing my homework though. I had a big research paper due for Psychology 389 - Learning Disabilities and I worked on it during the day while Wade went to help his dad move something at his dad's shop. I was sitting at the picnic table trying to get all my research papers in order and I was having a hard time breathing. It was like I was out of breath. I felt terrible. My belly was badly bloated and my weight had increased from 132 lbs to 150 lbs. I felt like I was pregnant. I also noticed my body shaking in tempo with my heart. It was the weirdest thing. I brushed the way I was feeling aside. I was probably having anxiety. I reminded myself to breathe and take in the beauty that was around me.

Wade's Aunt Colleen and Uncle Vic were visiting and stopped by the campsite to see us. We had a great time with them and we all prayed for my health. I had accepted that my fate was in God's hands but it didn't mean I didn't worry about my daughters and Wade. I wondered if Shaylynn would go through the same things as me and I prayed she wouldn't have too.

I let go of trying to be in charge. If I hadn't received a heart from Dawn, then I would have passed away a long time ago. I had lived past the age of 14 and had been blessed in so many different ways. Perhaps you don't remember my favourite quote but it gave me strength when I was a girl and strengthened me as a woman:

We set our eyes on what we see, not on what we cannot see
What we see will last only a short time, what we cannot see
Will last forever.

2 Corinthians 4:18

Monday came fast – too fast. I arrived at the hospital in the morning and was prepped to have a central line inserted for plasmapheresis. The central line went into the left side of my neck (the right side was saved for biopsies and there were definitely going to be more of those). I would be having plasmapheresis a couple times a week. I had gone back to work with Healthy Minds/Healthy Children program but after the doctors put the central line in for my plasmapheuresis, I realized I needed to take more time off. I called Harold and let him know that things were not going well with my health. He was understanding and let me take a leave of absence. At the end of the week, someone from work dropped off an edible arrangement for me. It was a nice treat and so thoughtful.

We were nearing the end of July and things weren't looking great. I was extremely bloated, a sign of congestive heart failure. My face was swollen and my stomach ballooned out. My biopsy results still read AMR. At this point, I was having a biopsy every two weeks because they wanted to see what the rejection status was and also to see if the IVIG was helping and easing off the fight against the heart. School was still on my radar and helped me take my mind off of what was happening. I could keep up with my reading for school. I studied while I was getting plasmapheresis if I was feeling okay. The girls spent a lot of time with my dad as mom was usually chauffeuring me around to all the doctor, IVIG and plasmapheuresis appointments. Being sick didn't exactly make for good times but everybody was holding in there. I didn't tell Coral and Remi about Dawn's heart failing. What do you say to the parents of the heart you have beating inside you? I didn't want to worry them. I think they knew something was up anyway because Coral sent me a message to say they were thinking about me.

The second week in August we were supposed to go on a family vacation to the Okanagan Valley in B.C. It had been booked for six months in advance as we had put the girls into a ringette camp near Osoyoos. I was looking forward to going on holiday and getting away from doctors and hospitals. I was also excited that we would spend a whole week in our trailer because we had never used it for that length of time before. Wouldn't you know it – cardiology put a leak in our plans and told me not to leave the province because I was in heart failure and things hadn't been going well.

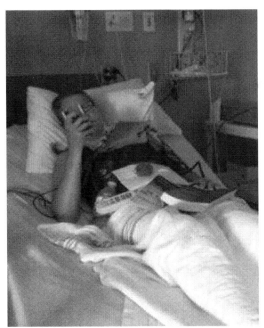

Doing school work while having plasmapheresis.

Saying I was devastated to miss the holiday would be an understatement. I was beyond upset. I had been looking forward to the break for a long time and now we couldn't go. I didn't even care if we couldn't get our money back from the ringette camp, I had only wanted to go and spend time with my family. We had also invited a few other people to come including Billy. (He ended up going on his own.) I realized waterskiing or air chair (instead of standing on skis or a board in the water, you sit) was not going to happen for me this summer. I continued with my IVIG and instead of going to BC, planned a weekend camping at a park near Medicine Hat, 40 Mile Park, with family for the August Long Weekend (August 3 to 6, 2011).

While camping, my cousin Jen and Aunty Terry (both nurses) cleaned my central line that was put in my neck for plasmapheresis. This weekend was a significant one for me because it was the weekend I realized things may not be going in my favour. My HPV had become extremely uncomfortable and was the worst it had ever been. I know I have said that before but it was incredibly bad here. It came back because of the prednisone (the steroid was weakening my immune system). (It was hard to reflect on changing my medication back to tacrolimus from sirolimus to make my HPV better when the medication change was possibly what caused the rejection in the first place. That was just my own opinion then. Later, doctors did suspect we hadn't bridged the sirolimus properly. My body responded differently on sirolimus and I required a higher dose than what I was on with tacrolimus.) I also noticed I had a bulging cyst inside my vagina, which caused a lot of discomfort.

I was 30 and this was not what I had envisioned for my future as an adult. I had been contemplating the "what ifs" for some time: "What if I die?" or "What if I need a new heart?" The saddest part about thinking all of this was that my kids were so young. They would be 12 in a few weeks. I worried about how they would deal with my death. I worried about Wade and my mom and dad. I worried about what Coral and Remi would do if I died. It wasn't only Dawn's parents I had kept in the dark about my health; I hardly told anyone I was sick. (Janine knew a little bit but she didn't know all that was happening.) I felt like me being ill sounded like a broken record and most people who knew me were desensitized to the phrase, "Kristy is sick." I continued soul searching and talking to God and one day I threw my hands up in the air and said, "Jesus, take the wheel."

Only so much medical intervention could be done for me and God had a purpose for my life. Letting go of control made everything simpler. I had a conversation with my Aunt Terry while at 40 Mile. I told her I was feeling overwhelmed with all the things that still needed to get done even if you are sick and tired. She said if people offered to help me, I needed to accept their help. That was tough for me to hear. I could give God control but it was hard to do that with tedious tasks like cleaning. That sounds peculiar but I liked cleaning because it was something I could control. I couldn't control my health and so cleaning gave me something I had power over. I turned people away when they wanted to help me. I thought, "I can do this." (I definitely turned to my parents for help. They took care of the kids and drove me places when I couldn't drive anymore. I never felt well enough to drive and was scared I would be somewhere and something would happen and then there would only be strangers around to help me.)

My cousin Jen and Aunty Terry just finished cleaning my central line site .

After that weekend, I accepted Audrey's offer to pay for a cleaning lady to come in once a week. I found an amazing woman named Pavlena. I cannot begin to express to you how joyous it made me feel to come home to a clean house after medical appointments. Mom would drop me off and I would walk in the door – the quietness was amazing and I didn't have to worry about doing the dishes or vacuuming. With the girls still at school and Wade still at work, it was just Breaker and me. I would lie on the couch and relish in the moment of peace – concentrating on my heart beat – and my body would sway to the rhythm. (Heart pounding was a side effect of being in heart failure and my heart beat rocked my body with every pulse.) If this was my time to go, then everything was right with the world: my house was clean and my family knew how much I loved them. I would slowly drift off to sleep with an amazing feeling of peace lifting me up and delivering me into my dreams.

CHAPTER THIRTY FIVE

In sickness and in health

My HPV was full-blown again. The warts were so bad that Dr. Ghatage brought up the possibility of having a vulvectomy. We had talked about it before but then the sirolimus had cleared up the problem for a while. The HPV was feasting on my body because of my weak immune system. It couldn't fight the warts. But my immune system needed to be lowered as much as possible to stop the antibodies from attacking my heart. It was a vicious cycle.

I spent a lot of time researching the vulvectomy, in which part, or my entire, vulva would be removed. I wondered if it would alleviate my pain. I had a lot on my plate at the time and I knew the timing wasn't fantastic. The plasmapheresis was done and I finally got my central line out but I was still going for IVIG and having biopsies every two weeks.

In the interim, I had a laser on September 12, 2012. While I was undergoing the procedure, doctors also drained the cyst at the same time. It took me a little more time to recover from the procedure due to the cyst. Eventually, I healed but the discomfort from the HPV continued and was bringing me down. I was sluggish and completely depleted of energy. I knew part of my loss of energy was from all the medical tests and procedures I was having from the heart failure, blood clot and AMR. The other part was the HPV.

My depression had never completely slithered away and it wasn't great again. It wasn't like I was sad though, I was more angry at myself thinking, "What the heck did I do? I advocated to change medications for the HPV and now look where I am: my HPV is worse than ever and my heart isn't doing well."

It was during this time I was sick that we realized how much of a hassle it was to live in Langdon, especially since I wasn't driving anymore. I usually didn't feel well enough to be behind the wheel. I was going into Calgary almost every day and spending hours on the road and in hospitals. Wade and I had talked about putting our house up for sale and moving to Chestermere. It seemed the place to be for us. The girls never switched schools when we moved in with Wade and had remained in Chestermere. My parents lived there and we did all our grocery shopping there so it only made sense that we lived in Chestermere. The timing didn't work though and we decided to wait until things settled down with my health.

***

Wade and I had been married for two years and the last year had been something of a grinding whirlwind. We took time to celebrate our wedding anniversary on October 2 by going to The Keg in Calgary. (We loved their garlic mash potatoes.) Wade was such a support to me and never wavered on his wedding covenant: *in sickness and in health.* That was good since I needed a blood transfusion two days later on October 4.

I was running on fumes. I had no energy and was beyond tired. My hemoglobin (protein in red blood) was very low and I was also getting bad migraines. The medical staff at the Rockyview said I was anemic (low iron) and gave me a blood transfusion to boost my red blood cell count. I hadn't had to have a transfusion since 1996 when I first received my new heart.

While I was having the transfusion, mom listed my symptoms to the nurse. Besides massive headaches, my skin was mottling terribly. The colour was changing in patches. It was as if my arm was in a tourniquet and the blood had been stopped to the area. The skin was turning white and purple.

I was glad mom spoke up because the nurse said that it sounded like I was having an allergic reaction to the IVIG. Thank goodness for that amazing nurse. The only reason she knew about the reaction was because she had another IVIG patient with the exact symptoms.

It was thought that the IVIG was being administered at too fast a rate. We slowed it down to see if that would help with the headaches but this meant that I would be at the hospital for longer than four hours. We also had to be careful because administering IVIG too quickly wasn't good for the kidneys and my kidneys were already not in the best of shape. As soon as the IVIG was stopped, my skin went back to its normal colour and the migraines went away.

Then something else came up. When I got my period, I was bleeding clumps of blood that were as big as my fist. I notified cardiology when it started happening in early August. I think we kind of thought that the blobs were because of the blood thinners and all the other things my body was going through. The large clots alarmed me as I had been on blood thinners before and never ever did I bleed like this. Now I was bleeding so heavily that I would soak a super absorbency tampon in less than 30 minutes. The doctors didn't have any advice for me and I thought perhaps I had cancer. I had to "wait and see" what would happen once more.

Next it was Shaylynn's turn to be sick. She had a fever and was throwing up. She was admitted to the Alberta Children's Hospital (Calgary's new facility on Shaganappi Trail) with a bad kidney infection. She was diagnosed with an E. coli infection in her kidney and treated with IV antibiotics. I was extremely ill and couldn't stay the night with her so Wade had to sleep at the hospital with Shaylynn. McKayla and I went to mom and dad's because I wasn't in any shape to drive.

I had been on medical leave from work for about a month and a half and I used the time to complete the school courses I needed to apply for the BSW program. The application for UVic was due January 2013 and the application for U of C was due in February. I could still apply even if I didn't have all my course work completed. I had finished 18 courses and would have the last two done by May 2013. The schools only needed to see the transcript and that I was enrolled in the courses.

At the end of October, I broke free of the cocoon that had kept me an ailing prisoner for so long. On October 27, I attended the 25th Anniversary of the Canadian Transplant Association at the Red and White Club at McMahon Stadium with the girls, Wade and our parents. It was the first time in a long time I had put make-up on.

The evening was fun and I felt like a real person again. The feeling wouldn't last for long.

One day soon after, I was doing some school work in the morning. I noticed Wade forgot his lunch, a peanut butter sandwich, so I ate it. A couple hours later, I started to have gut-wrenching cramps. I thought maybe my period was starting again. I decided to put the school books away and rest for the afternoon.

I woke up at about 4:00 p.m. and the stomach ache had gotten worse. I moved from the couch to my bed, hoping that would make me more comfortable. I squirmed around in agony until 5:00 p.m. when the pain became severe. I brought a small garbage can from our bathroom onto the bed as I had now started to feel nauseated. Then I started to throw up.

The girls and Wade came home and by this time, I had already called and notified mom about how I was feeling. By 6:00 p.m. I was throwing up uncontrollably. Mom came to our house to look after the girls so Wade could take me to emergency. Then I lost control of my bowels.

I'm serious when I say that I didn't have any control over my bowels or my vomiting. I had so much pain too that mom and Wade were trying to decide if he should take me to the hospital or if we should call the ambulance. Here I was, writhing in agony, constantly throwing up and not in control of my bowels. I couldn't sit in our vehicle without a diaper on but we didn't have one. Who would have thought I would have needed a diaper? Not me and I'm always prepared. (I usually have a small drugstore on hand at home. A diaper was definitely one thing I didn't have.) Due to my diarrhea and vomiting, mom called 911.

The Langdon Volunteer Fire Service was the first to arrive. When the paramedics came about 15 minutes later, they immediately started an IV. They didn't have a diaper for me to wear to the hospital but they gave me some medication for pain and some medication to help with the vomiting. The ambulance then took me to the Rockyview General Hospital in Calgary because, according to the paramedics, it had the least wait time. Wade rode up front in the ambulance and arrived with me at the hospital around 9:00 in the evening.

I waited for about an hour for the doctor to examine me. By then, I wasn't vomiting anymore and I didn't have diarrhea. Mom picked up Wade around 3:30 a.m. because I told him he should go home and get some sleep as he had to work that morning. I stayed in the emergency all night.

The doctor said I had a bad stomach flu. That was plausible and I was happy it wasn't an issue connected to my heart. At 6:30 a.m. the nurse came in and asked me if someone would be there to get me. Emergency needed my bed. They essentially kicked me out.

Usually I had no problems leaving hospitals but there was a bad snow storm that morning. Instead of taking Wade 35 minutes to drive to the Rockyview, it took him a little over three hours. The nurse was not happy and asked me a few times when my ride was coming. They had wanted me out of that room by 7 a.m.

Wade finally arrived and got me. Rather than taking me home to Langdon, he dropped me off at mom and dad's house in Chestermere. Then he went to work. That day I was feeling much better albeit exhausted from the events of the past evening.

My parents were scheduled to leave for Scottsdale in a couple of days and Wade and I were supposed to follow them a few days later. We had a short getaway planned. (Audrey was going to look after the girls while we were gone.) After contracting the stomach flu and the excessive bleeding while on my period, we cancelled our trip. We would have to plan something for the spring.

We said goodbye to my parents on Thursday, November 2, and they headed to Scottsdale. The next day, Wade and I decided to have pizza for supper at home. It was a typical Thackeray Friday night and after supper, we watched *American Horror Story*, one of my favourite TV series at the time. We went to bed later but I was having trouble sleeping. I was extremely bloated and uncomfortable but thought nothing of it. (Actually, I thought the bloat was from eating pizza crusts.) In the last several months, I had put on about 15 pounds. It was a lot of weight for me and was on top of the pounds I had already gained in the summer. Part of that weight gain was edema (fluid retention), especially in the stomach area. The fluid retention was thought to be from my heart failure and I had been put on Lasix (a diuretic brand name) by the doctor a couple of months earlier to help me shed the water weight. The drug was working a bit and the swelling in my legs and belly had gone down some. Still, I didn't enjoy feeling puffy and fat all the time.

I abruptly woke up at about 5:00 a.m. with an overwhelming urgency to go to the bathroom for diarrhea. I made it to the toilet just in time. Once there, I was hit by a wave of nausea and started to vomit uncontrollably. After I was done, I washed up and brushed my teeth and headed back to bed. I told Wade what had happened and then I began shaking: I was freezing all of a sudden. My husband encouraged me to curl up beside him and get some more sleep. I shut my eyes.

About an hour later, I woke up and it started again. I barely made it to the bathroom. It was a repeat of the hour before with vomiting and diarrhea. This continued for the next hour. I had better things to do this weekend other than be sick. I had been looking forward to watching McKayla play in a ringette game that Saturday morning but I had to skip it. Wade left the house with her and Shaylynn stayed with me, taking care of me and getting me fluids. The pain in my stomach was becoming intolerable: it was like somebody was continuously stabbing me. It was the same symptoms as the bad "stomach bug" from the other day and the same things began to happen.

I lost control of my bowels and started vomiting uncontrollably. It was *Groundhog Day*, an exact repeat of what had forced me into the ambulance and to the Rockyview. By now, I was crying because the pain was so bad. Between sobs, I asked Shaylynn to call her dad and tell him to come home because I needed to go to the hospital. I called Billy in Calgary and asked him to come look after the girls since my parents were away. He said he'd be right over.

Wade arrived home immediately and once Billy arrived, they carried me to the vehicle. Wade wanted to take me to the hospital in Calgary but I knew I needed something for the pain ASAP. I asked him to take me to the Strathmore hospital, about 20 minutes away. Thank goodness I had asked for a diaper from the hospital during my last ordeal – I couldn't hold in the diarrhea.

I lay in the back of our GMC Yukon Denali SUV sobbing, pooping my diaper and vomiting uncontrollably. When we got to Strathmore, the medical staff gave me some medication for the pain and vomiting right away. They also sent me for an ultrasound and then admitted me.

It turned out this wasn't a simple flu diagnosis – the ultrasound showed a large cyst on my ovary. What was happening was that the cyst was pulling and twisting my ovary and cutting off the blood supply to it. The twisted ovary caused such an excessive amount of pain that in order for my body to cope, it went into survival mode. That was what caused me to lose control of my bowels and throw up violently. I was discharged from the Strathmore hospital the next day and provided with a referral to see my gynecologist, Dr. Brain. I was a little annoyed with the Rockeyview medical staff and their flu conclusion.

I saw my gynecologist regarding the cyst on my ovary. Given the risks of surgery and my complicated medical history, Dr. Brain opted not to remove the cyst. (Cysts on ovaries are not uncommon, especially during your period.) I think my cyst is still there but it hasn't caused me trouble again.

To update you on the rest of my health here, the heavy bleeding during my period didn't stop. There was some thinking that my body was going through so much with the IVIG, plasmapheresis and AMR that it caused the excessive bleeding.

The AMR came back negative. (0 AMR; 1 R. The 1 R means 1 for rejection.) That was very low and was, yet again, a "wait and watch" scenario. I don't think I have to tell you that the HPV was holding on but becoming less itchy (phew) and I decided not to have the vulvectomy. My blood clot remained and was measuring slightly smaller than what it had been in July 2012. That was good news. It meant the tinzaparin was doing its job. I was put on Coumadin and once that was working in my body, I could stop the tinzaparin. Coumadin was a pill while tinzaparin was a needle that I had to stick in my belly every day. My stomach needed a break as the tinzaparin was turning my skin into a giant bruise: black and blue.

I checked in with my friend Annelies around this time. I wanted to see how she was doing and also to let her know that I had a pacemaker. (She had a pacemaker too.) She was good and had actually been taken off the transplant list because she was doing so well. Sometimes that happens if the patient is stable and isn't sick. However, you're put back on if anything changes and your condition worsens.

I was always worried about not waking up in the morning and when I did, I savoured the hours. We spent Christmas 2012 with my parents in Chestermere. It was pretty low key but that was what I needed. For New Year's, we went to Whitefish, MT with Wade's family. It's a ski resort town and since I didn't want to sit in the lodge all day, I decided to take snowboarding lessons with the girls while

Wade snowboarded with his family. I had skied when I was younger but I hadn't been on the slopes for a long time. At first I thought hitting the pistes might not be a good idea since I was on blood thinners. If I banged my head or caused trauma to any part of my body, I would bleed internally. I decided to go snowboarding anyway and I was glad I did. It was a fun lesson and made all the better because I got to spend time with my girls. Maybe 2013 was going to bring some good cheer to our family.

***

My plans for getting into a social work program were solidifying. I submitted my applications in January 2013 to the University of Calgary and University of Victoria. There was nothing to do now other than wait to hear back from the schools.

Things were looking up for me. I wasn't seeing as many doctors as before. I started driving again and getting my life back. I didn't need Pavlena, our cleaning woman, anymore. (But I sure missed her!) The doctors tapered my prednisone. (I really advocated for this because I knew it wasn't doing anything good for my HPV.) My HPV seemed to be tolerable and wasn't causing the significant amount of discomfort it had caused the prior year. I had not been in a hospital for a couple months now – a record for me.

We attended a ringette tournament in Lethbridge at the end of March. We spent one night in a hotel and the second night we stayed at my sister-in-law Shannon's, and visited with her family. Throughout the weekend I had this weird feeling like my heart was pounding. It was a different feeling than the pounding from the heart failure. This time it was pounding and racing all at once. It was like I was running a marathon, except I wasn't. I assumed it was all because of anxiety; perhaps I was worried for some reason.

Back in Langdon as the week continued, I started to feel the pounding and racing every day. I told Wade and my parents what I was experiencing and they were keeping an eye on me. Meanwhile, I had returned to work several weeks earlier in my admin role at Healthy Minds/Healthy Children and it was going well. While driving to work though, I would feel the pounding in my chest and get a sense of urgency to jump out of my vehicle. (I think I was associating it with the vertigo spells I had in spring of 2012.) I never got out of my car. (I was on 16th Avenue, a busy city road, and Calgary drivers would have lost their minds! Traffic is already bad enough and when there's a collision or a stall, it creates chaos.) The only way I can describe the feeling I was getting is to compare it to a panic attack.

One particular day when I wanted to leave my vehicle, I overcame the feeling. I told myself that I was okay and I did some deep breathing to calm myself. Then while I was walking to my office at the U of C, I almost fell over. My legs felt like they weighed a million pounds each and I could barely walk. I was fumbling, losing my balance and really light-headed. That was when I knew something was wrong.

I called cardiology right away about my problem. They advised me to come to the Foothills and have an ECG done. I called Wade and he picked me up and took me to the hospital. There, they completed the ECG, which showed my resting heart rate was extremely elevated to over 150 bpm. My normal resting rate was typically anywhere from 90 to 100 bpm. The doctors said they would be admitting me immediately because my heart was in atrial fibrillation (rapid irregular heartbeats. My dad has frequently experienced this.) The pacemaker wasn't picking up on it because it only paces when my heart beats below certain beats – 60 bpm. I had the opposite problem now – my heart was racing.

To help with my racing heart, I was prescribed metoprolol, a beta blocker that helps lower blood pressure and conditions that cause fast heart rate. Doctors would have also prescribed a blood thinner to make the blood thin because with atrial fibrillation, you're at an increased risk for blood clots. Since I was already taking warfarin I didn't need another blood thinner.

About four days later, after the medication was prescribed and the dosing was determined, I was released from the hospital. This had all happened the weekend before we were scheduled to drive to Scottsdale for our Easter weekend. I was scared the doctors were going to tell me I wasn't allowed to go. However, cardiology didn't see why I couldn't go on my trip and provided me with a medical note for customs in case they questioned me about the drugs or if I had to go to a U.S. hospital. The doctor's note stated the medications I was on and that I was being followed by a cardiology team in Calgary. I made the executive decision to get our family to the States. Stat!

We went on vacation from March 28 until April 12. Mom and dad drove with us and we stopped in Las Vegas. They had tickets to see Shania Twain. They had booked the concert earlier when they hadn't known we would be joining them for Easter. I would have liked to have gone to see Shania but it was expensive. Oh well. While mom and dad were at the concert, Wade, the girls and I walked the strip. I was tired and feeling under-the-weather but happy to be with my family. I needed a break from everything so badly.

We went on the Grand Canyon Skywalk tour (a glass walkway built into the side of the Grand Canyon) and it was scary being on the see-through platform. We were high up and the ground was far below. McKayla was terrified and crawled the whole walkway. When we got to the end of the span, the other tourists clapped for her when she got to solid ground. It was an amazing holiday – much needed too.

Grand Canyon Skywalk with mom, dad, Wade, Shaylynn and McKayla.

CHAPTER THIRTY SIX

A good problem

When we weren't swimming or shopping on our Easter holiday, I was working on my Athabasca University course – Women and Gender Studies: Advocacy from the Margins. It was the last course I needed to have completed my 20 courses to get into school. I hopefully would hear if I got into UVic by May or early June. For U of C, I was hoping I'd get the news in June.

For Mother's Day 2013, we attended the Second Annual 2nd Chance Trail Ride. The money raised on the ride was donated to the GoodHearts Foundation to furnish apartments for people living in Edmonton before and after transplant. The ride was started by Arla Pirtle's family. We had kept in touch after the transplant games and Arla invited us to the event. (She knew how much Shaylynn loved horses too.)

The ride allows riders and wagons to follow the Iron Horse Trail (a rail line abandoned by the Canadian National Railway) between Lindbergh and Heinsburg, Alberta. Dawn's parents also attended the event in a wagon they brought from their farm, about 25 minutes away from Heinsburg. That was when I told them about having a pacemaker. They were understanding. We rode on their wagon for four hours and it was amazing. Later that night, there was a supper, auction and live music.

At the evening event, the host called up all the individuals who had heart transplants to come to the stage. I went to the front and Coral came up with me and gave a speech. She talked about how Dawn came home one day and said that she wanted to be an organ donor. At 17 years old, Dawn had made her wish known. Coral said that after Dawn's accident, she remembered what her daughter had requested. Coral then shared where all of Dawn's organs had gone and saved many, many lives. Coral paused…"and her heart went to a young lady who is here with us tonight," and introduced me to the group. Honestly, there wasn't a dry eye in the building. It's not very often you get to meet your donor family and I knew mine well. I will never forget that evening.

Shaylynn and McKayla with Coral and Remi at the
Second annual 2nd Chance Trail Ride.

We spent that evening talking about Dawn and I learned more about who she was as a person. We already had things in common but I found out she loved Reba McEntire too. In fact, she was Dawn's favourite singer! Life is funny. It was while I was on my wish trip to meet Reba that I got called for my new heart. Incredible.

That weekend was one of the best weekends of my life. I was proud to have Dawn's heart. The medication was stabilizing my heart and while it wasn't functioning at 100 per cent (more like 40 per cent)

I was able to do most things like walk. (I wasn't planning on running anywhere so it was okay.) Dawn made me want to accomplish many more things and live up to her potential. I wanted to finish my degree and finish this book! I wanted to leave a legacy in honour of Dawn. I wanted to make a difference in the world.

I knew my donor family but Shaylynn didn't know hers. I've always wanted to find them and to hold them and thank them for their amazing gift. Remi once told me how important it was to thank the donor family. They need to be acknowledged. I shamefully admitted to him that I hadn't written Shaylynn's donor family. Every time I sat down to do it, I fumbled. What do I say? How could I possibly express how I feel to have my daughter living because their child died?

I think about my donor family every day. It sounds cliché but it's true. My parents have me and my girls because of the Tremblays. It's that simple. I finally found the words for Shaylynn's donor family. I wrote them a letter and put it in a card. You know, I had the hardest time finding out whom to send the letter to. One person would tell me to contact this person and then I would be redirected to someone else. Finally, it was sent to the HOPE program in Edmonton. To this day, I don't know if it was ever sent on to the family. I would think the HOPE program would have let me know my letter reached its destination. I also shared it on Facebook where I'm part of some groups where donor families are looking for the recipients of their loved ones organs. Who knows? Maybe Shaylynn's donor family will read this book.

Mother's Day marked one year of living with a pacemaker. It was a way different year than the one prior. Things were going well health wise and I was getting a break from the cardiology folks. Now instead of being anxious about my well-being, I was getting anxious to hear about university. Every time I went to the post office I was excited and nauseous at the same time. I wanted to get into school so badly and get my degree. I did have a Plan B if university didn't pan out. I was going to take time off and finish my book. I remember reading a quote by Winston Churchill, a former U.K. prime minster: *Success is not final, failure is not fatal: it is the courage to continue that counts.* I probably would have applied to school again in a year.

In June, I had another laser. It sucked. One upside was, while the HPV didn't go away, the discomfort subsided. I could actually live with the warts. It was the constant irritation and pain that drove me crazy. That same month, I was sitting at mom and dad's when I checked my e-mail on my phone. UVic had sent me a message – I was in.

Yes! Woohoo! I did it!

I was ecstatic and couldn't wait for academia. This was something I had wanted for a long time and my dream was coming true at 31. Mom and dad were happy for me and knew I could do it. The girls (almost teenagers) were happy for me too. I got hugs from everyone. Wade never doubted my brains (I married him didn't I?) and we celebrated at a restaurant in Calgary.

UVic had written to say I needed to take two extra courses as some of mine weren't transferable. I had until the end of the year, December 2013, to complete them. (I took one course from Athabasca, Psychology of Women, and one from Thompson Rivers, Human Development.) As soon as I got home from mom and dad's, I collected the documents the school needed to state that I accepted its offer of admission.

About a month later, U of C offered me admission. I was in shock. I was good enough for the U of C too?! Gee. I didn't even have a high school diploma and now I had two universities to choose from. I was overwhelmed. What do I do? But I knew this was a good problem to have.

I had always wanted to attend university in person but provided my health history, I was worried about missing class time and on campus project work. I also worried about my family's financial situation, especially as I would no longer be working. I weighed the pros and cons of each school.

Pro: UVic offered the BSW online.

Pro: I knew a lot of people at the U of C. Plus, I had worked there for almost nine years. But knowing a lot of people at the U of C was also a con. I was nervous about writing papers for people I had known in a work capacity.

Con: The program at UVic was self-directed. Sometimes the biggest learning happens during coffee breaks between classes.

Con: What if I got sick at U of C? Would I be able to take time off to go to doctor and other medical appointments?

Con: Driving to U of C in the winter could be tricky. That brings up another U of C con: What about the costs of gas and parking?

Pro: If I "went" to UVic, I could go to class in my pajamas and have hot coffee always on hand.

Con: UVic only offered three convocation tickets per student. I had more than four guests who wanted to come to my convocation (Wade, the girls and my mom and dad.)

Pro: U of C gave you nine convocation tickets.

I had a lot to think about.

Wade and I took a motorbike ride to Calgary and I thought more about my options. Being on the back of a motorcycle cleared my mind. It had something to do with breathing in the fresh air as we rode along the highway. The only sound I heard was the whirring of the Harley-Davidson engine and I was conscious of the beauty of nature that surrounded us. I wasn't penned in by doors or walls. I was free. A bike ride was the perfect way to focus on making a tough decision.

My first hunch was to go with the U of C so I could meet people in my area and make friends. I never really had the experience of going to school and meeting friends. (I had lost a lot of friends after I got pregnant.) I asked McKayla what to do and she gave me some sage advice.

"Mom, go with who asked you first," she told me.

Her answer was so simple – I listened to her.

I decided to go with UVic because it offered me admission first and because it had a strong anti-oppressive approach. The school values looking at society and cultures and the systems within that are oppressive. It looks at how those systems influence people and groups. The philosophy also teaches how to challenge oppression and stop it. I have felt oppressed and marginalized in my life and it was something I wanted to help others learn how to reach past it.

UVic here I come.

My last day at Healthy Minds/Healthy Children was July 31, 2013. I think my co-workers were going to miss me but mental health and the helping profession is a small world. I might work with them again in a different capacity down the road, when I had my degree. They threw me a farewell party and bought me a nice present: a Willow Tree figurine holding a book.

It was bittersweet saying goodbye to my colleagues and job. I started with the program when it was only a year old. When I first started working there we had 40 people register for courses and by the time I left, we had over 800 people registering in total.

I spent the rest of summer finishing the courses I needed for UVic. My health was stable, there had been no major changes. It was time to relocate to Chestermere and we were trying to sell our house, which wasn't going well. It had been on the market since February 2013 and we had had no offers. The community of Langdon wasn't as popular as other places in the region. There were some downsides like it didn't have a grocery store. (Although one was being built.) I wanted the house off of our hands and to be settled in a new place.

I got to say, it was nice not having a job. I did work though. I worked my butt off hitting the books so I could head to UVic. Neither mom or I had ever been to Victoria and at the end of August, we flew to Vancouver Island for my first week of on campus face-to-face classes. Mom came with me because I was worried that I wouldn't feel good and if something happened, I would be alone.

On the Sunday when we first arrived, we went whale watching. It was cool seeing the whales in their natural habitat. Just beautiful. I was nervous on my first day of class. Mom and I went to campus and we made sure we were there early because the grounds were huge. Mom took a picture of me at UVic in front of the sign that read "Human and Social Development Building." That was the building that I would be in for the next week. I had to pinch myself to make sure I wasn't dreaming.

While I was in class during the day, mom toured Victoria. After I was done, she would meet me at the bus stop and we would go out for supper and do a bit of sightseeing together. I was having some anxiety about my ability to write papers but for the most part, I enjoyed learning and being in British Columbia.

I had been having bad pains in my abdomen for a few months. I sometimes worried it was another ovary twisting. I started to pay attention to the pain and realized it flared when I ate certain greasy foods. After that, I was careful about what I ate. However, in Victoria I had the excruciating abdominal pain every morning around 4:00 a.m. I took Tylenol, which helped some but it didn't totally make the pain go away. There was definitely something wrong but I had other things to worry about. I did think, "Ugh. Why now when I'm trying to focus on school."

My first day of class at the University of Victoria August 2013.

Shaylynn and McKayla started a new school too: Chestermere Lake Middle School. It was so scary but so exciting at the same time. They weren't little kids anymore. They were teenagers.

It was unbelievable how fast time was moving. September had come and gone. It was November 13 and I had been working on a project for my SOCW 311: Understanding Oppression class all day. It was about 2:50 p.m. and I had to take a break and pick up the girls from mom and dad's house. Since we hadn't sold our home yet, the girls walked to my parents' place in Chestermere after school. This week the girls were by themselves for a short time since mom and dad were in Scottsdale for their semi-annual vacation.

That afternoon I jumped into our Yukon Denali and hit the pavement. I typically take the back road, which is Glenmore Trail, to Chestermere. I was travelling westbound on Glenmore, approaching Highway 791 around 3:20 p.m. I got to the intersection of Glenmore and 791 when a vehicle appeared right in front of me. I grabbed onto the steering wheel and slammed on the breaks as hard as I could.

Too late.

I hit the vehicle travelling north on Highway 791.

I knew it was going to happen. I closed my eyes and kept my foot on the breaks. I smashed into the passenger side – between the front passenger and rear passenger area. The impact deployed my air bag and it punched me in the face. Square on the nose. My vehicle came to rest on the road, blocking the west lane. I opened my eyes.

I thought I had broken my nose from the air bag strike. My expensive sunglasses were hanging off my face and I thought they must be broken too. I couldn't see the other vehicle anywhere. I was shaking.

There was dust in the air. Smoke! The Denali might be on fire. I went to get out of my SUV when it started moving. I hopped back in and put it in park. Then I realized the dust was from the air bags busting open, not from flames.

The Denali was badly damaged. The hood of my vehicle was completely crumpled. My side mirrors were completely bent backwards toward the front of my car. Debris of plastic and glass and metal from the vehicles was strewn all over the pavement. I saw some kind of liquid dripping out of my SUV when I climbed out again, frantically looking for the other driver.

I spotted the vehicle nestled in the ditch. The driver, a young man with blood running down his face, got out of his vehicle. I ran up to him and asked if he was okay. He was alive but his car wouldn't be moving. I had hit his vehicle right in the middle of the front and back passenger area: the passenger side was caved in. If the man had had someone sitting beside him, his companion would have been dead or badly injured. The passenger door was touching the driver's seat. All I could think was, "Thank You GOD he didn't have a passenger."

The driver told me he hadn't seen me. He had stopped at the stop sign and proceeded through it. There I was. We were both calm when speaking to each other but I could tell he was as unnerved as I was about the collision. I tried calling Wade several times but I couldn't get a hold of him. He was at a jobsite where they weren't allowed cell phones. I just wanted to hear my husband's voice and cry.

I held back my tears. I was worried about my daughters being alone in Chestermere. They were young and not home alone often for any length of time. (Maybe half an hour at the most.) I didn't want to call them and worry them. I was on the verge of breaking down and wanted someone else, someone who was calm, to tell my daughters I was going to be late. Eventually, I called them. I didn't tell them exactly why I would be late getting them. They were upset with me as they were supposed to go to a girls' group meeting. (They meet in Chestermere to learn about things like self-esteem and applying makeup.) They didn't want to miss it. (They learned the lesson that sometimes life gets in the way of what we want.)

I got a hold of Wade and he was a good two hour drive away. I never thought about calling Billy until after that. Then I was like, "Oh! I'll call my brother to come get me."

Of course he said yes.

Billy took me to Chestermere and we waited there until Wade arrived. Then Billy left and Wade, the girls and I went to get something to eat. I was still really shaken up. When I think back on the collision, I'm relieved I didn't have the girls with me.

My Denali was a write-off but my nose wasn't broken. I did go to physio because my neck was sore. My chest hurt too. I felt like someone had kicked me. (I think that was from the seat belt restraining me in the accident.) I found out later that the other driver had the broken nose. He also had a broken wrist.

The collision scared me. For the longest time after the incident, I had terrible nightmares about it. I'm not sure if the other driver was ever charged. It was his fault but I have no animosity towards him whatsoever. Because he didn't run the stop sign I was able to have a completely different view towards him. He stopped. Didn't see me. Then proceeded. Vehicles have those blind spots. I hope he is doing well. I felt bad for him. He was much younger than me.

I had never been in an accident before. It was a scary thing to go through. It put things into perspective though. My drive had started out like any other drive and then boom! It all happened in an instant. I thought about Dawn and her accident. I thought about Coral and Remi. I didn't want to tell them what had happened because I was worried it would trigger painful memories. An accident changed their entire life course. I thought about me and how hard I had fought to get to where I was now. That could have all changed in a wink of an eye.

We had my SUV, a Kia Borrego, in Edmonton on a car lot because we were hoping to sell it. Since the Denali was a write-off, I would have to go back to driving the Kia. It wouldn't be a problem getting the vehicle though as we were headed to the city on November 18, 2013. Shaylynn was scheduled to have her pacemaker removed. It was a good thing. Her pacemaker was set to only pace if her heart went below a certain number of beats per minute (I think it was set at 60 bpm.) and tests showed she was using it less than one per cent of the time – she wasn't really using it often or if at all. It meant her heart was working great.

It wasn't going to be major surgery and that made Shaylynn happy although she was still nervous about the procedure. (Shaylynn is completely opposite to me as in she doesn't like being put to sleep by general anesthetic. If I'm going to have surgery, I'd like to be out, please.) The doctors at the Stollery Children's hospital (located inside the University of Alberta hospital) were going to remove her entire pacemaker and leave the leads in. She'd have an x-ray down the road to make sure they weren't tangled on anything.

While McKayla stayed at grandma and grandpa's so she didn't miss school, Wade, Shaylynn and I headed to the U of A hospital. Since our daughter was having surgery that required general anesthetic, we had to go to PAC (Pre-admission Clinic) first where we would see the anesthesiologist and a cardiologist. Dr. R, the cardiologist, was taking the lead on Shaylynn's pacemaker removal operation. (Dr. R had been completing her residency at the U of A when I had my heart transplant in 1996.) During our visit to PAC, Shaylynn was told when to stop eating and drinking. We were also given information on what time we had to be at the hospital the next day. Pre-admission Clinic can take anywhere from four to five hours. It really depends on how busy they are: meaning how many children are being seen for upcoming surgeries or getting ready to be taken to the operating room. The purpose was to make sure Shaylynn was healthy enough to have the surgery. The PAC nurses were fantastic and took time to explain to Shaylynn why she was having the surgery. The medical staff was amazing with both kids and parents.

Our PAC appointment was early in the morning, around 9:00 a.m. Everything was checking out good for Shaylynn and we were told to be back at PAC for 10:00 a.m. the next day (Tuesday, November 19). We left the hospital and went to the West Edmonton Mall for lunch and tried to make the day as relaxing and fun as possible for Shaylynn. We even went to the seal show at the mall and Shaylynn got a nice smooch on the cheek from the slippery mammal.

The next day we made our way to the U of A hospital from our Best Western hotel room on the outskirts of Edmonton. Unfortunately, there was a delay getting Shaylynn to the operating room. I guess the cases before her took longer than expected. This sucked because she couldn't eat or drink anything (only a sip of water to help her medication go down) and must have been hungry and thirsty. We tried to help by not eating or drinking either until she went into surgery. (Something my parents were pros at. They must have taught me well!)

The nurse pulled back our curtain and gave us the nod that it was our turn: the operating room was calling for Shaylynn. She already had an IV (Emla numbing cream helped lessen the "ouch" from the needle poke) and was wheeled down on a stretcher by the porter. By this time, Shaylynn had huge crocodile tears running down her face. She was scared and didn't want to go through the surgery. I rode the stretcher with her and Wade walked beside us in an attempt to calm her fears. I shared some of my surgery stories hoping it would help knowing that I had been through some of the same things.

We arrived at the destination. Shaylynn gave Wade a hug. My daughter and I were wheeled through the operating room doors. All my experiences of being in an OR came sweeping into my head: a hundred flashbacks of every time I had been there whether for me or Shaylynn. It honestly didn't matter who it was for, it was hard each time. You would think experience would make it easier. It didn't, at least not for me. What I do know for sure was it was a lot harder to see my daughter go through it than to go through it myself. This definitely gave me an understanding of what my parents had gone through with me.

The surgery team was busily getting everything ready. Shaylynn was transferred from the stretcher to the operating table. The table was tiny, there was pretty much only enough room for her. Our little patient was sobbing and clenching my hand as hard as she could. I reassured her again that everything would be okay. I wiped the tears from her eyes as I whispered in her ear how much I loved her.

The medicine given through Shaylynn's IV started to work as her eyes circled the room quickly, then slowly, than eventually... they closed. She was off to sleep and I was escorted out of the room. The surgery would take only a couple of hours.

I made a point to be in her room when they brought her back from recovery. I remember seeing my parents as soon as I got back on the floor of the hospital and it was reassuring. Shaylynn did well in surgery but she didn't do well with the anesthetic. The first few days she was nauseous. Wade's mom and dad came up to provide support so Wade bunked with them at their hotel room while I stayed at the hospital.

While we were at the U of A, I showed Audrey and Barry around the hospital, my old stomping grounds. I had spent a lot of time there. I also took the time to connect with Judy Dahl. I tried catching up with Dr. Coe but our schedules didn't match. (He's an incredibly busy man!)

Shaylynn was discharged on Friday, November 22. She still has those leads in and is doing fine with no pacemaker.

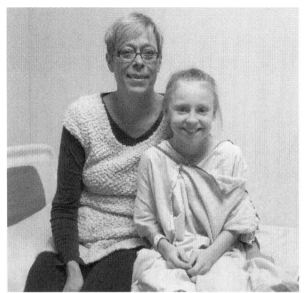

Shaylynn with her pre-admissin nurse.

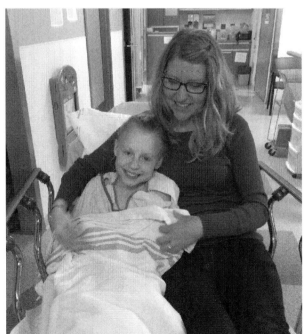

Shaylynn on her way to the OR.

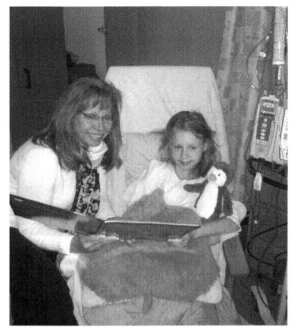

Grandma Thackeray reading to Shaylynn after surgery.

Shaylynn visiting with Judy Dahl after surgery.

Standing in the Cardiology department at the Stollery.
All the pictures behind me are pictures of heart patients.

While we were in Edmonton, we had a showing of our Langdon home. Then we had an offer. Yes! We accepted the offer. It was exciting hanging the red sign with the capital letters SOLD written across it. Once we sold our house, we looked for a place and found a home for us in Chestermere.

Christmas 2013 was hectic. We were organizing going away for the holidays while trying to pack up our house. I don't like having stuff and I'm honestly not one to keep things but packing made me realize how much stuff I had accumulated. We were going to British Columbia to spend Christmas with Wade's family and I didn't want to unpack all our decorations only to pack them back up to move them. That year, all we did was set up our fake tree. (I think we only put lights on it.)

We spent a few days in B.C. and then headed back home as soon as we could to finish packing. We had our entire garage to put into boxes. That Christmas was overshadowed with the moving. My parents and Billy pitched in to help us get our things over to the new place and Wade's mom, dad and uncle came for a couple days too. Leaving Langdon was bittersweet but I knew we'd be better off in Chestermere.

Moving was extremely stressful but we were settled in early January, 2014. I didn't like the new house at first. I hated it. This was also the start of a new semester for me and while writing papers in the office during the cold months of winter, I heard a dripping noise. It was water torture. (I think it was the air ducts compressing.) The noise remains to this day and I don't notice it anymore.

I may have hated this house for a few months but I eventually came to love it. I love the character and I love how all our pictures fit perfectly on the walls. It's our home.

CHAPTER THIRTY SEVEN

Because of Her

Remember those pains I was having when I first started classes at UVic? A year later, I found out what was happening with me. The excruciating cramps were caused by gallstones (solid material formed in the gallbladder) blocking my gallbladder. Certain foods do bring on gallstone attacks so it was no wonder that when I ate spicy, greasy foods, I was in pain. However, the attacks eventually came all the time and it didn't matter what I ate. I had to cut ties with my gallbladder.

On March 5, 2014, I said goodbye to it and the gallstones. I wanted to keep one of the stones but the doctor said I couldn't. I was pretty sore for a week after the procedure and then I had these horrible phantom pains. My body was so used to the gallbladder attacks that I had cramps for a few days after the surgery.

When I had the gallbladder surgery, we had to switch me back to tacrolimus as sirolimus would stop my incision from healing properly. This time when we changed medications, the doctors made sure it was bridged properly. We didn't want to have to go through the same issue as last time – rejection. After being on tacrolimus for a while I realized how much of a difference sirolimus made on my HPV. The itching from the warts was barely noticeable when I was on sirolimus: nothing like what it was on tacrolimus – constantly annoying. Thankfully, about a month after my surgery I was able to switch back to sirolimus. We made sure we bridged the switch and I had blood work done frequently (weekly compared to my usual monthly) to make sure my sirolimus levels were good.

In May of 2014, the blood clot in my heart dissolved. After being on Coumadin for years, it kicked in and kicked the clot out. The only thing to remind me that I had once had it was the fact I was still taking the drug and going for blood work every couple of weeks to check the Coumadin levels. Considering my clot was gone, I told the cardiology doctors that they should stop my Coumadin altogether. They said they would think about it.

The problem with being on Coumadin was that I couldn't participate in certain activities like waterskiing and snowboarding because I was at an increased risk for bleeding and bruising. (If I ever fell, I could be facing internal bleeding or even death.) My life had been somewhat restricted for the three years I had been on Coumadin and if the blood clot was gone, why did I need to take the drug? We already knew the clot had been caused by the minor heart attack. What would be the chances that would happen again? Pretty low.

That same month, we saddled up and attended our second 2nd Second Chance Trail Ride. My parents came with us and we all rode in Coral and Remi's wagon just like we had the year before. It was another amazing weekend with my donor family. We talked about Dawn a lot. It was important to know what she liked and how she had lived her life. I was learning more about her and becoming more and more comfortable with her family.

I started my first social work practicum in May and finished at the end of July. My work experience was at a long-term care centre in Calgary and I learned a lot during those months. It was the first time I learned about the Green Sleeve. The Green Sleeve is Alberta Health Services way of keeping track of advance care planning documents such as your personal directives (you name an agent to make personal decisions for you, including health care, but not financial decisions. Financial decisions are done with a power of attorney) and goals of care (which used to be known as DNR - do not resuscitate). I learned about goals of care, personal directives and power of attorney. I met interesting people at my practicum and my learning experience broadened my knowledge of senior care in Alberta. While I completed my practicum, I also completed two courses. I wanted to be done school in the summer of 2015. University had been dragging on and I needed it to be finished so I could move on to finishing this book.

Meanwhile, I continued to advocate stopping Coumadin to my doctors. In early June, cardiology agreed. I was able to be active again and skim over the lakes on my water ski, something I hadn't done since the summer of 2011.

It was the long weekend in August by the time I got back on the water. We went camping in B.C. with some friends at Moyie Lake Provincial Park. Our friends brought their boat and I brought my water ski. This was going to be the weekend!

I was changing in our family trailer and I found myself shaking when I tugged my body into my wetsuit. To say I was a little nervous was an understatement. I was scared but I was ready for the challenge. I couldn't wait to feel the wind blowing in my hair and be splashed in the face by fresh Moyie Lake water.

I made my way to where our friends were waiting for me on the beach. I was partly walking and partly jogging with my lifejacket on, my water ski (I slalom ski so I use one ski) under my right arm and the sun beating down on me – a perfect day. My black ski gloves were making my hands sweat but I didn't care. As I hurried down the beach, perspiration beaded down my back. I walked into the cool water and it was refreshing. My hands were no longer sweating as I trudged deeper into the lake, floating my ski along with me. I was now waist-deep in the water and it felt good to be cooled off.

Wade got in the lake along with me. He was as nervous as I was. He knew I hadn't waterskied for a while but I think he was more concerned about my heart. He had noticed me shaking and could tell I was anxious. He gave me a playful hug and reassured me that I didn't have to go.

"I know," I said. "I want to ski."

"I know you do," he replied with a smile. "I'm proud of you."

Our friend interrupted our playful banter to tell us that the rope had been sucked into the boat's pump. My day to prove that I could still waterski came to a screeching halt (or a tangled mess). The boat wasn't going anywhere and had to be put on the boat trailer and hauled up to the campsite so the rope could be retrieved.

It was a crappy situation, really crappy. I was left standing in the waist deep water in my wetsuit. By now, I had unzipped it and popped my arms out of the sleeves so the top was hanging limply. The water that had been refreshing seconds earlier was becoming cold. I stared down at my ski, bobbing beside me, and felt sad. I had wanted to do this so badly. I had been nervous but that wasn't unusual, I was nervous every time I skied. Right now, I had no feelings of anxiety and I was ready to go. That was unusual. There wouldn't be any chance for me to ski that weekend. We continued on our camping trip but I was bummed about what didn't happen.

I always say to you, it's funny how things work out – or how things don't work out but then you find out that was probably for the best. We spent the week camping in our trailer and travelled back home as I had an echo scheduled. I wasn't feeling any differently about this echo. It would be like the rest of the recent tests: no news to report.

My appointment was on August 18, 2014. I arrived at the Calgary clinic where I typically have my echo's completed. In my mind it was going to be "echo as usual" so I didn't bring mom or Wade with me. Wade said he would come along but I told him there was no need for him to miss work. (Mom offered as well but I declined her offer too.)

The usual appointment exchange happened. I gave the lady at the desk my Alberta Health Care card and confirmed my information. She politely told me to have a seat and wait for my name to be called. I didn't even have enough time to skim one of the magazines on the table when I heard my name.

I was ushered into a room with a stretcher and handed a gown. I was told to take everything off from the waist up and put the gown on with the opening facing the front. All standard procedure. After the lady left, I did what I was told. I neatly plunked all my belongings (shirt, bra and purse) in the corner. I set my glasses on top of my shirt and then kicked off my shoes and plopped on the stretcher. The lady knocked and I told her I was ready. She came in and quickly checked my vitals: temperature, blood pressure and weight. She confirmed the spelling of my first and last names and entered all the data into the echo machine. She then said the echo technician would be with me shortly.

I lay on the bed as I had done many, many times before. The technologist entered the room and prepared for the echo. He settled into his chair and gave me orders on how to position my body for the best pictures of my heart. He grabbed a tube of gel and squeezed a big gob of it on my chest area. The gel was warm, which was actually comforting as I was chilled in the room. (They keep the temperature low so the echo machine doesn't overheat.) The technician pressed down firmly on my chest with the ultrasound wand and started the process of taking heart images. Business as usual.

The technologist was asking me a lot of questions about blood clots. I shared the details of the previous clot and that I had been on Coumadin but was now off it. His inquiries were annoying me. Why bring this stuff up?

"I need to have the doctor come in and review the images," the technician said and he handed me a towel to cover my exposed breasts.

"Ah, sure," I replied. I didn't know if I should be worried or if this was protocol to make sure the pictures were fine. (It had happened before.) I wished it had been the latter scenario.

The doctor came in and proceeded to scan my chest. He also probed me for information about my former blood clot. I told the physician about it and as I talked, I craned my neck to see the screen of the echo machine. I saw my heart, something I had seen many times, but I also saw something else, something that was not supposed to still be there.

Little did I know that the doctor had been asking me about my previous blood clot as he was measuring my new blood clot that had formed in the exact same place as the last one. I knew what a blood clot looked like (cardiology had showed me before) and there it was, on the left ventricle, a round dark clump – a new blood clot.

My eyes began to burn. I really wanted to cry but I wouldn't do it here. Not while I was lying on the stretcher getting an echo. I would hold in the hurt until I was in my own private space. I couldn't believe I had another blot clot. Another one.

The tech and doctor were done and I was free to go. After everyone exited the room, I sat up in disbelief. I hurriedly dried my chest with a towel and quickly got dressed. As I readied myself to walk out the door of the echo room, I was becoming angry. I was mad at the world. I was pissed off. At the same time, I was trying my best not to break down. I knew I just needed to make it to my vehicle. It was going to be tough since I now couldn't breathe. I needed fresh air immediately.

I opened the door and rushed off without making eye contact with anyone in the waiting room. I made my way to another door that brought me to the hallway. I then proceeded to the stairs and when I reached them, I ran down them as fast as I could. The world was closing in on me. The sky was collapsing on my head and the ground was swallowing my feet. I felt claustrophobic. I felt like I was drowning. I reached the last step and sprinted to the door that led outside. I swung it wide open.

The blue sky looked as blue as before I went into the echo. Nothing had changed here. Nothing had changed outside. Everything inside me had changed. I got in my vehicle and switched from my eyeglasses to sunglass. As I was doing this, the tears burst out. I couldn't hold the tide back anymore. These weren't only tears of despair, they were tears of anger. I was mad. I had a blood clot again and I knew what it meant. It meant I would be back on Coumadin. I would be back to not waterskiing or snowboarding. I would be back to a life of restriction.

I called Wade and told him the news. He was upset and wished he would have come with me to my appointment. I called mom. She was upset too. The clot would need to be confirmed with cardiology but I was certain about what my eyes had seen. The blood clot was confirmed Thursday, August 28 at my cardiology clinic visit. I was put back on Coumadin. The doctor told me my left ventricle was damaged from rejection and I would need to be on blood thinners for the rest of my life. The blood clot has never completely gone away.

I thought about the day I was supposed to waterski. What if I had gone out on the lake? Would my heart have been able to handle the physical activity, especially with the blood clot? Now I knew there had been a reason why the boat sucked up that rope. I didn't know if it was God or Dawn who made it happen but I definitely had a loud cheering section looking out for me.

***

Later that summer, I received a call from Jennifer, my former U of A physiotherapist in Edmonton. She asked if my family was willing to go on a once in a lifetime train trip on the Rocky Mountaineer (a company that takes people through the Rocky Mountains on trains).

The Rocky Mountaineer had begun a "train ride for heroes" in 2013 for wounded war veterans and their families. This year, the trip was extended to organ donor families and recipients. Jennifer also wondered if my donor family would be willing to come along on the journey in September. It sounded like an awesome adventure and I said yes.

I called Coral and Remi and asked if they wanted to go. They were never ones for the spotlight and I wasn't sure if they would be up for it as the media would be following us during the trip. Dawn's parents thought about it and then called me back a few days later. They agreed to go with us. I was so happy and looking forward to spending more time with them and getting to know them better.

Wade, the girls and I flew to Vancouver on September 14, 2014 and spent an entire day in the city along with Coral and Remi. Then we boarded the Rocky Mountaineer train on September 16. There were 13 families onboard from Canada, Australia, United States and United Kingdom. We rode the train to Kamloops where there was a welcome party for us with champagne and hor d'oeuvres. We spent one night in a hotel there and then headed on the rails to Lake Louise where we spent the day. We ate our meals on the train and any drinks and food we had was covered.

I cannot begin to tell you how amazing the trip was. Oh my gosh, the mountain views were spectacular, but most of the time I was so absorbed with talking to Coral and Remi and other families that I didn't look out the window that much. We talked about Dawn often and some of our train travel coincided with where Dawn had been as a child. Coral and Remi went on a family trip to Lake Louise with their kids when they were young and our Rocky Mountaineer train had the last stop in Lake Louise.

I talked to Dawn's parents about why they hadn't come to my wedding. They shared how hard it would have been but also, they didn't want to take any of that day away from me. I told Coral that I had wanted to ask Heather to be my maid of honour as she never got to stand up for Dawn and so in a small way, she would be standing up for her at my ceremony. Then I said that I had wanted Remi to walk me down the aisle along with my dad. After they had declined my invitation, I didn't want to push it. I think they were shocked but grateful when I told them about this on the train ride.

Shaylynn and I were interviewed by the media but we weren't the only ones with transformational stories. Elaine Yong, her husband Aaron McArthur and their daughter Addison live in British Columbia and shared their transplant journey with us. Addison was three weeks old when she suffered from heart failure. She received a heart transplant after only two days on the wait list. Addison's heart was donated by a mother in Reno, Nevada.

Elaine and Aaron are both broadcast journalists and spend a lot of time advocating for organ donation. They created the Addison Fund to raise money for research and to ensure their daughter and other organ recipients live long and healthy lives after transplant.

Brian and Margaret Benson are also from British Columbia. Margaret had a double lung transplant about 17 years ago. Margaret is very involved in organ and tissue donation and competed in both the National and World Transplant Games. She spends a lot of time reaching out to people and showcasing the importance of talking to your family about organ and tissue donation. Margaret is on the board of directors for the Canadian Transplant Association as the provincial director for British Columbia.

We met parents Heather, Terry and their daughter Emily Talbot from Ontario. On March 8, 2009, Heather and Terry's son Jonathon was in a tragic car accident. After the collision, he was put on life support. Emily told her parents about a conversation she had with her brother regarding organ donation and it was something he had wanted to do if the circumstance arose. Knowing this helped Heather and Terry make the decision to donate their son's organs and Jonathon saved four lives on the Ontario transplant waiting list. The Talbot family was selected as the feature story for the Rocky Mountaineer Train for Heroes and continue to advocate for organ and tissue donation.

Australian Max Mohr received a liver transplant. After the transplant he battled depression but sought counselling and exercise to help him get his life back. He's a personal trainer and helps people, specifically individuals with mental and physical challenges, get their health back. Max is very much involved in Transplant Australia. During our trip, Shaylynn presented him with an honorary medal from the Canadian Transplant Association. The medal was one she had won competing at the Transplant Games in Calgary. We were asked to bring something to share with the other individuals on the train and Shaylynn wanted to give her medal to Max. We gave away a couple of pins too. Other people brought pins from their country or from their organ donation program.

We met American Chris Klug who was diagnosed with a terminal liver condition and required a liver transplant. He received his liver six years after his diagnosis and went on to win the Bronze medal at the 2002 Olympic Winter Games in Salt Lake City, Utah. His experiences inspired him to start the Chris Klug Foundation, an organization dedicated to promoting organ and tissue donation and providing resources for recipients.

Jackson Beattie, from Superior, Wisconsin, was three years old when he was on the Train Ride for Heroes. His cousin, Brett, was 22 years old. They share a bond far deeper than just being blood relatives. Jackson was born with a condition that affected the development of his kidneys and he required a transplant shortly after his first birthday. Brett, a college student, was Jackson's only hope to live without dialysis. Brett agreed to the procedure immediately. The Beattie family continues to advocate for organ and tissue donation by sharing their experiences and encouraging organ donation.

Scott Rutherford, from the United Kingdom, was now an adult in his 20's but he had his first surgery only hours after he was born. During his childhood, he went through multiple procedures and then a heart transplant at the age of 16. His experiences inspired him to spread the word about organ donation. While at one of his speaking events, Scott's donor mother, Freda Carter, happened to be in the audience. Freda knew Scott was the recipient of her son John's heart.

John Carter passed away within four weeks after being diagnosed with a brain tumor. John never spoke to his family about organ donation but after much discussion, they decided to donate his organs as that was what John would have done. His parents, Freda and John, and sister Julia believe it was the best decision that they have ever made. Scott Rutherford received John's heart and it was by chance at that event, that Freda would feel her son's heart beating for the first time in five years. We met Freda and Julia Carter.

Scotland's Marc McCay was suddenly fighting for his life just two weeks before his 16 birthday. His heart was failing and he needed a new heart. Within two days, the McCay family received a call that a 16 year old boy's heart was available.

Martin Burton was a healthy 16 year old when he suffered a massive brain hemorrhage and died. (The Burton family eventually learned that Martin had a rare condition that made him vulnerable to brain hemorrhaging.) Sue, Martin's mother, felt organ donation was the right thing to do. It was the only positive that came out of this tragic situation. Martin's heart, liver, kidneys, lungs and corneas were donated. Marc McCay received Martin's heart. Marc and Linda, his mother, met Nigel and Sue, Martin's mom and dad, for the first time on the train ride.

We had all come together to showcase how life giving organ and tissue donation can be. On Thursday, September 18 at 8:00 a.m. there was a Remembrance event on the shores of Lake Louise. We honoured those who were not with us on our journey. It was a poignant moment. Each person tossed a stone into the water and the ripples signified how the actions of organ donation can cause a huge impact on many lives: not only recipients. It was touching and many tears were cried that morning.

For me, the most memorable moment of the entire trip was when Remi and Coral felt their daughter's heart beat for the first time in 18 years. By now, we had spent some great quality time with Dawn's parents. We had toured parts of Vancouver together on Sunday when we first arrived in the city and Wade and I talked about how we felt like we were safe because it was like Coral and Remi were our parents and would protect us. The girls liked being around Dawn's parents who were almost another set of grandparents. On the train, I had been talking about Dawn and sharing things with her parents that I hadn't shared before like my wedding vision of Remi walking me down the aisle. Then Coral asked if she could put her hand on my chest and feel Dawn's heart.

It just came up. Out of the blue. I would have done anything to give her a stethoscope right then and there so she could listen to Dawn's heart. I was beyond words and couldn't express exactly what I was feeling at that moment. It was hard to keep the tears in. We couldn't. Me, Wade, Coral, Remi and the girls were all crying.

We associate so much of our life with our hearts: love, feelings, etc. The heart is actually the most recognizable shape in the world and I know our hearts as organs look nothing like the shape of a heart but everything we do, we associate it with our hearts. When Coral and Remi felt their daughter's heart beating in my chest for the first time in 18 years, it was like time stood still. It was like there was no one else on the train except us. It was an incredibly personal experience. The only thing I regret is not asking Coral and Remi sooner if they wanted to listen to Dawn's heart. I can only imagine that feeling her heart beating was like touching an angel's wing. It was probably the most beautiful thing to feel in the entire world (these are my words not theirs) but when Coral and Remi laid their hands on my chest and my heart (Dawn's heart), it beat perfectly in rhythm. It was beautiful.

Remi feels Dawn's heartbeat for the first time in 18 years.

Coral feels Dawn's heartbeat for the first time in 18 years.

Spending time with Coral and Remi at Lake Louise, Alberta.

McKayla and Shaylynn on the Rocky Mountaineer Train.

When we boarded the train in September 2014, I was in my third full semester of courses at UVic. I was halfway to my BSW degree. It had been one year since I had been on campus in Victoria. I couldn't believe how fast time was moving. I took some of my books on the train with me, thinking that if I had any downtime I could work. I did do a bit of studying, enough to make sure I wouldn't fall behind.

***

The first Christmas in our new house was fun. Wade's mom and dad came for the holidays as did my parents, Billy and my maternal grandma. It was low key and we ate and watched movies and played games together as a family. I relaxed because January was going to be a busy time for me school-wise.

My last semester of school began when the calendar changed over to 2015. I was doing my final practicum plus one course. My work experience was at a rural domestic violence centre that provided short-term shelter for men, women and children affected by abuse. This practicum experience was powerful: crisis is a different specialization for sure. I gained a lot of valuable information while working at the Shelter. (Once my practicum was completed in March 2015 I was hired on as casual staff.)

At the end of May 2015, we made plans to meet Coral and Remi for lunch in Camrose, Alberta. (Camrose was the halfway point between their house and our house.) I had mentioned to them last summer that I wanted to wear something of Dawn's while I crossed the stage at my convocation. During this visit, Coral and Remi gave me Dawn's pride ring (a ring set with birthstones.) They had given Dawn the ring on her 18 birthday and it had her birthstone in the middle with Coral and Remi's on the outside. They told me I could borrow it for my graduation. I was grateful for having something so special to symbolize Dawn.

I had something permanent that symbolized my organ donor. I showed Coral and Remi my new tattoo that I had inked on May 19, 2015. I knew for a long time (at least 12 years) that I wanted to get a tattoo. (In the past, people with tattoos couldn't donate organs but this has changed. They're allowed now.) Previously, I wanted to get a red heart with a green ribbon (green ribbons signify organ donation) wrapped around the heart. At the end of the ribbon strings, there would be an M for McKayla and an S for Shaylynn. In the middle of the ribbon, there would be a D for Dawn. I had wanted to place the tattoo on the left side of my chest, just above my left breast. When I started thinking about it more seriously, I wanted a tattoo that I could look at every morning and it would remind me to keep going. Something that was personal. Something that no one else would have. Something that was meaningful.

I knew I wanted to incorporate Dawn somehow. I had thought about getting the heart and ribbon on my leg, maybe my ankle, and I went to see my tattoo artist, Jenn, in Chestermere at Obsidian Rose Tattoo. I told her about my plans for the heart and ribbon. After that initial visit, I realized I wanted the tattoo on my wrist. I have always wanted to get a small heart inked on my wrist but then I changed my mind. I would save that idea for another time. My first tattoo needed to be powerful and say a lot with one glance.

I searched Pinterest and realized what I wanted. After all I had been through with the rejection and HPV and pregnancy – one thing always remained the same – I had Dawn's heart alive and well beating inside me.

I was going to get my ECG readout. There are times when my ECG is perfect. Those are the best days. There are times when my ECG is less than perfect and those are bad days. I wanted to be able to look at my tattoo and remember to be hopeful and stay positive through the bad days and remember this is all for Dawn and because of Dawn. When I'm having a good day, I want to look down on the tattoo and smile and feel humbled because good days are possible because of her.

My tattoo is copied from my ECG taken on May 7, 2015. The ECG is perfect: in perfect rhythm. The tattoo also contains a heart, Dawn's name and the date May 26, 1996: the day I got Dawn's heart and her birthday.

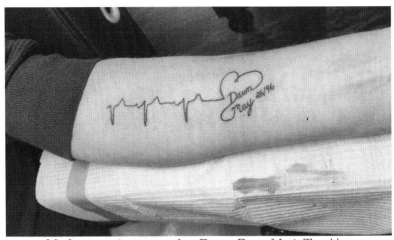

My first tattoo in memory of my Donor: Dawn Marie Tremblay.

About a week after the visit with Dawn's parents, Remi called and told me that Coral had been rushed to the hospital. After several tests it turned out that Coral needed a valve replaced in her heart. We took some time and went to Edmonton to visit her. While there, we were able to see Heather too, who had come to see her mom.

I prayed for Coral and Remi. Seeing Coral in the hospital was very hard. It was like seeing my own mom in the hospital because Coral and Remi feel like parents to me. There's a love there that's unconditional. Coral received her valve replacement and is doing fine. Now we have matching scars.

On June 11, 2015, I finally crossed the University of Victoria stage and received my Bachelor of Social Work degree. Wade, McKayla, Shaylynn, mom and dad were in the audience. The dream I had begun 10 years ago had come true. None of this would have been possible without Dawn. I wore her pride ring with more pride than I can begin to tell you. I realized all dreams are possible if you put your mind to it and work hard. I wanted my girls to know they could achieve anything they want. I was proof that things can be stacked up against you but if you want, you can move mountains and succeed. I did it because I was really stubborn and I wanted to prove that there was nothing I couldn't do. That thinking evolved into showing my daughters that life is worth living to the fullest. I have a mighty drive to succeed and it comes from my heart, Dawn's heart.

Graduation day with my mom, dad, Wade, Shaylynn and McKayla.

EPILOGUE

Now here I am, March 23, 2016. There are still ongoing doctor appointments and medical tests. Every now and then I have health hiccups or Shaylynn isn't feeling well. Life is busy and constantly moving forward. I know this is cliché but I say this because it's the truth – there seriously is not a day that goes by that I don't think about Dawn. I once told Coral and Remi that it's my hope that I can improve the world at least half as much as Dawn would have. I try every day.

And as I type this last chapter in my book, I hope you have enjoyed what you've read. I also hope that you have taken moments along the way to contemplate organ donation. Perhaps, after you turn the last page, you may even find that organ donation is worth discussing with your family. Everybody in my family knows my wishes: organ and tissue donation first and if that isn't an option, then I want to donate my body to science. If I can't save someone by donating my organs, maybe I can help with research. Every little bit helps.

My life today is possible because of my donor family. I'm working as a community resource coordinator for a non-for-profit organization that provides housing for low-income seniors in Calgary. I love working with seniors although I don't know if this will be my forever job. I really do want to work with donor families somewhere down the road.

The girls are in Grade Eight. They're full-blown healthy teenagers. I am so proud of them every day. I cannot believe how big they are. They truly amaze me.

Well, it's off to bed. It's getting late and that 7:00 a.m. med time comes pretty early.

Coral: Dawn's mom

My name is Coral Tremblay and I'm a donor mom. In 1996, we lost our daughter in a car accident and her organs were donated. This is our family's account of what happened during that time.

For many years, we sat back and kept our story to ourselves. The reason for this was because our experience was not a good one, to say the least. However, we don't want to deter anyone who is considering becoming a donor.

Organ donation is a very worthwhile cause but numbers are down. Even after all the years of promotion and spreading the word. Our experience gives us a firsthand look at what might be part of the problem. We'd like to tell you our story.

Looking Back on the Memory (Garth Brooks lyric)

Our daughter, Dawn Marie Tremblay, was born May 26, 1973 in Edmonton, where we lived at the time. She was the eldest of two girls. Her sister, Heather, is three years younger. They were typical sisters growing up; telling secrets one minute, fighting the next. One time in particular, my husband Remi and I, came home to find them chasing each other down the hallway. Each of them with a squeeze bottle of mustard in hand and the evidence of what had gone on, running down the wall and splattered on the carpet.

Dawn loved sports and was competitive. Whether it was softball, volleyball, hockey or swimming, she gave it her all. When some teenage boys at the St. Paul swimming pool (where she was a lifeguard) challenged her to a five lap race, the result wasn't even close. She had outdistanced them by a full lap. At home in the water, she had a unique ability to make little kids comfortable in the pool. This was something the parents appreciated. They would try to make sure their kids were put in her swimming class. But Dawn wasn't only athletic, she enjoyed music too and like most of us, she didn't always get the words right.

When she was a young girl, about five, she liked to sing *Delta Dawn*, a song best known as a 1972 country hit. I guess she liked it because it had her name in it. Instead of the lyric: *walks downtown with a suitcase in her hand, Looking for a mysterious dark haired man...*

Dawn's words went like this:

She walked downtown with a suitcase in her hand, Looking for a sterious dog haired man

Another lyric in the song: *To take you to his mansion in the sky,* became: *To take you to his match up in the sky.*

Later in Dawn's story, I'll go into greater detail about how music and songs have come to show me that she's still with us in spirit.

***

"Come on, we gotta go. We're gonna be late!"

Those were the last words she spoke to Brad, her fiancé, on May 20, 1996 as they left his parents' house at Rocky Mountain House on their way to a ball game. In hindsight, I guess she had an appointment to keep. Shortly after that, Dawn and Brad were T-boned by a vehicle that went through a stop sign. Their friends arrived on scene soon after.

Back at our home in Elk Point we were getting ready to brand cattle. The neighbours were coming and the chicken was in the oven. Then the phone rang.

Our world was never the same again.

The call was from Brad's dad, whom we had only met once before. He had the unenviable job of telling me that our kids had been in an accident. Brad had face and head trauma and the doctors were having trouble stabilizing Dawn. They would be airlifting her to

Edmonton's University of Alberta Hospital from the Rimbey Hospital and Care Centre, as soon as possible.

I dropped to my knees and Remi heard my scream of anguish from outside. When he came in the house, I could hardly get the terrible words that I had just heard, out of my mouth. We were both in disbelief that something this terrible could have happened to our daughter. Through tears of fear, we tried to collect our thoughts as to what we must do next.

Heather had just left for work. We called her co-workers and told them to send her home when she arrived: there had been a family emergency. We didn't want to tell her what had happened over the phone.

As soon as she got home, the three of us headed for Edmonton. Remi was frantically calling the hospital on his cell phone to get more information. But nobody had any answers. We had no way of knowing how severe Dawn and Brad's injuries were and we prayed the couple would be all right.

When we arrived at the hospital, Dawn was not there yet. The staff put all of our family including aunts and uncles who had met us at the hospital, in a private waiting room. Prior to letting us see Dawn, a nurse came in and told us that Dawn was in critical condition and she was in a coma. For the first of several times that week, I went into shock. My body went limp and I stared into space, unable to respond yet hearing what was being said. My brain could not or would not absorb what we were being told.

When we were finally allowed to see Dawn several hours later, she had a breathing tube, her head was bandaged and her eyes were already bruised from the severe trauma to her head. She had other injuries but this, of course, was the most serious.

Later that evening, we had a conference with the doctor. He told us that IF she woke up from the coma, she would probably have brain damage. That was IF she made it through the night. From that point on, we walked around in a daze.

At the hospital that same day, we met a family whose loved one had suffered an aneurism and was on life support. His sister told us that everyone was saying their goodbyes to the young man and they were just waiting for another doctor to see him. I never thought that, too soon, we would be at that same destination. Later on, as I relived all that happened that week, this conversation would come back to me as another piece of the puzzle on how things were actually supposed to happen in an instance like this.

Day by Day

In her school years and as a young adult, Dawn's life had been filled with many friendships. She was known as someone you could confide in because of her kind heart. This was attested by all those who stood vigil at the hospital after the accident. There were so many family members and friends that if some of the medical staff had had their way, they would have been asked to leave. But instead, other staff brought us blankets and pillows. A nurse brought us a piece of paper to make a list of anyone who would be allowed into ICU to see Dawn. Well, I filled the first page and continued to fill page two. How could we leave anyone out who was there with us?

The following day, Brad signed himself out of the Rimbey hospital. He still required medical attention for lacerations from embedded glass and a concussion but he had to be near Dawn. Her doctor treated Brad as an outpatient as he lay on a stretcher outside ICU.

Dawn tried extremely hard to come back to us. Several times, when it seemed like all hope was lost, there would be another reflex response from her. One time, when a doctor was in the middle of telling us that nothing more could be done, her nurse came running out and said, "Wait, wait! She responded to a different drug!" It was a roller coaster ride of emotions with high highs and low lows.

During those five days in the hospital, every one of our family and friends took turns sitting with Dawn, talking to her, encouraging her to wake up. We only left to go to Remi's sister's to shower. Then we headed right back to the hospital.

About midweek, I was sitting with Dawn and I could see the drainage tube coming from her head. Then I saw small pieces of something coming down the tube. I asked the nurse what it was.

"Gray matter," was her response.

At that moment, I knew that if Dawn lived, she would have more problems than we could ever imagine. Still, I wanted to climb onto her bed and hold her like an injured child. All the while, begging her to stay with us.

I pulled Remi aside to have a conversation that was gut-wrenching. I told him that this may be something he might not want to hear but we had to talk about the possibility of donating her organs. I'm sure he had already thought about it but couldn't bear to discuss it. We had too. I was trying to prepare for the worst. None of the doctors had spoken to us about organ donation yet but my husband and I agreed about donating Dawn's organs. However, we prayed for a miracle.

It was roughly about this time that we first heard of the Plotsky family. The *Edmonton Journal* was covering Kristy's need for a new heart. Her mother, Margo, was trying valiantly to have her daughter double listed so Kristy would have a greater chance of finding a new heart. Sadly, she was coming up against many brick walls of bureaucracy and red tape. At the same time, the story of Brad and Dawn's accident was also in the news. The driver who hit them had charges of dangerous driving coming. Neither my family nor the Plotsky family knew our paths would soon cross in the bittersweet aftermath.

Permission and Consent

Over the years, many people have asked us how we made the decision to donate Dawn's organs while we were going through such turmoil. The answer was and still is: she made it for us.

When our girls were in high school, there must have been a speaker who came to the school one day. When our daughters came home, they both said, "If something happens to me, I want you to donate my organs."

Of course, as a parent, you put that thought out of your mind. It's not something you ever want to contemplate dealing with. But we did. That's why I say to all of you, have the organ donation conversation with your family. Let them know your wishes. I can't tell you the burden that was lifted from our shoulders at a time when we could barely put one foot in front of another, let alone make a decision of that magnitude.

Unfortunately, our tragic story does not end there. Thursday evening we were visited by a hospital pastor who happened to be on call that night. He was the first person who asked us if we would consider organ donation. We could tell he was very uncomfortable, hesitant and not very knowledgeable about the process. We do not blame this man. He was recruited to do a job that really wasn't his responsibility to carry out. He got off easy since we had already made our decision. You could see the relief in his face and in his body language. And that was it...

Nothing was explained to us about the process, the timeline or anything. Nothing! Nobody from the HOPE Program (Human Organ Procurement and Exchange Program) contacted us at any time while we were at the hospital. Remember, there was always someone from our family in the waiting room or with Dawn.

Before the accident, it was evident that Dawn and Brad would eventually get married. His plan was to propose on his birthday in August, when she would least expect it. When we knew her time of passing was drawing near, he asked permission and put a ring on her finger, to symbolize what would have been.

I then gave Dawn permission to leave us. I let her know it was all right to go, if that was what she had to do. That image of me saying goodbye still breaks my heart.

Brad is a wonderful man, who made our daughter very happy. He was by her side until the very end. His family should be extremely proud of him. I know we are. Brad has gone on to marry a lovely woman and they have two beautiful children. As we have told him many times, he is never far from our thoughts and he is always in our hearts.

Slap in the Face

Friday night, May 24, as we sat in the family room, the ICU brain injury unit charge nurse came in. I still have a hard time talking about this because of how we were treated: poorly. Without emotion or compassion, the nurse told us Dawn had been declared brain dead and we might as well go and say our goodbyes and go home. At this point, all I wanted to do was be with Dawn. As I quickly got up from my chair and headed towards the door, the nurse put her arms straight out and grabbed my shoulders to hold me back from leaving the room. That was when everyone's emotions boiled over. We were angry at her insensitivity. When we asked, "Where is the doctor? Why isn't he here telling us this?" The nurse's response was, "He's too busy."

What a slap in the face.

We understand that a charge nurse in the ICU brain injury unit is under a lot of pressure but that does not excuse her behaviour. At the opposite end of the scale, Dawn's individual nurses cared for her as if she was their own. Many times, these women went above and beyond the call of duty. For that, we cannot thank them enough. The charge nurse's actions hurt us when we were already in agony. Now you might think that we were just emotional parents but as you will soon see, we had every right to be upset.

How do you enter a room, knowing that this will be the last time you will see your child alive? I don't have an answer for that but somehow we did it. We were on autopilot as we stood around her bed and prayed. Everyone took turns kissing Dawn and trying, somehow, to imprint what she looked like in our minds. To remember and see the shape of her hands, the colour and feel of her hair because it was those memories that were all we had to hold on to.

We left the room. We left the hospital. We left our daughter behind in the hands of strangers. The next morning, we left Edmonton and headed home to start the next unbelievable task of making funeral arrangements. We were just going through the motions as visitors came and went.

I will apologize in advance for what I'm about to say because I know it will be hard for some of you to hear. This is the timeline of what happened next.

As I said, Saturday morning we came home from Edmonton, thinking our daughter had died the night before. On Sunday, we started making funeral arrangements. We thought what had to be done in the hospital in Edmonton, was being done. The next day, we received a call from the funeral home telling us the hospital hadn't released her body yet. We had to delay her service and Remi called the hospital to find out what was happening. They wouldn't put us in touch with anyone who knew something.

'We'll call you back," was the response.

There was no return call.

Remi called the hospital again. He was told, rather nonchalantly, "Oh, she's still here!" We were floored. They didn't know and wouldn't tell us or the funeral home when Dawn's body would be released. The service had to be delayed again. Only when Remi said he would be there in an hour and a half to pick her up, did things start to happen.

We had been told that Dawn would be treated with the utmost dignity and respect but how could we believe that when we weren't shown any courtesy. Remi thought, "What the hell did we sign our baby girl up for?" It made him want to throw up.

We had told our family and friends that her time of death was Friday night but it was the funeral home that let us know that it was actually 7:40 on Saturday morning. It was the day before her 23 birthday. After already telling everyone she died the night before, now we had to let them know it was actually Saturday morning, May 25th. Another slap in the face. How could Remi and I, as parents, not know when our daughter died?

It was Tuesday, May 28, when we heard that the young girl we had read about while we were in the hospital had received a new heart. Could it be? Was it Dawn's? The timeline fit but how could we get proof?

That proof came a month after Dawn's passing. We received a letter from HOPE listing where, but not to whom, her organs went. Among her other organs, her heart went to "a 14 year old girl from southern Alberta." Bingo! We had proof that Dawn lived on. We were glad that Kristy had made it through surgery and was doing well. It was the start of a new chapter, a new life for Dawn's heart.

While Dawn's heart beat strongly in Kristy, our ordeal with the way our daughter was treated snowballed. We found out many years later that after all the testing was done to determine brain death, that was when the doctor calls time of death. We came to realize that we had been deprived of 10 hours with our daughter. It stems back to that charge nurse (and I use the term nurse loosely) who told us Dawn was technically dead Friday night and that the doctor was too busy to talk to us. I'm sure the nurse just wanted us gone and she got her wish. Unforgivable.

We assume this nurse was highly accredited but she sorely lacked the compassion and social skills to perform her job. These skills cannot be taught. You either have them or you don't. All the education in the world doesn't mean you have common sense or empathy.

Now you can see why we were reluctant to promote organ donation for years. Even though we believed in the principles of organ donation and all the good that comes from it, we were left bitter over how the program was managed. Saying that, we never once regretted our decision to donate Dawn's organs.

Covenant Health, a Catholic health care provider that is a partner in cooperation with Alberta Health Services, clearly lays out expectations for organ donor families.

Human Organ and Tissue Donation Act November 7, 2013

Organ and Tissue Donations Aug 7th, 2015

Covenant Health

3.5 If the family or next of kin elects to go forward with organ donation, the HOPE / S.A.O.P.D. coordinator performs consent, medical and social history questionnaire, chart review, coordinates recovery and family follow up as per their organization's standard operating procedures.

I sincerely hope that this process is being followed today. I have my doubts.

All our hurt and confusion could have been avoided if we had been guided through the ordeal. Perhaps we fell through the cracks, then again, maybe that's why Alberta is ranked second last in Canada for organ donation. Please realize, we're not looking for praise or publicity. We only want the process fixed because it's definitely broken. It's the worst thing when you lose a child and then to have no help with the organ donation process it's unimaginable.

There is some insight into the low numbers of organ donation. The *Edmonton Journal* published an article on May19, 2015 titled *Albertans sign up in droves for organ donation registry, but much work remains.* It said Alberta's deceased donor rate in 2013, per million population (including N.W.T. and Nunavut) is 11.7. The Canadian average is 15.7.

Some experts suggest the low rates could be tied to a lack of leadership on the issue and failures in the health system.

Gerein, K (May19, 2015) Albertans sign up in droves for organ donation registry, but much work remains. *Edmonton Journal*

Making a Difference

About 500 to 600 people attended Dawn's funeral on May 30. We tried our best to make it a celebration of her life. In her eulogy, we spoke of her kind heart, her compassion and how she was a friend to all. By being an organ donor, she saved the lives of seven people and helped countless others improve their quality of life. She left our world but she lives on in so many others.

After the day of the funeral, that was when the real grieving began. We saw people carrying on with their day-to-day lives. I wanted to yell at them, "Please, stop! Don't you know our daughter just died?" But life does go on and we each had to deal with our loss in our own way.

One morning, when I looked in the bathroom mirror, I was shocked to see a relatively normal looking person staring back at me. I had expected to see a disfigured monster: a figure that only had three-quarters of a body because one-fourth had been removed. That was how I felt. My body was numb. Meanwhile, we felt we had to send a letter to the hospital listing our concerns and our treatment, or lack thereof. We did this a couple of months after Dawn died. We were then asked that fall by HOPE to take part in rewriting policy regarding organ donation.

The donor family needs an advocate to be with them from start to finish and beyond: weeks, months, years – whatever it takes. HOPE kept asking us as the new policy was being written, "What would you like to have been told?" All of that should have been in place already for donor families. They are the walking wounded. They don't know what to ask.

Provinces and countries that have high donation numbers should be examples of what to do right. Research best practices already out there. We have met coordinators from other provinces and from the United Kingdom. Use them. After all, your best advocates will be donor families who have been treated with the care and respect they deserve.

When HOPE receives consent, it has to realize the amount of extra stress this puts on donor families in an already heart-wrenching situation. Having someone to help the families through would be a Godsend.

When our family received a copy of the finished product, we saw that the powers that be, still did not get what we were trying to tell them. They went into great detail regarding all other aspects of the donation process but the broad statement they had regarding the donor family seemed to be an afterthought with no details given. Deep within the rewritten policy was this statement: *Make more contact with donor family.* This is why we stepped back. We had hit a brick wall and no longer had the energy to pursue it further.

During this time, our other daughter, Heather, was more or less left to deal with her sister's death on her own. She didn't receive the care and attention from us, her parents, that she needed and deserved. We could hardly look after ourselves, let alone her. We pray that she has come to realize that our actions had nothing to do with her or that Dawn was more special in some way. Had their roles been reversed, God forbid, our feelings would have been the same. We love you so very much Heather.

Luckily, my younger sister Maureen, came forward and has filled the role of big sister. For that, I will be eternally grateful.

An Open Wound

Grief for me comes in waves. You think everything is going along fine and then a memory, a smell, a song, pulls you right back under. It can leave you gasping, unable to breathe and not knowing which way is up.

The year of "firsts" came next. The first Christmas without Dawn; the first family gathering without Dawn; the first friend's wedding (Rhonda and Bill's) that Dawn should have been a part of set us back again. Having an open wound is another way to describe grief. You're not sure if it will ever heal. The wound festers as you inch forward in your grief and a scab forms. When a significant date arrives, the scab is pulled off. Eventually, you are left with a scar. A deep scar that nobody can see.

People say to you at the six month mark, "It's time to move on." Grief is uncomfortable for family and friends. They think if they mention her name, it will upset you when it's just the opposite. Yes, we may cry but we don't want her to be forgotten. My mom gave me a poem by Terry Kettering called *The Elephant in the Room*. It's about how death is ignored sometimes, especially the death of a child. Instead of talking about a loved one, we talk about the weather or baseball scores. Terry Kettering's poem lets people know it's okay to say Dawn's name and talk about her with us. Remember, we've already lived through the worst.

I do have some advice on how to speak to someone who lost a loved one. Instead of asking, "How are you doing?" Perhaps ask, "How are you doing today?" Today will be different from yesterday and not the same as tomorrow. My train of thought was always different. It depended upon where in the endless reruns of events, I was at that time.

There is no timeline for grief. Feel what you need to feel. Cry when you need to cry. Don't let anyone tell you otherwise. Take it one day at a time. Eventually, the sun will start to shine again.

Silver Linings

In November of 1996, we received another momentous phone call. This time it was welcome news. Margo, Kristy's mom, had worked up the courage to call us. She had taken the chance, not knowing how we would react.

After she introduced herself, I started to cry and said, "I'm so glad you called!" She filled us in on Kristy's progress and thanked us for donating our daughter's organs and in the process, saving her daughter's life. We talked about our daughters and asked each other questions that were safe. We were testing the waters. I didn't bring up any of our experiences with organ donation because I didn't want to upset her or make her feel bad. We agreed to keep in touch, which we did. She would call with updates on Kristy or I would call her.

We also had another source of information. A friend of a friend who lived in Medicine Hat, passed along any news they had heard about Kristy. This went on for almost five years. During that time, neither Remi or I were ready to meet the girl who had Dawn's heart. Our feelings were still too raw.

A few years later in 2001, we heard Kristy was pregnant – with twins! This brought me to tears: it was the same thing Dawn wanted. Now, only a part of her would get to experience it. A few weeks before the twins were born, Margo called with the news. It was then that I told her how we had been keeping tabs of their lives. She told us they knew Kristy was having girls and she wanted to know if she could name her first born after Dawn. We were astounded and touched that she would want to do that. Of course we agreed. Little did we know that this would be the first of many astounding acts this young woman would include our family in.

Margo called us when the girls were born. Shaylynn Dawn and McKayla Mona had arrived on September 30, 2001. They were a little early but everyone seemed to be fine. I was now ready to meet Kristy. Not that it would be easy.

Heather, Maureen and I went up to Edmonton to the Royal Alexandra Hospital where Kristy and her daughters were staying. So many thoughts and emotions went through my mind. Fear, joy, apprehension and excitement. What will Kristy be like? What will she sound like? Will there be any heart recognition? Will I hug her too hard? Will I feel Dawn's heart beat against my chest in that moment?

In the hospital elevator, on the way up to their floor, I thought I was going to be sick to my stomach. I was shaking. I told myself to calm down and took some deep breaths. Here I was, about to walk back into another hospital room, where our daughter's heart was now inside someone else's body. It was surreal to say the least.

I needn't have worried about meeting Kristy. We all seemed to be very comfortable together right away. The babies of course, were beautiful and our conversations came easily. In that first visit, we brought some pictures of Dawn. Kristy had many questions and wanted to know everything about her. What was Dawn like? What was her favourite colour? How tall was she?

I was happy that I had decided to meet Kristy that day. I had waited long enough.

Shaylynn Dawn wasn't the only baby to be named after Dawn,

there were a total of six babies named after her:

Mackenzie Leslie Dawn,

Tennille Dawn,

Ky Dawn,

Sasha Dawn, and

Kendall Dawn.

Our family was honoured for these wonderful tributes to our daughter.

The next few years, we got together with Kristy several times. Each time, she always showed her appreciation for the gift she had been given. I'd like to tell you about just some of these times.

As you know by now, Kristy gave many interviews over the years. Before each one, she would contact us to let us know what was happening and to ask us if we wanted to be involved with the interview. We said no to her offers many times but she always respected our decision and so she referred to us as "my donor family."

A few years ago Kristy and her family came to visit us and she told us she wanted to take flowers to Dawn's grave. She had already googled a picture of her headstone but it was important for her to see it in person. We took them to Dawn's grave, which is close to our house. At that same time, Kristy said she was anxious to meet Brad and any of Dawn's friends. To date, she has met quite a few and there are still a few meetings to take place, Brad being one of them. But it will happen.

During the Calgary Stampede parade of 2012, Kristy proudly displayed a picture of Dawn on the float that carried many other organ recipients. None of the others knew their donor families.

Kristy's family and ours were honoured to be asked to be part of the *Train of Heroes*, a train trip put on by Rocky Mountaineer. The passengers were either organ donor families or recipients. We are very grateful for the opportunity that this company gave us. It allowed us to have a lot of private, one-on-one time between our families. We found out from one another the feelings or thoughts that we had over the years. Nothing was off limits.

Kristy was surprised to hear that we worried about her. We were taken aback when she told us she wanted to ask Heather to be her maid of honour at her wedding and if Remi could walk her down the aisle along with her dad. You could have knocked us over with a feather. She had already incorporated Dawn's favourite flowers, daisies, and the colour yellow in the bouquets, as well as other touches.

On the train, whenever Kristy and Wade were off doing interviews, we would watch over the twins. Very quickly, we formed a closeness with Shaylynn and McKayla. They treated us like another set of grandparents.

Kristy hadn't brought her stethoscope with her on the train trip but when she heard we would like to hear Dawn's heartbeat, she made sure she had it with her the next time we met.

Kristy's caring and compassion shines through in everything she does. She would be a perfect national ambassador or advisor for all things organ donation related. She has lived one side and she understands the other.

Messages From an Angel

Earlier on in my story, I eluded to how music and song has shown me that Dawn is still with us in spirit. I understand that many of you will think I'm off my rocker. That's okay. This is my belief.

Dawn's funeral was the first time she made her presence known but I didn't pick up on it at the time. In the middle of the service, the tape recorder started playing music on its own. My sister said, "That's Dawn!" Normally, that wouldn't mean anything but there were other incidents.

On a Saturday morning, a few months after Dawn's passing, after Remi had left for work, I was still in bed. I was restless and agitated and felt something that I couldn't explain. I got up and said out loud, "Kid, if you're trying to tell me something, I will know by what song is being played on the radio or the very next one to play." I turned on the radio. The first song was *Today my world slipped away* by George Strait. The second was *I ain't one for living on past glory* by The Family Brown. I think it was her way of telling me that, yes, her life as she knew it was over but she was okay with that and that she had done her part by letting others live.

When I had a meeting with an Angel Reader, she asked me, "Did your daughter play an instrument?" The answer was no but the reader said she could see music all around her. I laughed because then I knew that Dawn had a hand in all these musical occurrences.

Here is the most astonishing one that happened. I was coming home from work. We live in the country with gravel roads that have many blind curves. That day, the county had laid down a cold mix (poor man's pavement) and the road was nice and smooth. As I was driving, a little too fast around the curves, a thought came to me that I better slow down in case there was a swather (a farm vehicle that cuts hay and crops) coming around the bend. A swather, not a truck or another vehicle or a piece of equipment, came to mind. Just then, a song that we played at Dawn's funeral came on the radio. I slowed right down, rounded the next blind curve and there it was: a swather taking up the full width of the road.

Delta Dawn always started playing on the radio when I was deep in thought about her. It has been a long time since any of these things happened. I guess she thought I got the message that she's always with me. However, the week Kristy and I were talking about this book in February 2016, Remi was trying to remember the name of a song that had hit home for us when Dawn died. Between the three of us, we finally figured out the name: *Nobody Knows* by Kevin Sharp. The next day, Kristy was scanning some pictures of Dawn at a copy store and do you know what song came over the PA system? You guessed it! I guess Dawn figures we're on the right track with the book.

There's Still Work to be Done

In 2014, we watched a documentary titled *The Ward* (ID Productions). It told the story of people who were waiting for transplant, either in the hospital or as outpatients. A segment of the program showed a re-enactment of a conversation between a hospital rep and a potential donor family.

From what was said on film, our concerns were realized. The family was not given all the info they needed or deserved. The HOPE organization still doesn't understand that this part of the process needs to be changed. Don't get me wrong, we're glad for the initiatives that have been put in place but so much more could be done.

To those of you who have not registered your intention to donate, remember you are more likely to need an organ that to donate one. Also, to donor recipients and those of you on waiting lists, if you're lucky enough to get your organ, please send a letter to the donor family. You don't know how much that would mean to them. This is all I ask.

When we see Dawn's friends moving on with their lives like getting married and having children, we wonder what could have been for Dawn. Then we think of Kristy and realize that this is the way it was supposed to be.

I could have missed the pain, but I'd have had to miss the dance, Garth Brooks, *The Dance*

Thank you to our family and friends who helped us through the darkest time of our lives.

Thank you to Heather for your love, your strength, your determination and just for being you...

Thank you to Brad for your love and support.

I'd like to thank my husband Remi. I never would have made it through this without you.

And last but not least, thank you to Kristy for bringing back the light.

Remi: My Life As I Knew It

I am the proud father of two girls: Dawn and Heather. They were raised to respect and have consideration for everything and everyone. I made sure they knew the same things as any good farm boy would know, whether it be feeding cows, running equipment, fixing fences or taking care of animals. That was to make them independent and confident so that they could handle anything that came up in life. I also taught them that if you're not going to give it your all, don't do it at all. That was why when Dawn's tragedy happened and I lost a child, I questioned my priorities. You say to yourself, "What was the point of being a hard-ass?" as I was somewhat accused of from time-to-time. My heart had been crushed and there was nothing to repair it in sight.

After the accident, things slowed down. Heather was young and wanted to venture out on her own but I couldn't let her go. This caused significant problems between us. I couldn't bear the chance that something might happen to her and I didn't want her out of my sight. I was going to protect her, no matter what. Over the years, I have learned to bite my tongue and pray for her protection and safety because I was causing a bigger and bigger divide between us. Things are good between us now. Heather understands me and I understand her but that does not stop the worry.

My girls are my all. When they were young, I would come home after a 10 to 12 hour workday and play ball or go riding or do whatever with them. Sleep could wait. It was more important to let them know I was there for them. That was why it took me years to meet Kristy after Coral and Heather had already met her. I was afraid of frightening her or something and I was still bitter about the accident and the loss of Dawn Marie. Before I met Kristy, I had to decide if I had the energy to deal with her or what might be.

I started letting down my guard by chatting to Kristy over the phone. We talked one or two times a year. I began to see how wonderful she was and I often thought to myself, "this girl gets it." Kristy's ability to relate is rare. She's wise beyond her years and a joy to be around. She has inserted hope into a very sad situation: our tragic loss of Dawn compounded by the fiasco with the organ donation foundation and that charge nurse (the rest of the hospital staff was wonderful).

Over the years, we have been to a few organ donation functions and benefits and I'm usually disappointed in the speakers. Whether they are doctors or organ donor reps or even recipients, most, or all, don't get what donor families are looking for. We know that donation is a never-ending saga and we feel we have a stake in the process too. We all would love to know how the recipients are doing, even when we don't know them. We only want the best for them and don't want to be an afterthought. My family doesn't want a personal acknowledgement, just respect for the donors. By honoring donors first, they honour us. After all, it all starts with the sacrifice of the donors and we need to acknowledge their lives.

My heart is still heavy at times when I think of what would have been if Dawn was still here. I wonder what her family would be like but I know she would have been a great mom. She had already been using her farm girl ethics on her fiancé Brad. For example, if he didn't do a good job cutting the grass, he would be reminded that if he was doing the job for her dad, he would have to do it over.

Now I think what if I had never met Kristy. What would have been? Whenever I see or speak to Kristy, I am pleased to see something of Dawn lives on in this beautiful young lady. If I had never met Kristy, I'm pretty sure I'd still be bitter about the loss of Dawn Marie. We have come to love the woman who holds Dawn's heart, her husband Wade, their daughters Shaylynn Dawn and McKayla, and Kristy's parents, Margo and Blaine, like our own family.

Made in the USA
Charleston, SC
12 June 2016